CLOWNS ANTHOLOGY

EDITED BY
MICHELLE TEA

Published by DOPAMINE
P.O. Box 363, Joshua Tree, CA 92252
www.dopaminebooks.org

Covert Art: MariNaomi
Layout & Design: Brooke Palmieri
Copyediting: Katie Fricas

ISBN: 978-1-63590-280-8
Distributed by the MIT Press, Cambridge, Mass., and London, England.
Printed in the United States of America

10 9 8 7 6 5 4 3 2 1

CONTENTS

INTRODUCTION
Michelle Tea

I imagined that the prompt *clown* would mean many things to many people, and I wasn't wrong. A loud figure whatever the sort, circus or killer, hobo or elegant, clowns are with us from childhood on up, showing us their many faces. People love them or hate them; rarely is a person indifferent or neutral about that greasepainted mug and patchwork attire. Clowns provoke feelings and opinions, and after collecting the pieces for this anthology, I get it: inside our hearts and psyches and souls, we are all clowns. And it's tragi-comic in here.

I did not initially understand the intense vulnerability of the clown; on the surface, they seem protected from the blast of their costume, from the terror they inspire. Hardly human at all but a mute, related species, like apes and aliens. But clowns are of course intensely human, inflating daily emotions—love, silliness, frustration, sorrow, rage—into caricature. Is it so we can laugh at ourselves, or displace our discomfort onto this colorful other? No doubt any individual's embrace or disdain of this icon is a fizzy mixture of recognition and repulsion; where you land in relationship to the clown says much more about your own psyche than the goofy persona you're witnessing.

Witnessing anyone's vulnerability can make us acutely aware of our own, and it's this site of discomfort that many of the contributors for *Clowns* reckoned with. On the surface, many pieces seem not to reference clowns at all, perhaps leaving a reader to wonder what this book is even about. But somersault deeper into and through the collection, and it becomes apparent how each and every story and poem is marked by clowning: our own. Our tender interiors harbor these cringe characters; indeed, we suspect we most authentically *are* them, applying our normal-person costumes each day to mask the clown within. Such an insight renders the actual clown a creature not costumed but revealed, a revelation; the fiction that tells the truth, our own.

The anthology's opening piece, the illustrated *Clown Nose* by Katie Fricas, sums this up with sweet, simple poignancy: the narrator applies her clown nose, as she does each day before going out into the world. Is the fact that no one notices it a relief at passing, or a sadness at remaining fundamentally unseen? From this we move into all the many ways we are forced or choose to embarrass ourselves, to feel our inherent clownishness—with Megan Milk's *Name Dropping #17: On Dog-Sitting for Alice Krock*, self-promotion, ambition, social climbing, the need to make a living, the thrill of celebrity, and humble human bumbling collide to cringetastic effect. Artist Vivek Shraya locates a sort of enforced clownness that gets projected upon marginalized artists expected to perform their trauma for media attention and institutional support.

Comedians and other performers who work with humor show up, often confronting the energies of shame that feed what we find funny; they are the ones who most occupy the role of the Holy Fool, the medieval clown permitted to speak truth to power, who lives on in tarot packs and open mics. Kate Bornstein's *The Fool at the Draft Board* is a genius tale of survival-clowning, as the trans icon recalls inhabiting—and lampooning—her own femininity to escape conscription into warfare. Gender—in particular feminine expressions, with its color, play, imagination, and occasional ridiculousness—can make one think of, or feel like, a clown, a tension féi iká shumarí confronts in *I Am Not a Drag Queen I Am a Trans Woman*. But gender normativity is the clown which does not understand its clownishness, as exposed in Riley Yaxley's *Gazelle*, wherein a femme ride share passenger is subjected to her driver's preening machismo.

Class clowns show up, such as Chris E. Vargas's *Tears of a Class Clown* and Marisa Crawford's *Class Clown GF*; high school, as the last gasp of childhood, is one of the final spaces overt clowning is permitted, recognized, rewarded—though for those whose aggressive humor masks marginalizing difference, what's being honed is truly a survival skill. Graphic memoirist Nicole J. Georges illustrates how parental control can make unwitting, disempowered clowns out of us in *Lies*. Samara Halperin's *Nougats and nazis*, also set in childhood, returns us to the Holy Fool aspect of the Clown, as a gang of mischievous children—the ultimate, innate clowns—bring a procession of inappropriate humor to the suburbs.

Artist and writer MariNaomi, whose dynamic work graces the cover, explores their fear of clowns, and the final piece, Jake Hall's *The Freak Revolution*, displays why perhaps certain sorts of people ought to. I opted to end on such a jagged note because, while I wanted this book to explore the Clown archetype, I never want to resolve it. The clown remains within us and without, on the edge of our dreams, turning somersaults in our psyche. Death is a clown, and so is love, and sex of course, and heartbreak; kids on acid are clowns, and kids taught by clowns at a formative age may pick up its rebellious philosophy and innovate the profession. Clowns are possibly inherently feminist, a stand-in for both the sly wit within each underestimated femme, as well as their fed-up fury. Clowns are inherent allies to trans folk and all who experience oppression, an embodiment of the radical queer practice of reclamation and confrontation; the anonymity the mask of makeup provides can encourage, allowing for brazen acts of revenge. If you're still scared of clowns by the close of this book, perhaps you ought to check your conscience.

The pieces in this collection work together, revealing the Clown archetype to be so much deeper and wilder, so much more vulnerably human than I had ever realized. The clown in me sees the clown in you and honks its crimson nose.

Michelle Tea
On a Plane, October 2025

Clown Nose
FRICAS
EVERY MORNING
BEFORE WORK,
I PUT ON A CLOWN NOSE.

I KNOW...
IT'S FUNNY.
USUALLY, I PUT IT ON RIGHT WHEN I WAKE UP.
OR I PUT ON THE NOSE AS I HEAD INto WORK.

OTHER DAYS, THE CAT WAKES ME,
AND I WON'T BE ABLE TO GO BACK TO SLEEP FOR HOURS.
SO I PUT THE NOSE ON.

NEXT THING, IT'S MORNING AGAIN
I EAT,
THEN I GO INTO THIS SPIRAL,
WHILE I'M LACING UP MY SHOES,

AND I SIT,
AND I THINK,
MAYBE I SHOULD TAKE IT OFF
SUBWAY
EXIT
FOR ONCE.

BUT I LEAVE IT ON,
PRETTY MUCH ALL DAY,
AND NOBODY EVER NOTICES.
DELI

OR THEY DO,
AND THEY'RE JUST TOO POLITE TO POINT IT OUT.
FIN.

LAST NIGHT
Stella Leoni

Last night, I put on makeup.

I probably looked a little *too much* to someone not minding their own business.

I was celebrating a one-year anniversary. One-year breakup anniversary with my first—and only—boyfriend.

Last night, I put on makeup.

It's not a poem, I'm just repeating myself.

Last night, I put on makeup. Besides that, everything was the same—just me, alone in my one-bedroom apartment. I opened the left kitchen cabinet and stared at the pills on the top shelf, the tea options on the middle shelf, the dried powder soup packs and rice pasta box on the bottom one.

I grabbed the pasta box, turned around, and filled the one pot I own with water—the same pot that sits on the burner day and night, dirty and clean. I waited for it to boil, thinking about the in-betweens. The times after something and before the rest.

After ordering a coffee and before getting it.

After sitting on a dentist's chair and before getting a tooth pulled.

After starting a hug and before letting go.

After filling a pot with water and before it boils. I rubbed my eye. Makeup. Do I usually rub my eyes? Was it itching? Was I allergic? I couldn't tell. Does makeup expire? I thought about checking it in the mirror but decided not to. I looked down and had brown eye powder and some black on my finger. Eyeliner.

I had learned these words—powder, eyeliner—in my late teens, with Clara. I tried opening my eyes really wide and closing them really tight, just to feel. There was no way to know if it was feeling normal or not since it was something new. I opened my eyes really wide and closed them really tight again, and again, until I realized the water was boiling.

I put two handfuls of pasta in there, and thought about Clara, who always weighed our pasta portions to 100g. I never picked up that habit from her. I did pick up standing on my tippy-toes while brushing my teeth as an easy everyday strengthening exercise—who knows.

I opened the fridge and freezer, decided on the frozen peas and some vegan pesto. I could have gone for the zucchini and baby spinach, but not last night. Last night, I went for the peas and pesto. I took the jade face roller from the freezer, too. I dumped the peas into a strainer and ran the sink on hot to defrost them. Nine minutes left on the timer.

I rolled the roller over my face.

The roller lived in three different apartments before I ever considered using it. It was a gift from Lucy; she always chose challenging gifts, ones that shook my habits. Now, I've been using it for one summer, one winter, and halfway through one spring.

Last summer I realized I didn't have to painfully wait during the in-between times, I could use things. I added things to do and things to stare at as distractions, like movie posters. Face roller, foot massage balls, coloring books. I rolled my face until the stone wasn't cold anymore and reached for the velvet pouch to put it away. Red on the roller.

It felt sticky between my fingers. Red and sticky. The lipstick. It came off the stone easily, but no matter how much I rubbed it off my fingers, the red wouldn't go away, it just spread. The timer went off.

I forgot to add the peas to the water, so I dumped the water and pasta slowly over them—hoping it would make them perfectly unfrozen—and transferred everything into the pink ceramic half-bowl, half-plate from the cabinet on the right-hand side. I added pesto and salt. I never find anything too salty—that's a conspiracy theory to me. The more salt, the better it tastes. That's all that happens.

I sat around my round, metallic table with melted wax all over it. At this point, I call this table a "work-in-progress art project" to justify keeping it. It's an abstract way of keeping track of time. A day, a candle. The wax makes it difficult to put anything down on it. If it's hot it sticks, if it's full it wobbles, if it's circular it slides. And it hurts my elbows and my wrists when I lean on it.

I usually love it. But not last night. Last night I hated it. All I wanted was a flat, compliant surface to put my plate and silverware down on. I put them on the floor instead and held the knife in my hand.

I thought I could use the knife to carve out a spot in the wax—a level enough place for the plate, at least. The carving out didn't go so well. Maybe the impossibility of surrender, the overthinking, the impatience were because I was eight days late on my period, or because of the date, or the reflecting back. Maybe it was all, or none. It's always hard to tell.

It was strange to be with someone who couldn't relate to periods. For me to care about what my boobs looked like. Strange to want to be seductive, to be attractive to a man. To feel like I was being looked at differently. To feel like I needed to lean into a different side of myself that wasn't safe. To imagine the image of a woman like we're fed: the perfect ass, the hairless body, the long nails, the makeup.

I didn't really get anywhere with the carving situation before the knife slid over the wax instead of cutting through it and bit my finger. I threw the knife across the room and cried. I went back to the left cabinet in the kitchen and stared at the top, middle, and bottom shelves again, searching for a solution.

I could use a Band-Aid but it didn't feel quite right, I was looking for a different kind of solution. A solution to fix me, not the cut. I took an 800mg ibuprofen hoping it would get me out of my brain and body. I found success in the placebo effect of taking any pill with the intention of calming my nerves down. No Xanax, no pot, no alcohol for me, just a good old ibuprofen or an allergy pill once in a while.

The mascara had stained my white sleeve as I dried my eyes and nose, although there were other colors, too: some beige/brown, some red, a little pink I had a hard time identifying. Surely the red was from the lipstick, not the blood though. Maybe snot was diluting the red, which could explain the pink. He was my first-and-only-ever boyfriend and it only lasted three months. I liked him. I don't like makeup. I don't have any answers.

The makeup bag was left behind by Clara, who had weighed our pasta portions to 100g, who I had broken up with years ago. The makeup bag has lived under the sink in every bathroom I've had since. Like it was with the jade face roller, I thought, "Who knows?" Maybe one day I'll want to wear makeup. I try to stay open to anything, to whatever might come my way. I'm an experiment. Everything is an experiment.

I wore makeup last night as a celebration of the unknown; it felt like an act in a play. Maybe every relationship is like a performance, too. I went back to my plate, on the floor, and sat cross-legged on my striped black and white carpet. I got my period sometime during all this—of course—and bled through my underwear, my shorts, and stained the white part of the carpet. Sometimes it feels like the end of the world, like nothing will ever be ok again, and I'll never feel the way I feel when I'm ok. I walk around with my internal chaos, invisible to everyone else.

I went to the bathroom and stopped in front of the mirror. For once, the chaos was visible. It was a relief to see it. I cried more. The lipstick had spread in an awful way, the mascara streaked long black marks under my eyes, my nose was red from the crying. The only untouched parts were the eyebrows. I used a greasy crayon to make them thicker and darker. I couldn't even recognize myself. I grabbed my phone and snapped a picture. I took my bloody shorts and dirty top off and went back to my cold pesto-pea-pasta half-bowl half-plate on the floor. I lay on my stomach, propped my feet up, and kicked my legs in the air, one after another, as I ate. It always makes me feel like a little girl to do that.

When I woke up this morning, I'd almost forgotten about everything—until I unlocked my iPhone and saw the photo of myself in the bathroom mirror. I laughed out loud.

Last night I probably felt like any other girl, once in a while.

THE ANTIDOTAL GHOST

Jennifer Hasegawa

The simultaneous
abundance and austerity
of a clown car.

Outlaw river
between tenderloin
and soup bone,
shapeshifter,
and dull clone.

A chain
of thousand-sided circles.

Hands
that talk better
than a mouth.

In two dimensions,
a right triangle.
Limbs, a ratio
of the rubbery torso
that storytells
for the shadows
squirming inside.

In three dimensions,
a thunderbird.
At dreamtime
anointing some

into the third-oldest
profession
after warmonger
and peacemaker.
A mirror
made of flesh
playing
the primal ribcage
like an accordion,
serenading us
in the history
of failure.

And what does it sing?

Honk. Mercy.
Boop. Grace.
Ahooga. Humility.

The key changes
based on location.
Even roach
is a freedom fighter
or terrorist,
depending on where
it drinks its water.

Moving across
the darkness
in a blip of light,
more like a mistake
than life.

What is this
void of voids
from which we spring
like clowns
from a cannon?

Modern clowning
is a cornflower negligee
and thigh-high stockings
in an office setting.
Doe eyes embalming
the conscience
of a nation.

Anonymity
+ fidelity
birth the lucky mutant
whose maker
burnt its gene map
along with the placenta.

Couplet of RNA,
proto-lasers scanning
the primordial
sous vide
to make life
from braids of mud
and electricity.

Vicariously metabolizing
individual violences.

Keep playing
and the birds
swarming on the horizon
come to live
in your own head.

Stretching your face
into a Vantablack beak
stuffed with
vinegared sponges,
ambergris,
and camphor.

Arms deploy
into wings.
Slapstick wands
cast spells
clearing the smoke
of knowing,
and in the clearing:
flush with potential,
the beautiful
red nose
of nada.

After *Autre Complainte de Lord Pierrot* by Jules Laforgue.

NAME DROPPING #17: ON DOG-SITTING FOR ALICE KROCK

Megan Milks

Dear Friends,

First, some announcements.

- I have a reading coming up next Thursday at Hivemind Books. I'd love to see you there.
- I finally published my essay about leaving my aesthetic home—that is, the school of "experimental literature." I've been talking about writing this bad boy for ages and finally did. I hope you'll read it and let me know what you think.
- I've opened registration for a new set of summer workshops. You can find out more here. I'd love to work with you!

*

I'm writing while dog-sitting for a celebrity who's away for the day at clown school. The dog, Sir, is a thick-necked French bulldog with mobility issues. He greeted me like I was the best thing he'd ever smelled then scrabbled onto my lap to slather my face in his drool. But as soon as Alice left, it was like Sir's spirit departed his body. He became a shell, a recalcitrant gargoyle perched on my thighs, displaying his quivering back. Alice had warned me he gets anxious—that's why she needed a dog sitter, not a dog walker—but I wasn't prepared for the nakedness of his despair.

You're ok, Sir. She'll be back soon. He lets me scratch behind his ears.

This gig was passed along by a friend I ran into last week at a party. When I told them I'd recently lost my cat (RIP Little Debbie Harry—see my last Name Dropping for more), they suggested I try petsitting. It would be an easy way to soak up some animal energy while bringing in some extra cash. In fact, they had a job I could take. They had agreed to dog-sit for one of their regulars, but the dates conflicted with an acting gig they couldn't pass up, not even for Alice Krock.

Alice Krock? I repeated. The name tugged on some file stored way back in my brain.

Yup, *that* Alice Krock, my friend supplied. From *Slinkys*.

A thrill ran through me. *That* Alice Krock was *famous*. I could be in her home. I could be with her dog. I could leave behind a signed copy of my book, which could be received with enthusiasm. She'd sit down to read it right then with Sir nestled beside her. She'd stay up all night to finish, shut the book—*my* book—with awe, and be moved to gush about it on all of her social media channels. *A life-changing work*, she'd tell her millions of followers. *And FUN!* **Order here.** Soon I could be famous, too.

If not fame, I would at least get good material to write about for my newsletter. If you've been reading these transmissions for a while, you'll know that the name *Name Dropping* is kind of a joke. I'm hardly a gossip columnist. I mostly write about books and friends or publish short conference talks and content that won't see life anywhere else. But if I have a run-in with a celebrity like Alice Krock, I basically have to write about it. That's the rule of a newsletter called Name Dropping.

Yes, I was available. Yes, I could handle an anxious Frenchie. (I would not admit to not knowing what a "Frenchie" was and would look up this breed when I got home.) It had been years since I'd walked a dog—the last time was with my long-ago ex, Kel, a dog person—but how hard could dog-sitting be? My friend texted Alice my info and told me Alice would get in touch.

[Thanks for reading *Name Dropping*! Subscribe for free to receive new posts and support my work.]

*

You probably remember Alice Krock from the hit Netflix dramedy *Slinkys*. You'll remember that the show was instrumental to the company's successful shift from DVD mailing service to first major streamer. We can blame *Slinkys* for the rise of streaming TV and all the time we've lost to it.

Which is fitting, because the show is about time loss. It centers a character named Jeff whom we first meet competing in a Slinky manipulation contest—a cross between juggling and raving. Alice played Jeff's buddy and love interest. Her character, Lena, is an elf therapist who believes time travel can be harnessed as a method for healing. She's been looking for the perfect object—a tool she might imbue with magic to unlock access to other times. Watching Jeff practice his routine in the park one day, she lights up. The Slinky: it's perfect. Innocent, dumb, yet alive with potential. Watching Jeff fling his rainbow spring through the air, Lena surmises that if she can figure out the right finger spells to open the fourth dimension, she can use the Slinky's tubular force to forge a tunnel through time.

Because Lena, being an elf, doesn't understand that adult men who play with Slinkys are largely considered "uncool," she comes on too strong, and Jeff assumes she's making fun of him. But eventually they team up. Jeff teaches her to manipulate Slinkys, and he becomes her first test subject. Not her client—as he keeps reminding her. This is an ongoing bit. The more she comes to know about Jeff and the pain he carries around with him, the more she wants to use Slinky time travel to heal him—and the more he resists her efforts.

Consider the Slinky. It's the perfect metaphor for the ebbs and flows of time. Like time, it compresses and elongates. It slinks like a snake. It stops and starts. It reverses and spirals. Its velocity varies. It often seems to shiver of its own accord. But with enough skill and experience, one can learn to control it.

When the show premiered, Slinky manipulation was an obscurely subcultural art. Like jugglers, Slinky artists work with the Slinky's coiled body to do tricks like waves, twists, and flips, to surround bottles and cans without touching them, or sometimes to pull them up into the Slinky's orbit. Most, including Jeff, favored the plastic rainbow Slinky that was at that time only available in China—it had the perfect coil thickness, diameter, and length for manipulation. It was safer and less jangly than its metal kin; less prone to kinks in the Slink. It also created a pleasing psychedelic color show as it moved.

After a few episodes of troubleshooting, Lena finds the right finger spells. In the show's portal shots, the Slinky comes at the camera in slo-mo, a tunnel of rotating coils, initiating a rainbow fade into a new and surprising time period that is rarely the target time period (part of Lena's arc is improving her magical-tech skills). The visual logic is that as the Slinky comes at the field of the camera, it jostles loose time from its frame.

The characters have to move quickly to stretch open the portal the Slinky creates, so that they can follow the Slinky whenever it takes them. The camera then pivots to follow them into the past.

The show was beloved for its rudimentary visual effects, the quirky characters, and the sizzling opposites-attract chemistry between Lena and Jeff that neither could stoop to acknowledge. The Slinky manipulation community loved the outro clips, too: each episode ended with a real-life Slinky artist aka Slinker doing their best and most mesmerizing performance. The outro spot became prized among Slinkers, and the competitiveness attracted waves of new people to the sport, all of them vying for an appearance on the show.

So, Alice is really famous, a name I'm eager to drop. But she never became a star. In fact, it was Kit Collado who blew up. It's easy to forget that *Slinkys* was Kit's first role—they played Lena's nonbinary best friend Jax, a secondary character who'd pop in for a scene here, a scene there, then disappear for episodes at a time, generally when Jeff and Lena got stuck in time loops and lost time in the present. But Kit's appearances excited such enthusiasm that they were made a series regular and got to go through the portals themself.

Allow me some more historicizing. It was just the right timing for a nonbinary celebrity. Kit was an early adopter of Twitter, where they served up reliably witty and increasingly political, often pro-queer, sound bites. Surely you remember their satirical tutorial on how to incorrectly use they/them pronouns—early nonbinary canon. Alice, by contrast, tended to shun the spotlight. She was queer, too; but, if not exactly closeted, she was quiet about it. (The community knew.) When she accepted her Emmy for one of the middle seasons, especially the episode where Lena gets stuck in a psych ward in 1954 and Alice got to show off her considerable range, Alice threw out a nervous round of thanks and shuffled from the stage in what can only be called a glorified shift dress. At the same ceremony, Kit wore a show-stopping tuxedo gown and brought their trans lover as a date. Kit didn't win their category but, as presenter, managed to slip in a comment on the binary nature of the categories before their mic cut out and their co-presenter took over. Now Kit is an icon and Alice is something else, something more like a has-been, though that's harsher than is accurate.

I remember arguing about this with my girlfriend at the time. Alice Krock doesn't owe us anything, I declared while sprawled next to Heather on my bed, my laptop between us, the browser paused between episodes. She's an actor, not a political advocate. Heather shrugged. That's not the point, she said. The point is if you have a platform, you should use it, and it's disappointing if you don't. Because I was nonbinary and Heather was cis, there was perhaps something loving about me defending cis Alice and Heather celebrating nonbinary Kit. But if I'm honest, my defense of Alice was personal. Twitter was new and I was leery of it—yet I could see that it was making people's careers. I was an Alice who wanted but was too scared to be a Kit. (I have since found my lane, and it's newsletters, the longer-winded the better, published just often enough to remind you I exist.)

After the show ended, Kit got their own spin-off, *Slinkys: A Time for Change*. Alice and Michael Fishman, who played Jeff, occasionally turned in lackluster cameos. Michael transitioned to film work with little success. Alice's few post-*Slinkys* roles have seen her playing women who fear intimacy in mediocre sitcoms. In one, she's an aggressively bored, unhappy civil court judge. In another, she bitterly co-owns a frozen yogurt shop with her jolly ex-husband. Her best role after Lena (imo) was the voice of the donkey divorcée in that Lisa Hanawalt cartoon that everyone was into five years ago.

It sounds like I have stored up all this knowledge of Alice but it's just from looking her up last night, after learning some basics about French bulldogs, who are, I have discovered, as expensive as they are loyal. I wanted to remember what Alice looked like, and then before I knew it, I'd lost time: two hours, into the hole. My image search retrieved mostly stills from the show: Alice as Lena in the psych ward, Alice as Lena with Jeff and his Slinkys, Alice as Lena with Kit in a chocolate factory (a nod to *I Love Lucy*). Then there were the same few shots of Alice looking sheepish in cumbersome get-ups at awards shows. And one cover photo for Time, posed with a rainbow Slinky in a rainbow-shaped arc above her head, each end hovering above her lit-up palms. And then a few candids of Alice in sunglasses and a baseball cap, sweetly holding hands with Bronwyn O'Shea, her girlfriend at the time. Alice seems to move through the world with a private laugh frozen on her face. Otherwise, she looks like a lot of people.

*

When I met her this morning, Alice was not laughing. She was not the zany and lovable elf her character is. But it was early. She wasn't rude, just tense and steely, like a metal Slinky coiled and ready to spring. This may have been a reaction to the uncharacteristic and probably off-putting verve with which I greeted her. I was playing the role of competent dog sitter, which meant (I thought) approaching Sir and Alice with happy dog energy. I wiggled my body while emitting a stream of high-pitched statements such as we were going to have the best time together, weren't we, Sir, yes we were. I was probably overselling it.

Now Sir is gently snoring by my side on the couch. I just sent a pic of us to Alice to assure her Sir is alive and in good hands. She responds with a thumbs up. Heartless. Boundaried. This place has a joyless energy. The only wall art is a large, framed photograph of the New York City skyline. It's not as though I expected something screaming CELEBRITY and WEALTH, but maybe I expected something that whispered it. This beige basement unit in central Brooklyn is probably an Airbnb. I'm guessing Alice has a better, more permanent home in LA. Or maybe she's not as rich as I imagine her to be. I thought from the modesty of my $20 an hour rate that she might be one of those cheap rich people. Could she be, rather, a hard-working actor who landed a plum role that didn't ultimately pay well or result in a lasting material rise? Maybe she has an incompetent agent or blew it all on a house for her mom. Maybe Alice doesn't care about politics or material things—just her craft, and her dog, who is currently passing foul gas.

*

So, I took Sir out for a walk but couldn't get him to move more than a few steps. He looked up at me, ears back, whites of his eyes showing. Was I behaving in a way that communicated *heel*, not *walk*? Was I supposed to be ahead of and not behind him? I tried various commands. *Walk, Sir. Come. Go. Let's move. Pee? Bathroom?* I hesitated. I didn't want to say it . . . *Potty?* Sir was rigid and perplexed or obstinate. I'm not a dog person and he could smell it.

Sir did not go potty. We turned and came back inside, where Sir has continued to pass foul gas.

Maybe we'll play. Get the ball, Sir. I toss it past him, for something to chase. Get it, get it. He stares after the tennis ball dolefully. I try the rope toy, which is thick and knotted on both ends. Get the rope? I pantomime a tug-of-war without a rival. He lowers his head. Treat? Bone? Yum. Gnar. Get it. No?

I feel like a clown trying to get this dog to cheer up.

Sad clown. He's not into me or my tricks. He wants Alice. I can placate him with body heat and butt scratches but he's all the time pining for Alice.

I wander the apartment. It's a one-bedroom with an office space and three more examples of generic cityscape art (Manhattan from Brooklyn, Manhattan from the top of the Empire State Building, the Brooklyn Bridge). There is no color in this home. Alice is almost out of toilet paper. The only personal touch is a handwritten letter from Reese Witherspoon who loves what Alice has been doing for women in the industry, keep up this important work. It's stuck to the fridge with a dog-butt magnet.

I sink back into the sofa.

It's kind of strange, thinking of Alice in clown school from the vantage point of this cold, sad apartment. The internet tells me she's going through a breakup. She and her most recent girlfriend (a Tracy Turcell) are no longer together. Maybe that's why Alice was so steely today, barely a smile when I stepped inside. Maybe that's why she's here—to get out of LA, and the memories. Maybe that's why she's going to clown school—to cope, through movement and community, with crushing heartbreak. It must be difficult to be that kind of famous when you're in your twenties and looking for love, especially if you're queer and quiet about it. And then again in your thirties when you're still famous but forgotten at the same time.

Sir settles in his crate. We have three hours left together. I put on an episode of *Slinkys* to pass the time.

*

Now I'm writing from home. I fell so thoroughly into a time tunnel I'm starting to think the show casts its own spells. Comment below if you agree. I put on Season 1, Episode 5, one of my favorites because the subplot is a 1920s lesbian noir and, you may know, I love 1920s lesbian noir (you can buy my book **here**). But as I was watching it, a strange thing happened: the episode's portal scene didn't take me to the 1920s; it took me back to Chicago fifteen years ago, when I was first watching this episode with my then-girlfriend Heather, a huge fan who was excited to initiate me into the show. It wasn't a typical memory trigger—the experience was too vivid for that. I could feel my body sore and singing from a few hours of fucking, I could feel Little Debbie Harry warm and purring next to me on the bed. I could taste the gummy wheatberry salad we'd made again and again that summer. I could smell Heather's salty sweat and hear her scratchy voice, telling me this part is the best—there's so much erotic tension. Inside the episode, Lena clearly agreed. As she watched one lesbian graze another's palm with one sizzling, expert finger, Lena dropped her Slinky, inadvertently creating a new time tunnel.

Eventually Sir broke the spell. He'd woken to Alice's voice on my iPad and hopped onto the couch, his stump tail thumping wildly. Then disappointment. He whined. I checked the time. Two and a half hours had passed. I'd apparently watched four episodes. How?

My phone dinged. Alice wanted to know if I could stay longer.

I sighed. Sir let out a heavy huff, perhaps intuiting the situation. I told Alice sure, with no exclamation point. She gave me some new things to do: cart Sir to the park in a backpack carrier, try to get him to eat some wet food, try to get him to eat a pill. I started with the pill. I pushed it into the fold of Sir's cheek, and he commenced frantically swallowing and licking his lips, like he was about to vomit. He spat out half the pill, melted down, a chunk.

I gave Sir some water and he lapped it up, swallowing noisily. On my phone, I looked up "how to give a dog a pill" and saw many strategies, none of which I would have been able to employ had I thought to research them before administering. There was no peanut butter in the house in which to have hidden the pill. There were no human or dog snacks that I could find. The cabinets were bare, with the exception of two cans of dog food and many supplements for humans.

Sir was fine.

When I placed the backpack before him, he climbed in. I strapped him on and felt his weight settle against my back. I walked to the park with new dog goggles on. Before, most dogs had blurred into the noise of city life, but now I could identify some breeds. Ahead of us, a Goldendoodle. Across the street, a Corgi. I also noticed their owners with their fanny packs and treats, subtly rewarding their animals after every good pee and heel.

At the edge of the park a human animatedly hurled a frisbee for their—beagle? beagle mix?—to chase. It struck me that people who have dog energy may also be people who have clown energy. Is this true? My strongest data points are Alice, a dog person who is learning to clown, and Kel, my first girlfriend, a dog person who was anointed class clown of her senior class and went on to do stand-up for a few years before she fucked it up with drugs (she would say). But surely there exist some no-fun dog owners. Like Alice, for example, who interacted with me like a moody cat. I don't know. This is a stupid binary. I just know I have neither dog nor clown energy. (What do you think? Be sure to tell me in the comments.)

I unloaded Sir at the edge of the park and clipped his leash to his harness. We walked onto the path, where Sir stopped to take in a pee stain on the edge of the pavement. I let him lead us to the lawn, where a group of kids was Slinking. Nothing unusual about that—though the show was canceled six years ago, the Slinky's comeback has held fast—but it still seemed like strange synchronicity, me coming upon Slinkers after having binged four episodes of *Slinkys* from within the temporary home of the person who played Lena. It was like I summoned them, or Alice-as-Lena did.

Catching a scent, Sir pulled us toward what looked like a birthday party. A dozen kids sat criss-cross-applesauce on blankets and quilts, intently watching a clown. Next to them stood a table of cake and snacks—what had lured Sir. I let him lead us closer, but he was definitely not getting those snacks or that chocolate cake. Distracted by another smell, he snorted at the ground.

It seemed impossible, but this clown, too, was Slinking. She tossed a Slinky back and forth in an arc above her head while hopping lazily from one foot to another. Finally, she caught the Slinky in one hand and smashed the top of it with the other. A bouquet of flowers dropped to the grass. The party laughed and clapped. The clown handed the bouquet to a kid in the front row wearing a tiara, presumptive birthday kid.

The clown did this trick again, and a clatter of colorful uninflated balloons fell from her hand. She bent down to select a purple balloon, then stretched it out theatrically before lifting it to her lips. She took a big inhale and used it to inflate the balloon. Sir rooted around near a bush, then curved his body and began to evacuate one long slow solid shit. The clown took another gulp of breath, and another. Sir was still shitting. The balloon grew into a narrow tube that swayed in the gentle breeze.

"Make it pop!" one of the children yelled. The others tittered. Some covered their ears. The clown raised her eyebrows. Her face was turning red. She blew again. And again. And again.

The balloon popped. Sir jumped, barking. Startled, I dropped the leash and he fled, the shit still hanging from his butt. He was trying to escape it—which he did, then kept running.

Mayhem ensued. Sir tore through a number of picnic blankets, then barreled through a kids' soccer game, moving surprisingly fast for a Frenchie with mobility issues. Other dogs were desperate to follow him. A Shih Tzu slipped her leash and flung herself after him, yipping. No, Sir! I shouted as I raced after them. No, Sir! No! When lots of confused men and mascs turned to look at me, I was unsettled but used the attention to my advantage. Get the dog!

Dozens of park people were now collaborating in the project of apprehending Sir, which only made him more frantic. As I ran, I fretted. What would Alice do if I lost her dog? I would feel terrible. I would *be* terrible. And it would be worse because she's a celebrity. She'd post about it somewhere. Even if she didn't name me as the one responsible (I couldn't imagine her being that vindictive, but then what did I know about her? Nothing!), the whole story would come out. Bystanders were surely recording it. I'd get identified, found out as an imposter dog sitter. I'd be doxxed, cancelled, my legacy tarnished.

A nearby runner grabbed Sir's leash and slowed him down. (The Shih Tzu slowed, too, and went to find her owner.) Sir panted, wheezed. He looked dazed. When I caught up to him, he took one look at me and barked angrily. I still wasn't Alice. The runner turned suspicious. *He doesn't seem to like you*, he said with cop energy. *You sure it's your dog?* From my research I remembered that Frenchies are valuable and often stolen.

*

I got Sir home safe. I'm sorry I don't have juicier information to dish about Alice Krock. I had hoped to hear about her first day at clown school and whatever new role she must be preparing for. But she instructed me to leave a half hour before she was due back. Maybe she didn't want to pay me the additional $10 or navigate the awkwardness of hello/goodbye again. Maybe she just wanted to give me more time with which to do whatever I wanted. I went home. With my time, I've resisted the urge to binge-watch more *Slinkys*, and I've written this.

[Thanks for reading *Name Dropping*! Subscribe for free to receive new posts and support my work.]

Yours,
Megan

THREE POEMS
Harper Galvin

WHERE WE GO

When I feel you're wet, it's like waking up to new snow which I want to touch only a little more than I want not to do anything that changes it. A world wrapped in a new world whose colors emit their own light.

You said what if my red socks were more colorful, and we imagined colors that can't exist in real life, so bright they would make us roll on the floor moaning.

We imagined how the colors would make us go crazy

We imagined a place that doesn't exist, where I can touch everything as long as I want and return afterwards to the moment we left, as if I never had hands at all, as if my hands were the snow, too.

THE ATTIC

Booby Doo is the movie where a series of villains and monsters remove their masks to reveal they are actually breasts. In the sequel, all the breasts remove their masks to reveal they are villains and monsters. The movie's outrageously low-budget sets and costumes, the massive plot holes and non-sequitur dialogue are delightful to the percentage of the population who laugh at themselves when they walk into closed glass doors in public. Female nudity scares people because everyone is a *Booby Doo* movie, but nobody knows which one. Other movies are made only so that the audience can yell "Don't go in the attic!" as if there were anywhere else to live.

COMMERCIALS HAVE TOO MANY XYLOPHONES IN THEM

I'm angry because strippers are never fat enough and commercials are ruining xylophones. When I'm the mayor, every citizen will receive a free xylophone lesson while getting a lap dance from somebody with an ass that could suffocate them. Commercials for my campaign will just be silent footage of an empty chair, the discarded recliner where I once got fucked on a street corner, because people are advertised to relentlessly, but hardly ever have an opportunity to wonder where all that blood came from.

CIVIL WAR ENTERTAINMENT PRESENTS

Julián Delgado Lopera

It's the middle of a civil war, I'm bored and horny AF. Afternoon a beating sunshine, light streaming through the window inside my room on the third floor of an apartment building in Bogotá. It is the late 1990s. The stereotypical violence for which Colombia has won bloody popularity crowns around the world is in full swing. I've been robbed at gunpoint and my nineteen-year-old cousin Julio Mario had just been found dead, tortured. Women had been fainting all around me ever since.

My grandmother and I watch TV every day together, hoping for some entertainment beyond the usual massacres, kidnappings, and car bombs that already have us yawning. Give us drama! Give us tears! Give us a love that kills! We want entertainment and we want it now.

This week I'm off from school because it's April, the time every year where Jesus metaphorically dies (again) and resurrects (again), and I'm not allowed to eat meat or sit cross-legged or say a bad word because Papi Dios counts it as three times more sinful. It is the week where time elongates, piles on itself, sits on my chest suffocating. There's no playing outside, ever, unless you want to disappear, and even though there's a tearing pull in my chest that constantly shoves me towards the edge, even though at twelve years old I was already a motherfucker with a nervous system clickety clacking on repeat, a high frequency mind activated at all times, and a powerful desire to take in every single detail of the world, disappearing is still in the bottom of my list of ways to run away from here.

Every year, during Semana Santa, the local TV channel streamed footage from towns all over Colombia where people reenacted Jesus's death and resurrection, nails and crucifixion included. My grandmother and I spent said week praying rosaries, lighting candles at the feet of an array of Vírgenes, walking pilgrimages, and watching the live crucifixions together. The reenactment was a way of tele-transporting a 2000-year-old pain and metamorphosis into the present via dusty streets bloodied by Colombian performance. A break in time. Dragging Jesus's hands, yes, blood, yes, nails, yes, moaning, of course, through the time-space continuum into a burning placita Colombiana papá.

It was the time of the year that I felt closer to God. I already knew I was an outcast in the sea of compulsory normal people who didn't seem to want to hump every chair, wear outrageous outfits, and daydream about having a dick and running away. This was the time of year when God was like, my son will die and come back as a new body and it will stream as a reenactment for years all over your Colombian TV, and I was like yes, please.

What I mean to say is, crucifixion and resurrection fascinated me. First, you are an undesirable, misunderstood outcast (but a heavenly one carrying gifts from Papi God). Then as punishment, some hot Romans with delineated muscles flog you, you are crowned, crucified, left to bleed, while a hot sex worker with a mouthful of a name—María Magdalena—weeps for you. Some days later you resurrect. Come back as a new self. A new body. You've unzipped the old body, healed the wounds. An immortal body that changes the course of humanity. What is more transsexual than resurrection? I was obsessed.

What I mean to say is, I am sitting on my grandmother's bed wearing a bed sheet as a robe, Christmas lights around my head as the crown of thorns. Crimson streaks drip on my face, drawn by my grandmother's only lipstick that she never wears. I stare at the 1980s bulbous TV screen streaming the same images as the year before, the same images that will stream one year later: a Jesus parade of people flogging themselves bloody, lashes popping in the background, the sound of whip on flesh, whip on flesh, whip on flesh, open wounds dripping blood, magenta rivers running down backs and legs, a pious crowd of onlookers with pashminas and rosaries galore, all the outfits serving Crucifixion in the Tropics at the Holy Week Catwalk as the TV anchor interviewed a guy with nails hammered on his hands. Face dirtied by blood.

I want to feel what he felt, what he did for me.

With my crown of Christmas lights wrapped around my head, sitting on my grandmother's bed I bite on the arepa. My grandmother's specialty, arepa with cheese. My fingers greasy. I lick them one by one never taking my eyes off the TV, what seemed like hundreds of Colombian Jesuses in crowns of thorns, long brown robes, all walking in sandals or barefoot in some remote town just a few hours from where I lived. Dust. Palm trees. Small colorful houses. Blood running down their faces like a painting.

From the bed, I yell at my grandmother to come, she is going to miss the best part, the moment when the bravest daring Jesuses were lifted in their crosses, fully crucified. It's our thing, we must watch it together.

The excitement I feel is insane. My entire body activated and electrified by bloody Jesús after bloody Jesús zoomed in by the camera, showcasing the depth of the wound, from time to time one of their voices comes through in a moan or a prayer. More than that, I love holding my grandmother's hand, the only safety I know to be true, the excitement we both feel watching the TV together, the fact that I too am participating in this Crucifixion in the Tropics at the Holy Week Catwalk, as Jesus nonetheless, as male nonetheless, wearing my robe and all of my grandmother's rosaries around my neck as necklaces. My grandmother helped put together my Jesus outfit. She dug through the back closet for the Christmas lights and then safety-pinned the robe around me so that it was loose and perfect. It was also her, Alba Corina de Jesús Juan, who worked on my mustache in the kitchen with coffee grounds. Cross-dressing is, of course, a punishable sin in my world. But dressing up as Jesus doesn't count as cross-dressing, or if it does my grandmother doesn't let it show. When I asked for the mustache, when she reached for the crown of thorns, there's nothing but yes in her wide eyes.

The crosses are about to be lifted.

My grandma holds my hand.

We both cheer as the crosses are erected—*ay dios mío ay dios mío ay dios mío*—three or four bodies wobbling, struggling to stay up, nailed to crosses that were sometimes poorly designed. We prayed they wouldn't fall down, rip their skin, not before we had a chance to fully take them in. My grandma and I, our hands inside each other's. I remember the roughness of her hands from frying arepas and how our index fingers looked exactly the same, and the closeness I felt with her; with no words, I knew she understood this to be a moment that would change me. Metamorphosis was possible. Transformation was a divine gift. A few women, pashminas wrapped around their heads, kneeled at the feet of the crosses, placing flowers and candles. My grandma held onto her rosary and once the crosses were up, she led me in prayer. In between the Ave Marías I pray to be loved like Jesus, to be given a new body, to be taken away from here.

*

The next day my grandmother leaves to run errands. I watch the Mexican telenovela *Dos Mujeres, Un Camino* by myself. In my underwear and three rosaries hanging off my neck, I reenact the love scene streaming from the TV, kissing the poster of the 90s all-boy salsa band *Salserín Con Mucho Swing* that I have taped to the back of my closet. The constant tonguing of said lead singer has faded the mouth so that René is puro ojo.

I have memorized all my favorite lines from the telenovela: where have you been! Who were you with! Why won't you leave her! Leave her for me! I deliver the performance in my room to an audience of no one but the poster of *Salserín* staring back in all its silence. Above the closet a crucified Jesucristo, next to a Virgen de Chiquinquirá, blood tears pooling at the bottom.

That's when the phone rings.

Annoyed, restless, pissed that my performance bubble has been burst, I pretend like I wasn't just playing like a boy and put on my girl clothes again, my skirt and hoodie from school.

I pick up the phone in a fit, "¡Qué quiere!" I realize how rude I sound and it hits me that if it's my father calling I'm not gonna hear the end of how that's not the way his daughter answers the damn phone, was I raised in a circus? Te criaste en un circo o qué? Is he raising a fucking clown? For every ungirly thing I do—close the fridge with my legs, spit on the ground, wear a cap on my head—my father says he's going to return me to the circus, that I am no daughter of his. My father is what around these tierras we call a chistocito, a joker. Sometimes my father jokes he's giving me away to the homeless guy smoking next to the church, asking for money outside our building. Whenever I do an ungirly thing my father turns to me, te voy a regalar muchachita. And with my father you can't tell when the joke ends and reality begins, the line is fine and thin, because then he walks up to said homeless guy smoking by the church and asks him if he wants a bad-behaved girl? That one right there, I'm ready to give her away. I freeze. I want to apologize, take back my open-legs, the boots I love to wear, the way I speak like I have no education, like I was raised, yes, in a circus, in that moment I want my father to love me and want me back, then my father winks at me, grabs my hand and says, not today, not today. And then to the homeless guy smoking, maybe next week she'll be ready. My dad, el chistocito. He loved to clown around with my nervous system, roll it around like that, bum bum bum.

And then we'd laugh about it even though my heart was undergoing a massive coup d'état.

I stare at the phone knowing that after my "¡Qué quiere!," if it's my father on the other side he will surely hang up the phone and call again just so that I may reenact my girl politeness—we've done this before—make sure I can act like a good Colombian girl who wasn't just rubbing himself against a boyband poster and dreaming of running away.

Luckily it is not my father. It's another man calling who wants ransom for my father. I get my small twelve-year-old ass comfortable on the sofa, play with the cord of the phone. The man asks what am I wearing and if I know my father is in trouble and about to get killed? Right about now hijueputa, he says to me, I am pointing my gun at his gonorrhea face. If I don't want my daddy killed, I need to tell my mother tell my tías tell my abuelita to drop a few million pesos pero pa antier ASAP because this man is unhinged and hungry for blood.

The paisa accent of my father's potential sicario does something to my system.

I deep breathe.

First, I'm annoyed that I am pulled from my fantasy world of licking my favorite salsa singer in my boy clothes. Second, I am further annoyed that my fight and flight kicked in thinking it was my father (all that adrenaline wasted, for what). But then the paisa's breathing gets heavy on the phone, dare I say sexy, and in between the threats he keeps asking what are you wearing, niña? What are you wearing?

I remember the Mexican telenovela. Blonde Laura de León falling to her knees in a spectacular performance of over-the-top horniness and want. I remember the Colombian Jesus drenched in blood resurrecting.

The problem is I liked to perform. I practiced for the imaginary crowd first, my stuffed animals, the boyband posters taped to my closet, and then I enact my acting: at my all-girl Catholic school, to my grandmother. But I'd never had the opportunity of doing it over the phone, to an unknown caller.

Christina Sharpe describes "precarious" as a state of constant danger. Balancing a state of constant danger. The knowledge that one may fall off the edge. But what if you're not even aware of the edge in the first place? What if you never know you've been balancing on it? What if the edge is home?

But I digress.

Back to the hot sicario on the phone who continues his threatening rant in that gorgeous paisa accent.

The sicario pants and talks slow like he cares about the delivery of his performance, and in between threats he keeps asking me, what are you wearing? You want to see your father alive? What are you wearing? Are you listening to me, gonorrhea? He says the name of some pollo place in the south of Bogotá where someone needs to drop that coin.

The afternoon light falls right on my lap. A stream of golden radiating, warming my dick. I sit cross-legged like a good girl, like I've been taught, but since no one is watching I spread my legs as wide as I can, my ass and dick taking up every inch of surface. Something internally clicks. It occurs to me that I'm still slightly wet from my previous imaginary romantic telenovela showdown with the lead salsa singer and something about this sicario's paisa accent on the phone and the total activation of my flight and fight gets me slightly horny. The living room is empty, my grandmother is yet to come back. The quietness and boredom of the afternoon only broken by the sporadic honking outside.

The first time it happened I fell for it. The second time I fell for it, too. Wrote down all the information of said pollo place, said bank account where money needed to be sent before my father went bye bye out of this world with a bullet through his head. Then frantically I'd called my mother. Meanwhile my father was having lunch at work in his business suit as calm as a leaf, while over here I was already figuring out what I would wear to his funeral because nobody had bought me a black suit yet. At twelve years old I was connoisseur of these types of calls: men who wanted to get some money by pretending to kidnap my father. By this time, it's like my father had been potentially kidnapped so many times it'd lost its momentum. I already knew how it felt. My body and I had enough practice understanding his potential kidnapping, my father's potential death. What didn't lose its momentum was this particular paisa's want. This time the paisa added another flavor to the panic, he wanted me. It was a strange line he's walking: horny and aggressive and potentially lethal (my three favorites!).

"I'm only in my underwear," I lie to the deadly paisa on the phone. His voice shifts and I know I hit a note.

"I wanna lick you," the deadly paisa says in a different voice. Deeper, husky and I feel his voice licking the inside of my thighs, warmer now from the late afternoon sunshine landing on it.

Scanning the living room for signs of my grandmother I rub my dick on my underwear lightly.

What did I imagine could happen? Daily, all around me, the world seemed to be falling apart. I understood the danger, the risk of crossing any boundary with a man I didn't know over the phone: kidnapping, death, rape. And yet. The longing in his paisa voice pulled me out of the monotony, the daily expectation, the routine that repeated itself every evening: my father drunk, my mother desperately locking us in a room, crying. Me, bored out of my mind. What I mean to say is, I was ready to run away with this paisa's voice. I was ready to be taken.

What I remember of that moment rubbing my dick on top of my pink flowery underwear was a feeling. Pluck me. Rip me apart.

On the phone, deadly paisa breathes. I stare at the edge. Dipping my toes in it. I smile and giggle and cannot contain my excitement. I hear what can only be his wrists stroking his dick up and down. A circular wet dark stain on my underwear.

FUCK MARRY KILL

jaz papadopoulos

masks 1, 2 or 3
a french yoga teacher

with an extremely tight asshole;
a beatboxing vagina;

and a sprite, long-haired and leggy.
we barely acquainted because it kept

wanting to masturbate in public and I was a bit shy
for those antics. if I'm being honest I regret

not knowing it more.
relax

your butthole. every day, relax your butthole
again and again and again. rigorous

butthole
repose.

fuck marry kill
butthole diaphragm the strings

vibrating inside muscles
pelvis-tittering groin-flittering

a little deep clit razzle dazzle
your keening swinging to laughs swinging

to freaky fun depending on whether the cohort is laughing
or crying or gasping or coughing or nearly nothing at all,
a soft *a ha*
a ha
a ha à gogo, accordion-pumping
the diaphragm like arrhythmia like surprise
that jolts you into momentary multi-vision.

interruption, the first step to
imagination, he instructs––
the man in the rainbow suspenders.

we rehearse unencumbered path
from impulse -> output. no.

intuition -> impulse -> output. no.
connection -> intuition -> impulse -> output.

yes. the man in the rainbow suspenders
and cheshire cat grin

secures a blindfold over your eyes.
he circumambulates the class,

ties the next, and the next, and the next,
you assume, your ears spread like a fan.

he gives the prompt. something
esoteric. the timer begins.

fuck marry kill
a clown a buddhist subspace. one hour

to press your palms into the cold cube of clay.
your hair knotted in the blindfold and it's unbalanced

over the ears but part of mindful presence
is breathing through the things you want to change.

just notice. ear discomfort, easy
to notice. you press

thoughts away from yourself. you knead. you squeeze
honk honk like if your tits could talk

honk honk they would say. *honk honk* leads you to great
mountainous expressive eyebrows, a magnificent furrow.

your thumbs meet in the middle of the humped slab,
pressing a crease, a dioramic mountain range.

now, two creases meet in the north
surrounded by valleys. you remove the blindfold.

you have sculpted an enormous vulva
which you will now papier mâché into a mask and wear

on your face. *seems like you're working through a lot of gender stuff*,
a friend muses.

before, you'd watch yourself from above and it was dissociation.
now you watch yourself from above and it is the most mindful

presence observing your total immersion in a tactile experience;
the ringmaster––you––spiritually surveilling as you––you––play in risks.

ringmaster you and you you snap between perspectives like magnets:
supervision/immersion. you can snap out of it and use your full brain to respond

to an emergency or give someone an extra sweater.
now, these parallel minds happen often. you're clowning or meditating

or fooling around with a tinder dude knuckle deep in your literal pussy––not your pre-language vulva––enjoying your hanky panky while still supervising

groans swinging to a quick
more lube and back

to groans again fuck marry kill
hypervigilance dissociation a secret third thing.

the trick is to sink into the whole feeling.
to both know and not know you're doing it.

limbs folded
shins kissing
floor. calves beneath
hammies under
quads cuddling
tummy. *a ha*
a ha
a ha
curve of spine
pie-smushing face
down.
black shine
laced leather
boot pressing
into spine,
pennywise plump.
not funny bone
spine.
pump
pump
pump the accordion
glees
squeals
feels

fuck marry kill
ha ha ha ha ha ha

HOW DID THE SUFFERING OF MARGINALIZED ARTISTS BECOME SO MARKETABLE?

Vivek Shraya

The first art I made was inspired by heartbreak and loneliness. I wrote songs about the boys who would never love me, about the beauty I would never possess, with a healthy serving of Jesus metaphors. Typical angsty teenager shit. Like most musicians, these were the themes I continued to sing about when I began recording albums. But when only a handful of people were interested in these songs, I needed to find a way to continue to be creative without the pressure to "break in" or to "make it." I switched gears and wrote my first book, *God Loves Hair*.

When my mom asked me why I wanted to write this book—which details the complexities of growing up with Hindu immigrant parents and my experiences of homophobia, suicide ideation, and sexual violence—I told her that I wanted to give young, brown gender-creative kids the kind of book I didn't have growing up. Much of the art I have produced since has been inspired by a desire to address gaps in the representations that shaped my childhood in hopes of minimizing the kind of loneliness I felt.

What I didn't express to my mom, perhaps because I didn't fully know how to express what was happening, was that I began to feel unburdened. In short, writing—and later reading aloud in public—about childhood and teenage experiences of trauma was healing. Once I clued in that art had the capacity to set me free, I wanted to relieve my entire body and its history of every ounce of pain I had experienced through any medium of art available. I also hoped that if I shared my experiences of pain, my art could perhaps even set audiences free from their stereotypes and biases, elicit different behaviors and reactions when they encountered difference off-stage and off the page.

What I didn't know was that by writing this book and creating subsequent art projects that explored my encounters with racism, biphobia, and misogyny, I was walking into a trap.

When I reflect on my career, it's hard not to notice the ways interest and institutional support (in the form of art contracts, funding, awards, invitations) have increased as I've shared more of my traumatic experiences. While my ability to survive as a working artist depends in part on interest and institutional support, the correlation between trauma and "success" is disturbing. Have I unknowingly been typecast as a trauma clown?

Unfortunately, this seems to be a common experience for marginalized artists: our value often seems inherently tied to the suffering we portray in our work. What is it about the suffering of marginalized bodies that's so appealing?

In 2013, I saw *12 Years A Slave* in a theater packed mostly with white people. As I listened to many of them cry, I wondered if watching this film was somehow cathartic for them, and perhaps even for me as a non-Black person—offering the opportunity to momentarily feel guilty, cry, and then be absolved. As I left the theater, I overheard a couple sorting out their dinner plans, as though seeing a movie about Black slavery was a kind of appetizer. I was grateful to later read Black writers who discussed their significantly different perspectives about the film, including Kara Brown who wrote in Jezebel: "I'm tired of watching Black people go through some of the worst pain in human history for entertainment, and I'm tired of white audiences falling over themselves to praise a film that has the *courage* and *honesty* to tell such a *brutal* story. When movies about slavery or, more broadly, other types of violence against Black people are the only types of films regularly deemed 'important' and 'good' by white people, you wonder if white audiences are only capable of lauding a story where Black people are subservient."

When I consider the long history of marginalized suffering being used as a form of entertainment, whether through public lynchings, the egging of queer people on Yonge Street on Halloween, or the consumption of "trauma porn," I wonder if the demand that marginalized artists repeatedly perform trauma—becoming trauma clowns—in our art is a way to contain and oppress us, politely or indirectly, from the comfort of a seat, hands clean. What happens when the kinds of traumas I have experienced aren't trendy or traumatic enough to "sell"?

The more the pain of people from marginalized groups is repeatedly and consistently consumed as a form of "entertainment," the less potential these images have to effect necessary social change.

In the years since I wrote my first book, when I've pitched art projects that were not explicitly tied to trauma or experiences of oppression, arts institutions have attempted to steer my focus back toward trauma, encouraging me to revisit issues and experiences I have explored in previous projects, because this is the kind of work that they believe is marketable and that audiences are most eager to consume from me.

For example, when I was seeking a publisher for a children's book I wrote about raccoons taking over in urban settings—a cheeky homage to Toronto's beloved trash pandas—the feedback I've received has seldom addressed the story itself or the quality of the writing. Instead, I was told that the problem with the book is that it doesn't explicitly tackle sexuality, gender, race, and the corresponding forms of oppression. When white, straight authors fail to include these themes in their books, is their work rejected?

More importantly, I have already written a children's book that celebrates gender creativity. In "The Circus of Cruelty: A Portrait of The Contemporary Clown As Sisyphus," curator Didier Ottinger observes: "One of the standard devices of the art of clowning is endless and unbearable repetition." Must I keep creating the same art, featuring the same themes over and over again? What happens when I run out of "new" stories of childhood, immigrant or bodily trauma to tap into and share? These questions are at the core of my photo series *Trauma Clown*.

In 2019, actor Jussie Smollett reported to the police that he had been the victim of a horrific racist and homophobic attack. The news of the attack produced an outpouring of support from celebrities and the public. Smollett was later accused of staging the attack as a way to boost his career and charged with sixteen felony counts. While the charges have now been dropped, my friend Michelle pointed out that if he was lying about what had happened, it is a devastating statement about the pressure that marginalized artists feel to perform trauma publicly in order to be valued.

Arts institutions and audiences can play a formidable role in eliminating this pressure. To give arts institutions the benefit of the doubt, perhaps one origin of the trauma clown can be traced to a misunderstanding of the concept of "diversity." In response to ongoing calls for more diversity in Canadian arts, some institutions have been actively looking at ways to add more marginalized artists to their rosters. This is a fine action, but it falls dangerously short when "diversity" gets conflated with "oppression" and "trauma," and when marginalized artists aren't allowed to express stories beyond our traumas.

Focusing exclusively on images and narratives of trauma severely limits representations—and by extension, consumers' perceptions—of people from marginalized groups by failing to show a wide range of experiences, perspectives, interests, and abilities. More importantly, the more the pain of people from marginalized groups is repeatedly and consistently consumed as a form of "entertainment," the less potential these images have to effect necessary social change. And for people in marginalized communities, only having access to trauma narratives can create a narrow sense of their life opportunities.

A deeper commitment to diversification must not only include diverse voices but also create room for those diverse voices to tell diverse stories, whatever they might be. Any argument that stories that are not rooted in trauma are less marketable is ultimately lazy, inaccurate (see: *Black Panther, Crazy Rich Asians, Call Me by Your Name*) and negligent, especially when institutions play a significant role in shaping what audiences consume.

In 2019, Arsenal Pulp Press published my first comic book (illustrated by Toronto icon Ness Lee) called *Death Threat*, which is a meta response to a series of unforgettable hate mail I received. Trauma? Check. And yet, I never felt like a trauma clown while we were creating this book. This project allowed me to turn hate into art, an alchemy that runs throughout my career, and which has been personally and vitally restorative. The key difference here is choice—that I chose to tell this story and to tell it in this form. Marginalized artists have the right to explore our pain in our work, but it has to be our choice, not our only choice or opportunity. Because sometimes we would rather choose to write a book about raccoons.

A WALK

Christina Catherine Martinez

bell hooks wrote *I came to theory because I was hurting*. I came to art criticism because I wanted to know what the fuck was going on, and to find out by which inexorable flaw had I been excluded from the whole thing. There is a love story, between me and several men, and several disciplines, and several versions of myself, some of whom I think were actually crazy and some who just pretended to be. Being too long on a healing journey is one type of insanity. I'm doing my best to sit quietly alone. No grand metaphor here—just leaving my boyfriend's house and coming into my apartment without the urge to clean the window sashes or put on music right away—and feel around inside for the twitch of authentic impulse.

It rarely leads where I want it to.

Last night I had the impulse to create an image of a magnolia floating in a pool of milk. I have not made the image, but I have not brushed it away, either. Today I had the impulse to sew a back stitch of red thread diagonally across a small piece of white cardstock even though I was in the middle of reading an article about the benefits of going on a walk.

I'm going on a walk. Dylan asked me for advice over breakfast the other day. His manager asked his opinion about a comedian on the rise. The way she asked implied that this comedian was on the rise in a way that Dylan specifically is NOT on the rise. He shrugged, said, "he's not my cup of tea," which felt diplomatic. Later that night the comedian was spotted across the room at dinner, a dinner explicitly arranged to discuss the slant of Dylan's rise, and the manager told Dylan he should go over to the comedian's table and make nice because she wants to sign him, and if he makes nice perhaps Dylan can open for him. Dylan declined, and the manager ignored him for the rest of the night.

Did I do something wrong? he asked. I feel like you have to choose between two games. Do I double down on what I really think, or do I just eat shit and play nice?

I think you can play another game entirely. I have been warned about this. I have been told "Play stupid games, win stupid prizes!" by people who have no thoughts of their own. Maybe I like stupid prizes. I often talk to myself when I walk. I practice what I'm going to say in interviews that have yet to take place. I picture myself with the prize.

I heard a successful comedian on a podcast of an even more successful comedian, and he asked her if there was a specific smell that she associates with her childhood. She replied that when she's stuck in traffic in LA there's a blend of weed and smog that wafts into her car and she *mppppphhhhh!* huffs it up "and it feels like home." I felt a stab of envy—like when the person in front of me at the coffee shop orders the last chocolate croissant. Like I'd wasted hours in line for whack-a-mole at the fair because I wanted the giant stuffed unicorn, because I wanted the stupid prize, and none of the other game booths had the unicorn in that particular color, and I inched forward with glee, watching the players ahead of me lose, or choose something else, until there was only one girl in front of me, and she won. She took my prize.

And she deserved it. The comedian on the podcast didn't try to make a point or subvert the question. She just hit the three big buttons that would make the word LOS ANGELES light up inside the heads of her audience: traffic, weed, smog. I was in the car at the time listening to the podcast and took a big breath in spite of myself. *Pffft!* I've lived here my whole life and never have I ever smelled weed on the freeway. Los Angeles is so hard to capture, even those of us who grew up here start inventing shit to prove that we exist in the place we call home. Plus, now if I ever get on that podcast, and the more famous comedian asks me the same question, I can't say weed and smog. It was hers now, signature, like a perfume. I have to think of my own smell.

I once had a writer friend from Canada message me asking for help with something she was working on for *The New York Times*. It was a story about a forgotten starlet and she wanted to open with a description of the 1957 Emmy Awards ceremony in Hollywood. She wanted to say something like, *Jacarandas perfumed the air*, but jacarandas didn't bloom in the winter and she's not sure if there even were any planted around the award show venue that year. So, if it wasn't too much trouble, what, in my Expert Native Angeleno opinion, do I think maybe the air smelled like in Los Angeles in 1957? I looked up a jacaranda map. Then a jacaranda heat map. Then I got angry. Angry at being expected to help someone thrive in a space I wasn't invited into—this was her byline after all, her prize. Angry because she saw in me an answer, a correctness I couldn't access. She called me an Expert Native Angeleno, and I couldn't even tell her what central Burbank smelled like in 1957. I thought writing was supposed to grant me access to my own sensations.

I may have been mistaken.

Another writer told me he once spent nearly a month researching different spices and native North African flora just to write an opening paragraph that might situate the reader in a Moroccan bazaar. It was a commissioned text for an artist's monograph and the artist hated it.

Los Angeles smells like gas, I think, most of the year. Maybe that's just because I'm in my car and the car is old and has no roof. After it rains, we sometimes get a loamy scent sloping in from the San Gabriel mountains but that's about it and that's just where I live (I live at the base of the San Gabriel Mountains). If I lived near the ocean, I might say Los Angeles smells like the ocean. There aren't as many jacarandas as you think, and there's only one in particular I care about, and it's in Penn Park in Uptown Whittier, where I went to school as a child. Before entering public school at the age of twelve my mom had taught us at home, or at the beach, or after a morning trek through the Old Navy outlet at The Citadel to replace our grass-stained clothes at a discount. The Citadel is an outlet mall made to look like an Assyrian Temple. I didn't know the name jacaranda then, only that Penn Park had one tree at the top of a grassy hill that was covered in purple flowers and when the flowers fell they formed a perfect circle around the tree that my brothers and I called The Carpet. If it wasn't too cold, we'd ask mom if we could do school at The Carpet, and I'd lay down on my stomach and fall asleep while she read aloud from the Bible. The smell, even face down in the flowers, was very faint.

Every time someone writes about Los Angeles they are creating a new one. The intellectuals start way out in the surrounding deserts, or the Colorado River, creating an ecological entry point to further their ontological one: Los Angeles is the contingency of everything around it.

Theorizing The Desert, as a literary genre, has done more than the myth of Hollywood to put up an invisible membrane between LA and itself. Everyone agrees Hollywood is a myth and plays along. But start off at the San Andreas Fault, or the Hoover Dam, and I nod like the good student of my own home that I am—yes, that is Los Angeles—even though the latter isn't even in California. I'd be much further along in my career if I could just say yum yum weed and smog and get on with it. I'd have a stronger sense of self if I'd grown up in a place where people didn't go to invent themselves.

A university in LA offered me money to give a talk about my work and they said they'd double it if I did studio visits with the graduate art students beforehand. One girl mentioned that she is also from Whittier. We talked excitedly and at length about our strange hometown; a Quaker village ten miles east of LA, founded in 1898 and named for the abolitionist poet John Greenleaf Whittier, who never even visited the place. There is a statue of him in the middle of a grassy patch called Central Park. I spent many afternoons of my girlhood curled up in his giant concrete lap, reading or sleeping. The Whittier First Friends still meet every Sunday on Philadelphia Street, but Whittier has since become home to a rising Latino (Latinx?) middle class, Catholicism, a Korean evangelical community, skateboarding, lowrider culture, and rockabilly style. In the Uptown area it's not hard to find a T-shirt of Marilyn Monroe throwing gang signs. Richard Nixon met his wife Pat when both were cast in a production of *The Dark Tower* with the Whittier Community Players. Yorba Linda, much to the chagrin of elder members of the Friendly Hills Country Club, eventually became the site of his presidential library, but we do have The Nixon Steakhouse, indefinitely closed but still flapping a large American flag out front. The art student said her family owned a restaurant in Uptown Whittier. I told her my family had been going there after church since I was a little girl. Oh, the place has been in my family for generations, she said. Incredible, I said. I grew jealous at this mention of her deep and particular connection to our hometown and changed the subject. Tell me what you're working on with these multimedia performances, I said. Well, I've been trying to get in touch with my roots, she said. I nodded. I mean my indigeneity, she said, and began to show me photos of clay pots. When I think of my roots, I think of tourism.

I met Sid on Tinder in the spring of the vaccine. We took masked walks for hours around the hills of Los Feliz, where the jacaranda heat map sprouts dense purple dots. He told me stories about being an actor and what it means to be an actor. I liked the firm, gentle pride he took in his work. We talked about books and heartache and how bad Tinder is. He had a cinematic view of the world, not as a form of escapism, but a way of getting closer to it. He read widely and would recite whole chunks of books while we walked. I loved that he leveraged his skill as an actor to be a better reader. I didn't even know that was allowed. He kept tabs on the flow of emotion in the text and used it like a map to chart his insights. Movies are not an intellectual medium, he said to me, bent over the bags of grapes at Ralphs, surveying them with his hand. His manner was gentle, knowing everything around him was capable of response. Twenty-six hours after we matched, he was cast in a Martin Scorsese film. In the six weeks it took to pack up his life and decamp to an apartment in Oklahoma the production had set up for him, that's when we walked. I did not do FaceTime dates then, or picnic dates, or walking dates for that matter. I had brief and intense encounters with other reckless people. One man's opening line on a dating app was, *I want to bring you a roast chicken tonight*, and so he did, and stayed for three days. Sid could not risk getting sick ahead of this opportunity, and I couldn't bear the responsibility if he did get sick, uncast, outcast, as a result of us touching, though I sometimes I fantasized about how shameful and powerful it might feel. So, six feet apart we stayed. I enjoyed, for the first time since I was a God-fearing teenager, visiting the hinterlands of erotic transgression. It had been so long since sex, writ large, simply wasn't allowed, and I liked the charge that hung in the air and mixed with the light soapy scent of the jacarandas, happy they were dense enough to achieve olfactory purchase.

Things were still weird, vax wise, when Cookie and I made the drive out to the Margaritaville resort in Palm Springs. The property was originally called The Riviera, allegedly a favored hangout of The Rat Pack. But there are two more Rivieras just down the road, and little else to designate this Jimmy Buffet-themed pleasure dome as a site of historical significance other than a giant statue of a flip-flop standing upright and royal blue in the lobby. An obelisk, a portent of leisure. In the hallway near our room there was a driftwood sign that said,

The weather is you here/ Wish you were beautiful. All of the decor, in fact, is executed according to the concept of clichés mixed with alcohol. I don't know how much more itself the Margaritaville resort can be without invoking Jean Baudrillard, whose work I'd been flicking through on my phone, the purpose of our trip being to attend an opening for my friend Ben's new paintings at gallery near the Palm Springs Museum of Art. The paintings were all of Joshua trees, which was a departure for him. They seemed split up and Cubist, and even the sky, supposedly open and blue, was shaped into angular areas where it's night in some of them and daytime in others. The press release quoted Baudrillard, proposing that the paintings echoed an idea of the desert "as a condition of extraordinary emptiness that offers a natural extension of a profound inner subjectivity." The trees bundle together in the corner of the frame. I liked them, knowing how Ben usually paints pictures of friends in their homes. Joshua trees have always looked uneasy to me, critched over in the open air like they sleep under the staircase or wait for a blow. Ben cutting up the sky, fracturing the landscape they call home, seemed like a fitting response—or some kind of response, anyway—to all that ecstatic emptiness.

I tried to call dibs on the ocean, even though it's rarely taken me less than an hour to get there, testing a brag on a friend from the Midwest: Oh, I could never live in the middle of the country, I said. It'd feel positively *claustrophobic* being so far from the ocean.

Have you ever been to Montana? He replied.

No. But I remember when Captain Vasily Borodin dies in *The Hunt for the Red October* because he spends most of the movie talking about how he wants to see Montana. Russians in movies were caricatures in bad pointy fake beards. It felt odd to me, tingling in a way, to hearing someone coo about Montana in a Russian accent—it was my first encounter with what I would later come to recognize as a type of cosmopolitanism. It would come to visit me full circle when my grandmother muttered under her breath, shortly before dying, that I speak Spanish with a French accent, and my pride at this could not bridge her disappointment. By the time Borodin dies, you really love him, have come to feel that his fealty to this image of America is touching and deserving of our sympathy. This disjunction of language and voice tapped through my consciousness like the breaking of sugar on a crème brulée. So of course I burst into tears as he choked on bubbles of his own blood, down there in the submarine where everyone has to critch themselves over just to get around. And his last words are,

I would like to have seen Montana . . .

It's weird to me only later that me and Cookie's Palm Springs weekend was spent at a resort built to replicate the beach we had just spent two hours driving away from, that we were there to look at paintings of trees not even found in Palm Springs. Everything about the built environment there meant to place us somewhere else, even though we giggled to one another that we were *doing* Palm Springs, we were really doing it. We took pictures of us humping the legs of the twenty-six-foot tall Marilyn Monroe statue downtown and everything. We did not ask why Jimmy Buffet built a hotel in the middle of the desert to make you feel like you're at the beach. The pool didn't have a ledge or ladders but a white plaster coastal shelf so you could wade in. Sand was scattered all around the deck chairs. Where did the sand come from? The desert? I've been to the beach when it's gray and windy and the water has too much fecal coliform to be swimmable. I know what it's like to have the wind ruin every sandwich, to be shit on by a seagull, to have trash whipping at your knees. Knowing that, it makes perfect sense to go out into the ecstatic emptiness of the desert and compress the idea of Beach into being more beach than Beach itself. Some people don't meditate because they can't stand the silence. We build whatever amount of noise we need to make the silence of the desert tolerable. During our trip, I made time to visit all of the places I tell myself I don't go to—H&M, Sephora, and Free People are all within one short mile of Margaritaville. Vacations are at times, for me, opportunities to visit chain stores that don't vibe with the consumer portrait I've painted of myself back home. They *feel* like home, a noisy emptiness that could be anywhere. Once, after weeks of European jaunting on account of the Venice Biennale, I went into the McDonald's near the Vatican and wept. That's how I knew it was time to go.

On the drive back from Margaritaville, Cookie and I made a game of guessing the names of what towns we were going through. We passed one compound after another of white stucco condominiums with red clay roofs. Each had a name like SOLARIA or IMPRESARIO. They should have a sign out front that says if you lived here, you'd be home by now, she joked. They should have a sign, I replied, that says if you lived here, you'd be nowhere at all.

The desert is a crawling kind of openness. Baudrillard is right to think of it as a screen.

But it is a wrinkled one—it holds our projections, but also fractalizes them. Waves of grain don't stand still enough to hold a fantasy. There is something about the openness of the desert and the way we impose our will upon it that is very American, and I hate that I have looked to Baudrillard to figure this out. Sometimes I hate the way people look to writers to know how they feel, like a little kid who falls down and must scan her mother's face before deciding that it's safe to cry. The French are not my mother. I'll write it on the bathroom mirror if I have to, though my mother used to talk about America's greatness by virtue of French opinion. They came here to learn about democracy from us, she'd say, citing de Tocqueville's *Democracy in America*. She never quoted it directly, just referred to the fact that it was there. I inherited this oblique national pride, and came to theory because I, too, was hurting. Theory became the Shield of Perseus to help me face the Medusa of my own country. I still freeze in the face of openness. I still wring my hands over every personal and professional decision, try on every outfit for my boyfriend and crumple in the perceived vacuum of his desire. And after I have polled every friend and lover for guidance, one of them inevitably says, well what do you want? And I turn to stone.

I'm on my walk now. A woman is standing in her drought-tolerant yard, having been reduced, unlike the citrus-laden lawns on either side of her, to gravel and succulents: a tidy approximation of the desert, complete with larger-than-life sand. She's holding two flaps of cacti in her fingertips like steaks. Her husband is standing on the front porch, laughing. Someone has been in our yard, she says, presenting the steaks one at a time. This one is broken, and this one is broken. That's what they do, babe, he says. Sometimes parts fall off. No, they don't! she cries. They don't just break for no reason.

Babe, he says, smiling less now.

They don't just break.

I'm starting to have ideas again, but they're fragile, like the gummy baby birds that would fall out of the palm tree in front of my grandma's house. I remember watching them bake and wriggle on the sidewalk, unsure of what to do. Once I saw one, still alive, covered in hungry ants crawling all over and into its mouth. My brothers poked them with twigs. I just stared. My mother would come out of the house and shoo us inside to let nature take its course, letting the cat out on the way in. My grandmother's scream was the signal that it was now a bloody splat left at her kitchen feet. An offering, from the cat.

Who's stupid enough to build a nest in a palm tree? Lots of us. That's what I'll say when I'm on a podcast where a more famous comedian asks me about home. I built my nest in a palm tree, I'll say.

VALLEY OF THE HOGS

Bethy Squires

What follows is an excerpt from my screenplay, Valley of the Hogs. It's a classic "rise and fall of a Hollywood starlet" story, starring Miss Piggy. She is swept off her feet by hotshot producer and secret scumbag, Kermit the Frog. Now he's moved on to her greatest rival, the only woman in Hollywood with the charisma and tits to rival Piggy's own: Sydney Sweeney.

In this scene, Piggy is comforted by her DSA-affiliated writer friend, Gonzo the Great. He tried to warn Piggy—about Kermit, about the Hollywood machine—but when has Miss Piggy ever listened?

INT. MUSSO & FRANK - DAY

Piggy is drowning her sorrows with Gonzo, who's got plenty of his own. She throws a magazine ad for Anyone But You *on the bar.*

MISS PIGGY

I knew they were going to recast me. I'm not stupid. I'm just shocked that Kermie didn't fight for me at all.

GONZO

Let me tell you about Kermit the Frog . . .

FLASHBACK!
FLASHBACK!

INT. WRITERS ROOM - DAY

A young Gonzo futzes around with a Rubik's cube.

GONZO (VOICEOVER)

We were both hired on the all-male writers' room for the American remake of *Absolutely Fabulous*. The show starred Kathy Najimy and Nia Vardalos. It was canceled halfway through the first episode because nobody could tell the two stars apart.

A young KERMIT in a Harvard sweatshirt is ushered into the room by future Scrubs writer/serial predator ERIC WEINBERG.

ERIC WEINBERG
Gonzo, this is Kermit the Frog. Kermit, Gonzo the Great.

GONZO
Hey. Hey.

ERIC WEINBERG
That's why we pay you Ivy League guys the big bucks, your command of the English language.

He leaves. Kermit and Gonzo exchange eyerolls.

INT. DRAWING ROOM - NIGHT
Kermit and Gonzo are shooting the shit after work.

GONZO (VOICEOVER)
We trauma bonded on that job, until he felt like a brother. Which is when I made my biggest mistake. I shared my million dollar idea.

GONZO
So, one day, my dad sat me down and launches into this hours-long story about how he met my mother. With way too many tangents, and the last part of the story seemed to be him trying to justify sleeping with my Aunt Robin.

KERMIT THE FROG
That's crazy, man.

GONZO
Yeah, I'm thinking about shaping it into a pilot.

KERMIT THE FROG
Yeah, maybe . . .

BACK TO THE PRESENT

INT. MUSSO & FRANK'S - CONTINUOUS

GONZO
He would end up stealing that idea, about MY dad and how he met MY mother. He shopped it around to all his little Harvard friends and he sold it. And that show wound up being . . . *House MD.*
(*beat*)
It changed a lot in development.

INT. TIKI TI - LATER
Gonzo is going full DSA "what's it all for?" spiral.

GONZO
I used to tell myself that I was comforting people with my art. Something for the real activists, for the oppressed. Maybe changing a few minds here and there with my stories. But what if that's bullshit? What if I've been nothing but a distraction? What if I'm the circuses in the man's bread and circuses plan? The main thing holding back the revolution is that too many people are too comfortable.

MISS PIGGY
I think the impressive military arsenal at the government's disposal is probably also a factor.

GONZO
But if you look historically, things never get better until they get way, way worse.

MISS PIGGY
So where does that leave everybody who lives and dies during the "getting way, way worse" period of history?

GONZO
Oh, they just fucking die.
They both stare into their drinks.

INT. DRAWING ROOM - LATER
Piggy and Gonzo are discussing all the predatory men in LA.

GONZO
Oh, yeah, he's a total sex pest. Fully CK'd a woman he was mentoring.

MISS PIGGY
Of course he is! Add him to the pile, why not? Fuck me for admiring someone's work, right? For letting it, and by extension him, into my heart. For thinking someone who writes so empathetically would also *be* empathetic. What a sucker I am.

GONZO
A rookie mistake, for sure.
They click glasses.

MISS PIGGY
Maybe these guys, the ones who can write with feeling, maybe they're actually worse. Like, they use up all their empathy on stories, and they have nothing left for real people.

GONZO
Well, every character is an extension of the writer, right? So, he's just sympathetic to himself. It's easy to care about women if they're just an extension of you.

MISS PIGGY
You are really down on your profession tonight, Gonzo.

GONZO
You have no idea.

MISS PIGGY
Then there's the whole apparatus designed to protect these guys. You find out one guy is a perv, and that casts a shadow on everyone he's friends with. What do they know? You write them off. And if someone doesn't write them off, then that's guilt by association with guilt by association. The world gets smaller and smaller and meaner and meaner. Until you're completely alone.
She fights back tears as Gonzo negotiates some to-go drinks from the bartender.

GONZO
One more stop! Allons-y, baby!

MISS PIGGY
Gonzo, don't call me baby or I'll have to kill you.

GONZO
Hey, as long as somebody kills me, everybody's happy.

EXT. HOLLYWOOD FOREVER CEMETERY - NIGHT
Gonzo and Piggy are sneaking into the cemetery. They drop down from the wall, scaring the peacocks. Piggy is blackout drunk, but Gonzo seems to be holding it together.

GONZO
Hot tonight.
He cracks open the last beer and pours it over his head.

MISS PIGGY
Why are we here?

GONZO
I want to show you my favorite grave.

They walk to the tombstone for Carl Morgan Bigsby, which is a recreation of the Atlas rocket in limestone. Piggy leans down and reads the inscription.

MISS PIGGY
"The Atlas, pioneer in space, here symbolizes the lifetime activities of Carl Morgan Bigsby. A recognized leader in many phases of the graphic arts. He too was a pioneer." What?

GONZO
Yeah, you see a big rocket grave, you think astronaut, right? Or scientist, at the very least. But no, this guy was a graphic designer. The rocket is a metaphor. For designing, uhhh, graphics. I guess.

MISS PIGGY
Rockets are a good metaphor. For lots of stuff, not just dicks, lots of really important stuff.
Gonzo stares up at the moon.

GONZO
Like escape.

MISS PIGGY
Or . . . dicks.
Gonzo pulls a bottle of Casamigos out of his pants.

GONZO
Rande Gerber himself gave me this bottle. At Richard Kind's sixtieth birthday. I've been saving it.
He opens it, takes a swig, passes to Piggy.

MISS PIGGY
(*mildly disgusted*) Yum, body temp tequila.
She drinks it anyway. Starts to wobble and falls down on the grass. She can barely keep her eyes open.
Through her eyes, we see Gonzo as he drinks and monologues.

GONZO
Isn't there something inherently selfish about a career in the arts? The "look at me, listen to me" impulse? Watching yourself and your friends and family, how they act, keeping it to use for copy later. You can't be there for people, you don't have the time.
The page, she calls! We make up little stories that hurt our feelings, then pat ourselves on the back for having feelings left to hurt. And to succeed in this business calls for such a coldness, a mercenary edge, that a *really* good person can't even fake.
You know I used to be a teacher? Now that's a job that does some good. At the very least, I kept kids safe while their parents were working. Strip away the idealism, the children are our future bullshit, if nothing else, I kept them safe. For eight hours a day, kids were safe in my care. Who have I kept safe since? Not you, that's for sure.
Piggy finally passes out.

EXT. HOLLYWOOD FOREVER CEMETERY - DAWN

Piggy wakes up to a peacock pecking her. She looks around, but Gonzo is nowhere to be found. So, she stumbles back home.

INT. MISS PIGGY'S MANSION, BEDROOM - AFTERNOON

Piggy is trying to sleep off her hangover. Her dog steps on the remote, turning the TV on. It's a newscast from GUY SMILEY, with Gonzo's face on the screen. Piggy sits up and watches.

GUY SMILEY

Tragedy struck the normally happy Hollywood Forever Cemetery early Saturday morning. The body of Gonzo the Great was discovered by the morning yoga class, in the Douglas Fairbanks reflecting pool. Gonzo was the writer of such films as *Antony & Cleopatra, The Maze Runner 2: Still Maze-y After All These Years*, and the Camilla the Chicken vehicle, *Police Suspect Fowl Play*. Police do not suspect foul play, as Gonzo's blood alcohol levels were at what the coroner called "full-on tree-tackling-Kiefer-Sutherland" levels. Hollywood Forever assures the public that tonight's Cinespia screening of *Sunset Boulevard* will proceed as planned.

LOVE MACHINE

Joseph Earl Thomas

after Mamoru Hosada's *Summer Wars*

seems like something
we should have made
happier. In-game, I recall
Delany's suggestion around the sucking of a good dick
as a rather polite
mode of sensibility. ain't everybody else
marching to the tune of Family Fun or otherwise
abusing their AI girlfriends? we could be
beached out endless in the polysexual sea of data
baby. so what you were born with this bomb in your hand,
my "strange" resistance
to the Oak Bluffs residence is just . . . form,
how I wish freaking out
could be mined for meaning, still,
texture develops me a little beyond
the scope of Jack & Jill or just sitting that one woman
on the bathroom sink
for eating. what
was I supposed to do, cry? I am an incredible cook, for which I
apologize never. Life, as it is presented to us
contains hardships best overcome through taste;
we are surrounded by everything except our needs:
helicopters & TERFS,
radiation & repossessions &
homonormative plastic bags, containing,
among other things, the labubu
whose central force—after moe, after market—remains,
pleasure, on the horizon of every gaze: how what you

want is always more than what you wanted,
or heard
through a first reading: meaning to be taken apart by meaning
& so you'll never *be*
president of a corrupt oligarchy,
have the toon world tonal confidence of a *true* writer, but
hey, you can touch something excellent

just there, if you slide your fingers
through the screen

MY BETH FRIEND

Tara Jepsen

Beth Lisick—one of the best women ever—and I entered a play contest at The Chameleon bar on Valencia Street in San Francisco sometime in 2008. I don't remember why, because we didn't write plays.

I think The Chameleon was called something else then; every renaming felt like a capitulation to the tech workers who had so blithely flooded the neighborhood. We pretended to miss the updates. Even now I feel like I'm cosplaying an inability to remember, as though my rejection pushes back against predatory capitalism. Je suis ding dong.

The Chameleon had wheezed along with vibes the outsider 1990s revered: anyone could bottom out there, no judgment. Only a dick would be a dick to the addicts smoking and shooting up drugs ("drugs"—a word only a dick would choose) in the basement.

I just remembered that the bar was called Amnesia in 2008. A prophecy fulfilled! Time is a charred tortilla!

I scoured my brain for the year we entered the play contest and found it on the dipshit's faultline (i.e. my romantic history) of dating an alcoholic idiot, an idiot so alcoholic, really the wig on a wig of a career dating alcoholic idiots. I remember I was still gasping with pain from our abrupt breakup. I thought I loved her, even after I found out she read pages from a published author and called them her own at a Sister Spit reading. She was so good-looking! She was a willowy Métis butch dumbass. She decided she was in love with someone else while I was on tour for a month. That was 2007, and the play contest was after her. So, 2008.

Beth and I wrote a lot of sketch comedy, all predicated on the idea that the earth's original joke was the human body. The second joke, of course, was farts. We performed naked as often as possible.

The night of the show we were dressed in large T-shirts and shorts, a short-lived nod to local laws. "Let's take our pants off," Beth whispered, right as we were about to walk onstage. The way she said it, I remember very clearly, was as though the divine spoke through her. I was raised Lutheran, so I respond to such seemingly blessed transmissions. She pulled her pants down. I dropped my shorts.

"Undies too?" I asked, to be sure; we hadn't trotted our beavs around onstage before. The regions had been abundantly present in our short films and slide shows, but not live, not without planning, not several feet above the audience with its attendant view.

"Yes," she said in the same hushed and holy tone. I yanked down my drawers.

Our T-shirts ended, like sidewalks, right at the southern edge of the vaginal coastline (the vaginal dawn?), so our undercarriages were visible like static-y radio stations, going in and out of view. Our play opened with our personas watching the 1970s game show *The Joker's Wild* in our apartment, so we needed to sit down on a couch of sorts. Our labial folds met with the unwashed cold of two beige, metal folding chairs. The live piano player man, hired just for this contest, played.

*

Carole and Mitzi were characters deeply beloved—mainly to us and, like, ten feminists of varying genders. Most of the world seemed not to care, which was/still is a familiar feeling for women. Beth was Carole Murphy, I was Mitzi Fitzsimmons, and our backstory was we were best friends who shared an apartment in San Francisco's Castro neighborhood. We had one broken Murphy bed that we never slept in, because we always passed out in our respective divots in the couch, worn-in from picking at the fabric and general butt movement while drinking lowest-shelf booze from Big Gulp cups. Details from our infinite mise en scéne included: a steel drum of pancake mix on the fire escape and a dustpan to scoop it out (that way it could also be employed when sweeping the floor—why have two implements where one will do?). We ate pancakes for every meal, and at Christmas every year, we added blueberries. A treat!

Carole and Mitzi worked at Eros, the gay men's bathhouse and sex club on Market Street. They were two people who never judged others, through a combination of philosophy and myopic nesting in their peculiar existences. They cleaned the interiors at Eros, weaving through TVs playing porn to sop up a puddle; among throaty orgasms to spritz a leather sling; across humble thresholds to dust an indolent glory hole; past glass doors to swab the game-y steam room. They were paid in cash, as a duo, and if you were bored enough to do the math, you'd realize they were making about $2.19 an hour (Total, not each. We figured this out during a performance at Claremont College). But their expenses were covered, and that's all they cared about. Details were a man's game.

Beth and I created Carole and Mitzi in the spring of 2003. My brother had died of a multi-pronged overdose that March, in a motel room at the Travelodge on Valencia Street. Soon after, we decided to write our second short film. I lived in Beth Stephens and Annie Sprinkle's attic. Beth would come over once a week, and we dreamt up a story about Carole and Mitzi going on a comedy writing retreat at Orr Hot Springs.

Our weekly writing plans gave me so much joy during that surreal time. How do you really ever understand a person existing in a body, and then not? I remember laughing so hard I couldn't speak every time Beth and I worked on the story for our short.

The narrative was: Carole and Mitzi decided to go on the comedy writing retreat at the hot springs. They were stand-up comics, devoted to the afternoon comedy open mic circuit at Lutheran churches in the greater San Francisco Bay Area. They took an average of three buses to get to any open mic. Carole's dad Carol had a VW Scirocco he let them borrow sometimes, but only in-town, because of the girls' capabilities, not the car.

Carole and Mitzi checked into a room at Orr Hot Springs outside Ukiah, a small town in Northern California. They had saved money for about ten years, all in change, all kept in large glass jars in lockers downtown at the Greyhound bus station. They roller skated down to get it, just to save bus money. On their way home, unfortunately, Mitzi fell with one of the large containers and it scattered all over Market Street at Guerrero. It took hours to retrieve all of the coins and stash them in Mitzi's backpack, but the goal of a joke writing retreat with a working bed and abundant hot springs was worth it.

Once installed in their cabin, the creative juices started flowing.

"If it has tires or testicles, it's going to give you problems," Carole declared in her signature contralto, to uproarious laughs from Mitzi. She didn't have the presence of mind to realize she had read that on a bumper sticker and instead enjoyed knowing herself as the author of this remedial genital-based joshing.

"A woman needs a man like a fish needs a bicycle," Mitzi rejoindered, soaring despite the embarrassing weight of her own prefabricated genius.

I believe we shot Diving for Pearls for two or three days at Orr. None of the guests had been notified that there would be a film crew present during their stay. One of those guests traded us an eight-inch joint for a few meals because they had forgotten to bring food. We called it "the pencil." The only people angry to see us were two lesbian cops from Pinole. They were charmed neither by our comedy nor our queerness. They interrupted as many takes as they could during a scene where I was swimming the breaststroke (the stroke that opens the vagina) past a straight couple having sex in one of the pools. Mitzi had decided she wanted to get pregnant.

*

After the show at Amnesia, Beth and I stepped out onto Valencia and chatted with the piano player. I remember looking down at his warm and smiling face while we were onstage. I think he had chin-length soft curls and seemed both talented and possibly familiar (a wonderful pairing!). He mentioned that he had played piano when we performed the week prior at the San Francisco MoMA as our characters Don and Phil, two gay gentlemen we portrayed in baby blue sweatpants, tan mandals, and no shirts, so that we could push our boobs aside and tuck our hands in our armpits, creating flat man chests on which we drew nipples to complete the illusion of simply being a shirtless silver fox gay man (our wigs were short gray hair). And so it was that we had given the piano player the experience of seeing us perform topless one week, and bottomless the next. A complete set!

Valencia Street was never marred for me by my brother dying there. It was a stretch of road mapped inside me, part of my life in San Francisco, a regular route to my therapist. I had driven down Valencia to therapy the very day his body was found, probably hours later, maybe as the motel receptionist was leaving me a voicemail at home. She hadn't had to. She told me later that she just thought he looked like he had people, and I was listed in the phone book as T Jepsen. She'd thought she was calling his house.

Beth and I live across the country from each other now, so we make meditation dates and share an obsession with the supernatural. Much (exactly?) like our matching skin tags and food allergies, we have both lost brothers in senseless early deaths. Our bodies are bigger jokes than ever. Nothing has changed for Carole and Mitzi, who forever live in our imaginations, the best place on earth.

BARFING UP COLORFUL SCARVES

Lizzy Cooperman

I put my napkin on my lap, tucking it slightly between my legs so it wouldn't drift to the floor. I'd told Caitlyn to take the better seat—the cushioned bench—since she'd driven all the way from Studio City. Her baseball hat had a tiny, meticulous font that matched her personality. I now remembered how, next to her, I felt like a gigantic clown, barfing up colorful scarves. Everything about her was muted, controlled. She was a terrarium girl, the kind who shops at Madewell and switches the knobs out on dressers. She'd ordered a vegetarian wrap. I'd opted for an egg and cheese sandwich that could not be contained by its bun. A little metal tin of Sriracha teetered at the edge of my plate. I knew I'd leave with a splotch of red somewhere. I also wore a splint on my right hand, which made me feel even clumsier. We were now in our forties. I hid my face with my long blonde waves. Her bright eyes gleamed from under her brim.

"I'm moving back to Raleigh," Caitlyn said, taking a clean bite out of her wrap. She had leaning-back energy. I had leaning-forward. Leaning-back is when you make people come to you. It shows restriction and self-respect, whereas leaning-forward is reactive. It's leaky. It crawls on all fours and suggests a history of riding mechanical bulls.

I'd prepared for this dynamic by reminding myself that I always did this—assumed the way I was living was wrong. After the fires, I'd started sleeping on my sofa, which worried me because my mom had slept on our sofa, away from my dad. She didn't use a blanket. She slept with a winter parka pulled up over her body, like a vagrant on a bench. She'd bolt upright when I came downstairs, fabric indentations marking her face. "Why don't you sleep in your own bed?" I'd ask, already knowing the answer. She'd muster a smile and say, "I like it down here. It's more comfortable."

On the days I left early for choir, she'd still be sleeping, and I'd creep toward her like a scientist who'd discovered her on the beach. It was her in her truest form; no front-facing performance. I could finally be alone with her on Earth's maroon carpet.

Sleep also gave her a break from her jarring, thundery cough. She'd sit at the dining room table, surrounded by Jolly Ranchers and crushed out Carlton 120s, playing Solitaire and erupting into violent bronchial fits.

Over the years. she'd developed a repertoire of disjointed behaviors to deal with the cough in public—one of which was to act as though it had come as a total surprise, and that she had never so much as cleared her throat before this. She'd playfully pat her chest in the same way a courtesan might fan herself to attract a suitor. Sometimes, following a longer jag, she'd sneeze over the cough as if to cloak it in another, less fatal, affliction. *Excuse me!* she'd exclaim as though taken aback, blinking like Betty Boop.

Eventually, I was able to predict how she'd react to each cough based on its duration and phlegminess. I became her supporting actor, rubbing her back in soft circles, or, if she ignored a cough, I'd ignore it, too, and rummage through my backpack. If anyone seemed startled by the severity of the cough, I'd act like they were the weird one, as if to say, "What's your problem? All moms sound like ice machines."

Once, in high school, after an epiphany in the bathroom mirror, I ran downstairs with news: "Mom! I just realized, I want to be a comedian."

She took a long drag of her Carlton 120 and said, "Women who are comedians are fat and depressed. Just look at that Roseanne Barr."

One morning, I got to the hospital early and her eyes had just creaked open. "I had a dream about what a good friend you are," she whispered, as the sun appeared next to her bed. The mood was then broken by a nurse who rolled her cart through the jangling curtain.

She never saw me perform comedy live—just once on TV, and I'm guessing maybe on YouTube. When I came to visit her during her final weeks in the hospital, she narrowed her eyes and said, "I've seen what you do, and it's crazy."

MOUTH TAPE

Erin Markey

You are a disembodied hand. There is precedence here. Thing from The Addams family—although Thing has flesh, and you do not. But bare bones seem more efficient for underwater movement. It takes bones much longer to decompose than flesh and soft tissue. Thing would be naked without the skin and subtle musculature on its tubby fingers, but you don't feel exposed, you feel hard and determined. How do you get to New York City via the Great Lakes? There is a map, but you are doing this by feel, fingertip stride by fingertip stride over the silt at the lakes' bottoms, avoiding predators, attacking predators, crushing predators in your grip, squeezing the life out of them, making a fist and slamming it down in underwater slow motion, the way you would emphatically make a point, the way you might fight when you want someone to know that you are right there in front of them.

"Can you please put on the Hostage Tape?"

Reese, waking from her mid-read, pre-sleep doze, mumbles, "I can't find it." She is naked on her back, her freckled belly beaming up at the bedroom's peeling ceiling paint.

"Then just use Scotch tape."

She doesn't respond. Within a few seconds, it starts again. The thick sound of air struggling to move in and out of Reese's respiratory system. You can't focus on the Mexican honeymoon taking place for the two people on your screen. They are just seeing each other's bodies for the first time after committing to marriage in separate pods: two Wayfair decorated rooms divided by a wall made from the light of a trippy screensaver inside of a windowless warehouse.

"Reese, please." You hear yourself in stern mommy contralto. Reese stops breathing entirely. You hear the faraway voices of the fiancés gossiping about each other in tropical outdoor confessionals on your lap. Then, closer, you start to hear the grunts of a piggy, a ruddy-throated, friendly monster.

"PLEASE."

"I can't find it!" Reese wakes, sits up, and swings her feet to the floor. You watch the grimaced Shel Silverstein-illustrated lines of her butt cheeks move towards the bathroom. The sounds of hinges, papers, a gentle pee stream. She returns with an XL box of Band-Aids.

"What are you doing? Can you please use the tape?" Your pitch has shifted, you're in a mezzo space, the understated desperation of a second fiddle.

"I am, I'm using this."

"A Band-Aid?"

"Yes, just be quiet." Reese has drawn some kind of a line here that you know not to cross. You watch her take a pair of scissors from the drawer. The micromovements of her shoulders working and pulled up towards her ears. The resting click of the scissors placed on the dresser. Reese walks back to the bed, unchanged, with nothing in her hands and nothing on her mouth. She picks up a half-read *New Yorker* and takes a swig of canned Pamplemousse La Croix. She leans herself into her reading position, chin on chest. You can already see the kink in the hose of her throat, but you know better than to say one word. You take the iPad off your lap, swing your bare feet to the floor, your butt swaddled in the thick cotton of Reese's large CK briefs and a T-shirt that reads "Penis" in heavy metal cursive across your chest.

You go to the dresser to investigate her handiwork. One big Band-Aid, the kind you would use for a bad skinned knee on a gravel playground, was cut into two. "What is this? What are you doing?" You ask a question you already know the answer to.

"That's what I'm using."

Guided by your liver, which is in its rush hour of processing three glasses of chilled red, you put out an Amber Alert. "This is not going to do it."

"What."

"The way you cut this, it leaves too much space."

"It's fine."

"No, it's not, do you even know how this works?"

"How what works?"

"Mouth taping!"

"What?"

"What do you mean, what? Are you alive right now?"

"I don't know what you're talking about."

"What it is is literally what it's called. I'm going to cut out a new shape that will work."

"Ok."

You cut a new Band-Aid into a shape that makes the adhesive the star, rather than the white part meant to cover a wound. "Okay, I'm going to put this on you right now."

"No, I'm reading, I don't want it yet."

You sense that you have to be very careful with your words, but also efficient. You know she will fall asleep within a matter of seconds, as she does every night, leaving the lamp on, the *New Yorker* on her belly, the iPhone on her chest, the hose kinked, the monster scoring your sleep. You want to remove the accessories, turn off the lamp, scoot her naked body down the mattress, lay the pillow flat, pull her shoulder blades away from her ears, and situate her in a way where she isn't fighting the natural curvature of her spine, particularly the cervical spine. Yes, you know every nuance of how this person falls asleep, when it will happen, and how she resists the inevitability of it.

"I'm just going to do it, it's fine, you are about to fall asleep."

"I'm still drinking water and stuff."

"That's fine, you can take it on and off."

"I don't want it yet."

"Reese, can you please take literally any initiative in this department. I have been sleeping next to you, STRUGGLING to sleep next to you, for six years, and you know this, and I do not have an issue sleeping. Can you be curious about this on your own? Must I always initiate every single thing? Do you give a shit whether or not I sleep? Do I need my own bedroom? Because I will put a bed in that other room again. I need to sleep. I've needed to sleep for years. I'm drowning in psoriasis. Please, give a shit about this. Pick up your phone and just research it. MOUTH TAPING. It's not hard."

Reese picks up her phone.

"And don't just look up the products, look up what it actually is and what it means."

You are so angry. You don't want to feel this way. You regret it. You regret having the conversation that way but you don't know how to have the conversation in any other way that she will actually retain what you are saying. There has to be a wound. But even then, she forgets. You hate yourself. It's the wine. Just solve the problem, get another bed, do what you threatened to do. But you know if you do that, it's just an invitation for an endless parade of guests to come stay in that bed, entrapping you even further, icing you out of the office. You use your phone as a nightlight to guide you down the hall and search for an evening meditation. No. Your phone is at one percent. It's fine. You could get through a couple minutes of it. That might be enough. Because you cannot go back into the bedroom where your phone charger is. You cannot look at her, hear her move, imagine sleeping next to her. You want to threaten to leave the relationship, but you know that doing that erodes the integrity of the relationship. You know because you've done that in every other relationship you've ever been in. The stakes of leaving this one are much higher. You are married. You want to be married. Reese's laugh. Your mom's handwriting on a birthday card. You think about the bodies of the two lovers who died in a house fire, their arms and legs wrapped around each other. You and Reese used to fall asleep that way. You built a home together. It is an exceptional place to be, and when things are good, it is a kind of heaven. Cookies.

You wake up in the middle of the night to the sound of her snoring. It's 2:15 AM. There is a Band-Aid over her mouth. You reach around for your phone and paw at the glass with your fingertips, trying to open the Spotify app. Sleep drunk, you swipe type "White Nosie 3 hour." But the algorithm knows what you are trying to do. You fill the room with static. You try to box breathe.

You see a shipwreck. At the bottom of Lake Ontario. "TJ Waffle," it says on the side of the ship. The TJ Waffle is saturated in Zebra mussels, an invasive species. Little open mouths inhaling all over the boat, inches deep. You are hesitant to crawl onto the boat, it's the last place you would want to perish when you have travelled all of this way. You are sufficiently humble. You are just the bones of a hand, and you know it, but as you find the bravery to finger your way onto the ship, you start to feel gorgeous. Like Ariel, but the bones of a hand. You see her golden signature in cursive at the bottom of Ursula's contract. The contract is something like: *I'm going to give you legs instead of a fish tail so you can go find this guy you are in love with on land. In return, I keep your voice. If you do not kiss the guy by sunset on the third day, you turn into a piece of seaweed.* And then, using a fish skeleton as a pen, she signs in glittering gold ink that is more alive than the document it is saturating: ARIEL. You feel like the ink. Glimmering in the darkness of the water. You tippy-toe finger onto the deck of the TJ Waffle, a little steamer a hundred and twelve feet long. You finger the mast a bit, what a pleasure to climb the mast underwater. You cannot fall. You cannot be torn asunder in the wind. Those conditions already came to pass, and now that the ship is sunk and immobile, sailing is safe. It is a playground steamer. Stuck and full.

You find the door to the cabin and creep below deck. There on the floor of the cabin is a shiny flat little object. Your bones click against the wood or just invoke the memory of how that would sound above water, and you see that the shiny flat little object is a trading card. A glossy trading card. The image on the card is Joey from New Kids on the Block. You love those blonde curls, the Shirley Temple of the band. But then the image shifts. It is Reese. It shifts again, now Charles, now Q, now Tess, anyone you ever fell in love with flashing before you like a slideshow. You know what you must do.

Your bony thumb caresses the sleek laminate surface of their faces, traces their jawlines. You gingerly hold the back of the card with your fingers, but how can you kiss them? You are only a hand. You have no mouth, no jaw yourself, nothing but a hand. And you remember the Zebra mussels, the shape of their hinged shells, the soft dark between them. You lay the card down on the bed of Zebra mussels lining the floor. They are unbothered by the card. And using your fingers, you tug a mussel by its threads up from the thick layer of mussels stuck to the floor. Its shells are open, perfect for a kiss. You hold the mussel up to the trading card of rotating lovers and one by one, the mussel gives them each a kiss of true love. The slideshow rotates through the same group many times and the mussel lips start to become more flexible and supple, like human lips, like cartoon lips, a big bright bulbous heart with a hole in the middle for kissing, and all over again you feel what it was like to make out with all of them for those first few months. The warm full feeling, the melt in the cabin of the boat, by yourself. Lonely for someone and reaching as hard as you can into the trading card with lips that are not yours, but they are attached to you and so you operate them as best as you can underneath the captain's chair, below deck, docked on the floor of the lake. It is dark and you are full. You must save the card.

It's a long way to New York, just dragging a card across the St. Lawrence Seaway. Should you leave it? Will you find another card?

You leave it.

You leave.

It's a big lake. It's a long way. And you have no idea how to get there. The bones are still somehow maintaining the shape of a hand, and you know how to do a kind of walking, but you feel susceptible, vulnerable, at risk. You find a place to curl into a fist, another shipwreck where there is no golden ink, no contract. Just a dark place to rest until you figure out how to keep fingering your way along the US-Canada border to the Atlantic Ocean.

Before you were twenty-one, you and your friends drove to Canada, to Windsor, through Detroit, just to get drunk at a bar together. The legal age to drink in Canada is nineteen. After you had a few drinks, you waited out your sobriety in a casino parking lot and got some donut holes from Tim Horton's. That's all you knew of Canada until you performed at an academic conference with Holly and Charles and Jim at a theater called Buddies in Bad Times. You went to brunch in Toronto and you and Charles started to bicker in front of the other people you were with. Charles kicked you under a table, hard. You screamed. You told on him to the others. "He just kicked me!" desperately looking for sympathy but obviously part of the problem. You had been making fun of Charles. Making fun of all people was a family heirloom: an inheritance. A dried-up oil well.

You and Reese are heading to couples therapy.

The first therapist you had in New York was a lesbian. She had a wife and they were trying to have a child. You did not find that out until after you told her that people have kids because they don't know how to make friends. After failing to pay her twice, you ghosted her and never saw her again. You were twenty-four years old.

VOLCANO

Scottie Harvey

Was Susan really upset because the world fucking loved her? In the elevator up to the event hall, she looked out at the churl of workers, snarled up like summer ants on a fleck of stray cat food. They were here for her. To see her, to hear her. For, to her they listened. *Maybe*, she let herself wonder, just for the length of a floor, *it will always be like this, forever?* From her king's pedestal by the stage, she watched the lights go down, heard the narrator's voice growl:

"She isn't like any other businesswoman."

"So, they want to label me a slut?"

"Because she isn't a woman. She a genius."

"You're damn right."

Her name in big letters, growing on the screen. One flash of the lead actress, the most famous twenty-five-year-old in the world, coy as she stared down the lens. A date for a future summer. Suddenly, the camera peered over the proxy-Susan's shoulder, a seamless fade into a live feed the real-Susan, now. The screen looping back in on itself, she turned towards the camera's crosshairs, herself now the object of interest.

All these looping feeds, delayed by half a second, stretched on endlessly. As a child, she studied all the different universes in the mirrored hallway of her Tae Kwon do dojo, wondering which of all these lives, as they unfurled before her, was meant to be hers. But there was no answer, as the question could only be asked from that one angle; the moment she stepped back, it stopped making sense.

In the room, applause, screaming. Heads turning towards her, all at once. For she understood that the stunt was not on the screen but in her reaction. Yet she could not hold up her end of the deal. She checked her purse for her wallet. It was there, and yet its physical presence did not ebb the rush of adrenaline that comes from the realization that something important has been lost. Susan thought, *do their eyes leave a trace?* The whooping office workers warped into hollering beasts, the champagne flutes resembling improvised weapons, torches. How long had they studied her? How long had they deceived her? *No,* she corrected herself, *their eyes take away.*

In their stares, she felt their desperation for her approval, for her to say, *you caught the detail of my life I thought others would overlook.* A microphone was handed to her at some point, she wasn't sure when. She unlatched her jaw—her mouth open, though soundless—as the applause retreated, patiently waiting in the wings for its next cue.

Susan looked down at her notes, the bleary hand exposing her obliviousness. Phrases jumped out at her from the page, things like "in-house" and "pipeline" and "creators" and "next generation." Wanting to "tell the stories that mattered," and offering "opportunity for mentorship and growth." How "change depends on us" and that "we must prioritize accessibility." All just noun-ified language to give the illusion of something concrete.

A chant began, the name, the one that appeared on the screen just seconds before. On each repetition, the force doubled. The blood ringing in her ears crossfaded into this rhythmic call, her name, her name, her name. She turned to her underlings, all plastered with smiles. They had outperformed her. All the little snipes and jabs they threw each other behind closed doors, maybe the words were real, but not the end. More than they wanted her approval, they needed her pacified. How better than to be suffocated by her own self-absorption? The humiliating belief that her "genius," as they had labeled it, insulated her from the petty pursuit of power.

Susan had been rich; she had been poor (well, middle class in an upper-middle class context). But she would never be a loser. She began:

"I was going to read you a speech and tell you all the ways you have been and will be the future of this company. But after seeing this, and wow, what a surprise . . . "

Susan dropped her prepared notes. The hollow words offered no out.

"I recognize in this gift a request. You see, the Greeks—they understood the point of a gift, right? Take this big empty horse, we want you to have it. And the Trojans, maybe this isn't historically what they say, but—the Trojans took the big empty horse, because usually, in a horse, there's something inside."

Susan could see the crowd shifting. Hear it mumbling.

"Not just the meat of a living horse . . . Um, piñata anyone?"

Someone from the crowd shouted, "we love you," and applause sealed the sentiment, though Susan knew this was a polite way of saying, *what the fuck are you talking about?* She cleared her throat.

"The Trojans accepted the giant wooden horse because of a thing called *hope*. The Trojans had hope that inside would contain the giant horse-shaped thing that fulfilled their desire. For a company like ours: as big as ours, as innovative as ours, as powerful as ours—*the thing we desire* must be constantly defined, and redefined. Otherwise, risk accepting a giant wooden horse in the shape of your dreams from your worst enemy."

Susan turned to her underlings, those rats who thought they could force her hand, to expose her, to outdate her. They were still.

"Your generous gift of this film, this portrait of my life, reminds me that hope looks different for a company such as ours. And to define this hope, to give this hope a specific shape, we must first admit when there's only so much future left."

The cohesion of the traitorous little cell fell away, each concocting a speech with their own unique blend of deservedness-gratitude and unexpectedness-preparedness.

"To this end, there has been much speculation. I'm not an oracle; I cannot tell you what happens when the credits roll on my tenure. But I can say this: I believe our future here lies in our humble origin story. Tonight, you, my incredible CSCBN family, will hear it first, before anyone else on this stage: we will be divesting from divisive media and reinvesting in our communities. By this day next month, we will have opened fifty thousand Cold Stone Creameries around the world."

There was some confusion amongst the crowd. Realizing that most employees had been born in the age of Cold Stone as a media brand, she clarified:

". . . The ice cream stores."

And then she smiled so wide at the underlings that any doubt vanished—she would die killing them, and happily. Susan would not be made obsolete by anyone other than herself.

The room opened to her like popcorn: there was the first to explode with their declaration to Susan's business brilliance, followed by another, and another; one by one, until it was the entire room exposing their tender flesh to this woman, this god, this flame from which the projections flew. Susan had never witnessed such loyalty, ironic that true devotion such as this seemed always to exist in relation to the threat of exsanguination, as if the threat of failure made the promise of life even more real. In their eyes she saw the reflection of herself on the stage, waving, smiling; she wondered what those eyes saw when they went home, perhaps a house, then a spouse, and some kids. A lot of people can look, but not many can see—what made Susan remarkable was she could do both—as she looked upon the mass, she saw what was coming. At least from a certain angle.

*

When Susan showed up at Elfen's apartment, she had to remember what roommates were. Any hope for privacy was shattered by the person practicing theremin on the other side of an opaque privacy curtain.

"I missed you," Susan said.

"And?" Elfen asked.

Susan shrugged and got on her knees.

"Not like this," Elfen said, pulling her back up.

"Well, like what then?"

"I think you need to acknowledge the ways in which harm was done."

"What?"

Elfen looked around.

"You pissed me off. You ruined my kink event by being weird and sloppy and it was embarrassing. I don't care who you are in your real life—"

"This is my real life"

"I don't care who you are in the world outside of us. I don't care where you go or where you sleep or who you sleep with. You pay me well and on time, but that's basic. I can't see you anymore unless I know that you respect me."

Susan looked hard at Elfen, their stupid floppy haircut that just highlighted their dandruff. And the posters tacked on the wall. Posters, the worst form of self-expression, somehow worse than brand T-shirts, even worse than promotional office wares. At least you could use a pen. A poster, what can you do with a poster other than plaster it over the hole you punched through the drywall into your neighbor's kitchen? Posters as self-expression, might as well get face tattoos that say, "here are the things I like," and then list a bunch of things you like. Even worse, Elfen's posters were for projects she had greenlit, like the cursed reboot of that hokey mid-earth fantasy *Izzaruth's Aisles*. The ghostly and atonal theremin music passed between them. Then it stopped.

“Please don’t listen to me practicing,” the roommate said from behind the curtain.

“Heard and acknowledged. Listen Susan, we’re going to have to talk a lot to accommodate that request.”

“But I don’t know what I want to say yet,” Susan responded.

“Ok, well then, just say a bunch of stuff and none of it has to be right.”

Susan took a deep breath.

“Ummmmmmmmmmm. It’s just, well, I don’t know. I guess, do you know, well, you know, so it’s just, like? And I’m wondering if there’s any way for you to, um, well, see, yeah, it’s just, there’s so much, and I don’t know, but I think you can, I think you can, I think, well, I hope you can, you can, if you want, I mean, no pressure, but then, by the end of the day, end of the day, circle back, haha, circle, um, ha, end of day, you know, ‘at the end of the day,’ no, but really, at the end of it, and it’s just, there’s like, it’s like, there’s, theirs, there’s, their, no, sorry, I mean, and I just want, because I just want you to, or I want you to know, rather, that um, there’s this, well, it’s not, so, no, it’s not, there’s well it’s just, um, I was wanting, I wanted, I want, I want, I want to know if, you, um, you, um, you, do you, well, do you know, like, who I am? And stuff.”

“What does it change whether I do or don’t?” Elfen replied.

Susan was flattened. For the first time in her life she felt . . . kind of ugly? Like there was this big bulge in her clothes that only other people could see. A big sagging ass. Something was undermining her, and she couldn’t adjust into it.

Elfen stood and gestured for Susan to follow them and Susan meekly obliged. As Elfen parted the privacy curtain, the theremin player stopped to watch. Instinctively, she tugged her shirt down around her, to smooth out her backside and protect herself from the judgments of this man whose every molecule Susan found repellent.

They made it out the front door and into the hall of the apartment.

“Can something be done?” Susan muttered; each syllable more pathetic than the last.

“I think that’s a question for you to answer. For yourself.”

“I don’t get it. Yeah, I fucked mean. Like, I guess how I could see that I made a fun night feel bad, or scary. The dance of it, we all signed up for one thing, and I messed up the moves. And that makes people self-conscious. But you’re punishing me, Elfen.”

"You have your perspective. Mine is that I'm protecting my community."

"You don't know anything about community. You know about roleplaying. You know how to play a role. Of a master, the one who spanks. Or of someone who cares about other people. But you're full of hatred. You hate yourself, that's why you box yourself out of the real world. You look like a child, so lost in the supermarket it's insane."

Elfen's pale face was now a purple-ish red. Susan realized she was smiling. She couldn't stop the words from slipping out, as though to drown out the Roommate in her mind, the one that said, *you're being a huge bitch right now*.

"You think you are free, but you're reading lines from a tired old play. You will never reinvent, you will never invent, period. You will always be just a reaction to all the things you hate."

Then Elfen slapped her. Like real slap, not sex slap! But then because of the realness, it kind of became a sex slap? Elfen dragged Susan by the hair into the elevator no one uses because it fell once, like eight years ago, and not even that far, just half a floor. And then Susan was bent over in it, sagging ass draped over Elfen's knee, making a sound that indicated—no, there was definitely perk, no sag.

Then all the dance moves came back to them, and they did them there. Susan felt a creeping boredom, knowing exactly how she'd arrive from point A to B, all the way through the end really. Suddenly it all became so awful, so contrived—she was mortified to be relating to this person she had just realized the depth of her resentment towards. Susan jerked her head around to see Elfen's thin wrist raise and flung out a hand to catch it.

Holding Elfen's wrist, Susan could feel the poor thing trembling, bringing out the featherless baby bird qualities Elfen's parents had unfortunately bestowed. Susan turned around to find Elfen fully sobbing minus the sounds. Snot and tears and drool all seeping into their expertly distressed 80s band tee, the wet parts of their skin peeking out from the scissor-cut holes, glowing extra green in the elevator's fluorescent lighting.

A big wave of nausea ran over Susan who found the whole scene nightmarish. She extracted Elfen's other fist from inside of her and stood up. Susan wanted to do something good, to transcend this moment from the muck, find a little god in all this shit. So, she reached into her purse and looked for some cash. She only had thirty-six bucks. *Oof*, she thought, *it would look really bad to hand them a one-dollar bill*, so she gave them the flat thirty-five dollars, with the twenty on top.

"You just handed me a strategically arranged amount . . . "

"What are you saying?"

"I watched you do it. Pull the cash out, put the one dollar back, put the twenty on top."

". . . That may be so."

That made Elfen laugh, which surprised Susan.

"I only ever fucked you because I thought I could convince you to bring back Seraphate the Small."

"What?"

"Seraphate the Small. You killed him off in the reboot."

Susan tried to recall and then it came back to her. There was this one character on the *Izzaruth* reboot that had to be shot separately because the character was a dwarf, but to avoid political scandal they had cast a six-foot-tall actor. The whole series was a bit of a first pancake so to speak, seeing what it would be like to shoot their own shows. They had rebooted *Izzaruth's Aisles* because so few people had actually seen the first series—there could be no accusations of altering its integrity.

"He's the one who got his sleeping roll stuck on a dandelion, right?"

"And then Swarthmore the Raven flapped his wings for the first time after Gondal the Wet used healing magic to mend the break—"

Then they both said: "and the gust of wind from the healed wing caused the dandelion to fly into the mouth of the volcano Swarnee, which was active because of the dark magic released when Izzaruth unsealed the Fourth Gate."

The two stared at each other, in disbelief.

"So, you do know who I am."

"Yes. And I despise you."

Susan balked. Then spun around on her heel. Clicked her tongue. Did all the gestures to mitigate the energy flowing through her.

"Open your ass," Susan commanded.

"What?"

"Now."

And Elfen did.

And the two went through the dance again, this time in each other's roles. Though the beats had become quite stale, there was now this new awkwardness in the gesture. Lines not connecting. Circuits open, energy spilling out, electrocuting them both.

Then they squatted there in the corner, the kind of lovers who fucked as an excuse to share words. Words so precious in their proximity to dumb language, the kind that falls out.

"How were you going to get me to bring him back?" Susan mumbled.

"Resurrection. Like Jesus"

"But Jesus didn't fly into a volcano."

"You must've never seen the real show."

Real show, that bit Susan.

"Why do you say that?"

"The real show trafficked in allegory. I know it was cheesy, the special effects and everything, but underneath there were real truths. About our universe. The things happening here, now."

"Like what?"

"The volcano was never filled with lava. It was filled with portal. To Heaven."

*

When he revealed he had made a reservation, she briefly worried he might be dying. Or leaving her. His keen sense of value served very little purpose in their life anymore, like a vestigial tail. In fact, it slowed them down—she had even told him this once. He looked a bit surprised and said, "it's not that I don't like spending the money on a fancy restaurant, it's just when we eat at home, there are fewer intrusions." *That cheapskate, what a cover.*

It's not that he didn't have a point: Susan frequented places that practically guaranteed a run-in. A night out was the perfect nest in which to lay the egg of a plan, fertilize it. Nothing to be done now beyond sit and wait, martini in hand. Even if no head of state intercepted her, she enjoyed the bustle and din of service. People weaving in and out of each other, the way the busboys deferred to the waiters, the waiters to the managers, all conceded to the true king: the customer. It was her fantastical kingdom, and she employed a benevolent hand. When times were good, she shared in the harvest. If word traveled to her of a dishwasher's unfortunate carjacking, breathlessly the coffer was opened, accompanied by a word of guiding support. The business tycoons approached, bent their knee, and in turn she blessed their ugliest stepdaughters with speaking roles. Those in her court were relieved to know that the check had already been taken care of, and that they need not perform their jester's routine of knowing when to feign their search for a wallet.

He happily drove them in his coupe, the one extravagance that made him truly giddy. Pulling up at a stoplight, men would gape, for once not at her, but at him. His steed so ancient yet neatly preserved, like a woolly mammoth thawed from its permafrost nap. His joy on this matter transferred to her as efficiently as physics would allow; she liked how her gut dropped when he paradoxically sped up for an approaching speed bump, taking to it like a ramp.

They were led to her table, the one that presented the perfect perch from which to view the comings and goings. But, looking at her husband, she said, "no no, we'd like one a bit more secluded tonight," and he smiled.

The aperitif had not even been cleared before she blurted:

"Is it stage four?"

He nearly spat his sherry.

"You hate this place, so drop the shoe already. You know I'm no good at performing grief on a dime."

"Sweetie, it's our anniversary."

With that, Susan eased up. Her husband ordered a quite nice bottle of wine, based on the data presented by the sommelier. Maybe she was tipsy, but she felt this stinging pride watching the way he listened to other people, changed his mind when presented the better option. It drove her crazy, that part of her that took him for granted. Yes, he wasn't like most men, but he really wasn't like most people. He cared about things not out of some studied calculation, or the need to present on the correct side of the issue. No, he had some sort of thing inside of him that generated real patience, empathy. Her mind imagined this whirring blue crystal, gyroscopic in his chest, always upright, magnetically righteous. All this was confirmed when he presented her with a bracelet, a perfect reproduction of her beloved grandmother's, this family heirloom which was nothing but costume jewelry with a stubborn tenacity for surviving the ensuring decades.

"But this one is real."

Susan sat, mouth agape. No one had ever known her like he had. No one had loved her as he had.

"I didn't get you anything."

"Good, because I need a new wok, I left the mine at the Saint-Tropez compound, and I think in this case it's best to have two."

They were both too tipsy to drive, so Susan had her driver pick up the car and the two walked home. That was her real gift to him, a drunken stomp around the block. The sidewalk was like a slow heartbeat, gushing out revelers from bar to bar in spurts. In this anonymous way, they made it to the subway, deciding to chance it.

On the train, their bodies jostled into one another, some kind of public foreplay of a union so perfect that they could share a single coat and still have it be fitted. Strangers around them were dressed for some sort of game, coming or going she did not know, because time felt oddly suspended in this group anticipation of a return to the surface. She watched as her husband made easy small talk with a group of these men, as they untangled some statistical thread.

Watching him talk, the way Susan could anticipate the boyish smile that always followed behind his deadpan, that trailed just far enough behind to get someone good, the way she trusted him always to grant the fool his absolving smile, the way it made him much younger than his age, younger than even the newest born baby, his total innocence, she saw this in him now, and realized that the only thing stopping her from loving him was her.

The train screeched to a halt, exhaled and inhaled, and they were off again. His newest companions had left, and in their wake was a troubled man, ancient in the same unknowable ways that he seemed so new. Maybe he was physically twenty-one, twenty-two, but the way he lived exchanged a minute for an hour at an abysmal rate. The boisterous noise of before wilted as the man shouted. People listened to his words for signs of imminent threat. He bounced from woman to woman, a spoor of epithets. These people did not budge, as any strapholder understood the basics of deflation: look at the floor, trace the liquid rolling to your foot, find the source, and breathe.

When he finally arrived at Susan, her husband placed himself between them, while examining a candy wrapper at his right toe. As the man spat vicious words at her, she couldn't help but look into his eyes. She noticed the burst vessels, the way his pupils lacked proportionality.

The wild man did not relent—her gaze fueled him. She smiled.

He spat at her and charged.

Susan didn't flinch.

Her husband grabbed the man by the shirt, throwing him backwards. He landed headfirst, the sound of his skull reverberating all around the metal tube. Nothing like the tone of that bone xylophone from the Halloween cartoon Susan liked as a kid.

People were gasping, running, clumping into the other side of the train. The man's blood chased them down as they climbed up towards street level. Her husband ran to him, and some others did, too. Things were shouted. Finally, a young woman who had been selling candy pressed the emergency button, and then this stop became the last for the evening.

Susan was stuck against the wall, hands trembling, fingering her new bracelet in the depth of her coat pocket, thinking, *when we get home, I can't forget to order the wok.*

RULES FOR CLOWNING

Ely Kreimendahl

1. time does not belong to you

My cat was about to die. That's why I was rushing home, hurling my enormous purple clunker bike into the jam-packed subway car. I pushed bluntly through the rush hour throng when usually I was so polite, apologetic for my very existence. Today I could do whatever I wanted. I was having an emergency.

Hours earlier, I'd woken with my girlfriend Naomi into an already unusual day, our rituals gratefully interrupted by the presence of last night's visitor camped on the couch, my little sister's friend Jenny. Jenny was nineteen and had just come out, we were twenty-three and for months had been occupied by the gruesome death rattle rumblings of our dying four-year relationship. Every day I cracked open my crusty, red-rimmed eyes just moments before Naomi, taking advantage of the opportunity to stare freely into her freckled, midwestern face, her smoke-choked lungs exhaling tortured, stinking bursts of morning breath into the cramped space between us. *I hate you*, I'd mouth silently, lying there so rigid, trying to discern for the millionth time exactly when how and why I had fallen out of love with her. Once she had made me so happy, so disgustingly happy, and now it was gone. It seemed a terrible injustice, and I panicked in the face of it, resolved to punish her and myself forever.

2. your body is your instrument

But that morning Jenny kept saying, *you guys are so cute*. She inspired us, grinning her huge hopeful smiles and feverishly underlining in a book called *Woman: An Intimate Geography*. We got really into it, happily embodying her elaborate projections of a glorious queer adulthood.

Naomi slung her arm around my waist and lit my cigarette; I made coffee for all three of us and thoughtfully sprinkled cinnamon into the grounds, making my tiny apartment smell like a Dominican bakery. I listened to Naomi enchant Jenny with her long-winded monologues about poetry and politics, and I bustled around the kitchen trying not to roll my eyes, made toast, scrambled some eggs. I brought them their plates and sat with my knees touching Naomi's, and she made some awful sexy lesbian joke about what she would be eating later. *Badum-ching.* I was horrified but played along for Jenny's benefit.

The truth was we didn't have sex at all anymore. Naomi still wanted to, but I couldn't. My body kept rejecting her in the strangest ways, becoming insanely ticklish or shivering uncontrollably every time she touched this soft spot in the middle of my back. Even worse was when she'd try to go down on me. I would start laughing hysterically and wouldn't be able to stop, my bottom lip shaking with determination, a righteous little soldier jiggling its truth, refusing participation in my desperate charade. It really hurt Naomi's feelings. Eventually I would bite my lip and try as hard as I could to dissociate, this was the best goal I could muster, just leaving my body completely.

Naomi was this really humorless second-wave type feminist. She systematically subjected me to her self-righteous tirades on *female empowerment* and then shamed me for asking her to dominate and debase me a little. In the beginning I tried to inspire her to slap me around or at least try fucking me with a strap-on, but she would inevitably freak out and get all puffed up about it, hotly suggesting that if I wanted to be fucked with a dick, why didn't I just sleep with a man and blah blah blah snore snore. *I just cannot be a part of that*, she shrieked. *I love you so much. Why would you want me to be a part of that?* She would get really shrill. *Fine, I guess I don't*, I grumbled. I had organized my whole life around her, moved to New York City because I thought she would want to come, too, and now I was sentenced to sleep next to her for eternity, this girl who just wanted to listen to Jeff Buckley and gaze meaningfully into my eyes while she ate my pussy. I rolled over and forced myself to sleep, fantasized about hacking the bed in half with a gigantic dirty chainsaw.

But I need to tell you about my cat, this beautiful fat gray tabby named Madeline. I found her on Craigslist, this young girl was moving to Sacramento and couldn't take her on the cross-country train ride, and she was just completely bereft. Her posting had all these capital letters, exclamation points. By the time I got to her crappy apartment I was distressingly awash in the knowledge that I wasn't at all well-adjusted enough to be adopting an animal, a warm panic steadily rising as I clutched the torn bag of leftover cat food to my chest and attempted nodding responsibly, *yes, yes, uh huh uh huh*. Madeline hid under the bed the whole time. Quick glimpses informed me she looked something like an engorged science-fiction rat.

I was scared of her. I didn't have a whole lot of experience with animals. The previous two nights I'd been plagued by really graphic dreams of murdering her, one particularly terrible in which I strangled her little neck, calmly twisting matted fur in my bare hands into the rusty sink, watching streams of clotting blood run efficiently down the drain. I woke all sweaty and burst from my bedroom, catapulting to the coffee pot where I scooped beans into the grinder, my mouth a thin tight line.

I have always been afraid of killing someone, of smoothly and unexpectedly transitioning into one of those feral children who can't stop masturbating in public because they were locked in a basement their whole lives, can't stop hollering incoherently and drooling and maniacally humping the staircase. I just didn't trust myself with anything. But I wanted so badly to be someone who would feel comfortable adopting a cat, being responsible for a life besides my own.

Turned out Madeline had kitty HIV. I learned this at the end of the casual hallway adoption, standing awkwardly at the precipice of this girl's door. A neighbor flung out of his apartment and demanded, *are you adopting that cat??? Make sure you don't have any other cats, she has AIDS. Did she not tell you that cat has AIDS!?!* He looked indictingly at the waify, heartbroken Craigslist girl who'd just tenderly placed Madeline into my arms, and slammed his door shut in front of him, an action oozing with contempt.

She stared down at the floor, terrified and humiliated, like I had just caught her taking a shit in her sock drawer. *I'm so sorry*, she cried, *I didn't think you'd take her if you knew!* She crumpled inward like the saddest used tissue. *That's fine*, I said, scratching Madeline's ears exactly like she'd instructed me to, a signal nothing had changed. Honestly, I felt sort of relieved. If it didn't work out, maybe she would die soon. Plus, I had been hoping to become a person who could manage a cat. Maybe now I could become a person who could manage a cat with AIDS.

But what happened is I fell in love with Madeline instantly, tasting morsels of reprieve from my fear that I was an evil animal killer, a latent sociopath with a dark rotten core, a shell of a person incapable of doing anything besides lying and waitressing. We became a team; me and Madeline against my girlfriend. I shamelessly used her as an excuse to not have sex. *Madeline doesn't want to get off the bed*, I whined. *I can't fuck you with her just lying here, it's too weird*. I rubbed her soft belly, and she offered my palm the tiniest sandpaper lick. She looked so peaceful, uncomplicated and tender. *I don't want to hurt her feelings*, I'd conclude. I was happy I was a grown-up and could welcome her into my bed. I wasn't raised by animal people. The poor, mistreated childhood dog my sister and I had begged for was often confined to our laundry room, denied true membership into our family. *She is a cat*, Naomi would snap, turning her frustrated body to the wall with an exasperated sigh. Free from Naomi's gaze, I could finally smile easily and welcome Madeline onto my soft stoner belly, kiss her nose, and fall right asleep.

4. you exist to fail, and fail again

On the morning of Madeline's demise, Naomi and I had plans. We were going to take Jenny into the city, go to our coffee shops, lay in the decaying brown grass in Tompkins Square Park and eat giant orange triangles of bubbling greasy pizza. But Madeline was breathing laboriously and slumped heavily outside my bedroom door. She wasn't eating, her bowl of beige crumbles just sitting there untouched all morning. She seemed lethargic and depressed, just deeply, globally pained and uninspired. I could relate. *I know sweetie*, I whispered, *I know*. I wanted to inject myself into her fur, occupy her inside layer like one of those Russian dolls. I had nagging thoughts that I shouldn't leave her, but didn't linger in them. I couldn't. I was twenty-three and she was the only thing I loved, and she had to be okay, plus I had this whole fake day to go live out. *Bye, Maddy*, I hollered with a falsely easy bravado, leaving her to my empty apartment and chain-smoking roommate Krista, who was currently strapped to her own school of depression, drooped permanently on my parent's old couch watching *Degrassi Junior High*. It was she who called me hours later, interrupting my romantic day of lies. *You need to come home right now*, she said.

By the time I ran up the stairs and flung open the door, Madeline was dead. Krista was sitting on the floor beside her, carefully watching the door for my arrival, smoking. She hadn't wanted me to walk in and see her lying there, so she'd kept vigil in the long hallway, covering Madeline with a fraying white sheet, the tiniest suggestion of a former living being poking from under it. There was this sea glass green ashtray we'd had since college sitting placidly next to Madeline's corpse. I wasn't a crier, generally lugged landfills of unshed tears with me daily, cheeks pressured and bloated like teardrop purgatories. But I walked into that whole awful scene and erupted, letting years of hot, gorgeous tears finally push through. I clung desperately to Krista, my dear old friend I'd also enlisted to move to the city with me and then immediately neglected once we got there, abandoning her safe and genuine love for my masochistic relationship and burgeoning addictions.

Krista was really alone. Her dad was dying of cancer, and I'd left her home with my sick cat, had thoughtlessly let Madeline die in her arms. The cruelty of my obliviousness didn't occur to me then; I just collapsed into her scaly, soothing embrace, wiping snot on her familiar plaid bathrobe. It felt good to have something tangible to cry over. We clutched each other tightly beside Madeline under that terrible sheet. I felt so Shakespearean. I lifted the worn fabric and saw her tiny skull, contorted jaw, mouth full of sharp and miniature teeth. She looked scary, like a little monster, all the life pumped out of her, a deflated toy.

5. everybody loves a clown, until they don't

Suddenly I reached my feeling threshold and couldn't sit there anymore. I abruptly detached myself from a bewildered Krista and a still, frozen Madeline on the hallway floor, moving swiftly and businesslike to the couch while Jenny stood helplessly in between us. I'd forgotten she was even there. I felt possessed. Lit a cigarette, defiantly punched Naomi's number. After I'd gotten Krista's call but before beginning my desperate tear from the train to my apartment, Naomi had declared she would go home, too. *Madeline is a tough old pussy*, she cracked. *She'll be fine*. I stared coolly at her, betrayed. *I need to be alone*, she repeated plainly. *Call me if you need*.

If I need. We'd recently gotten into a 3:00 AM screamfest that loomed over us like a cartoon storm cloud. Naomi felt suffocated by my need for her, *needlove*, she called it, and she'd proposed something beyond reasonable, that we limit our time together to three or four days a week. I lost my entire mind, yanked on my hair and cried, *how could you want to impose a structure on our love, Naomi, it's love, what the fuck is wrong with you???* I was insane. She made me so miserable but I just couldn't let it happen. My insides were this pulsating shredding thing, a confused and heartbroken machine determined to equalize our suffering; plus, I hated being alone.

Naomi picked up on the fourth ring, sounding tinny and far away. *Madeline is dead*, I reported. Naomi sighed, *Do you need me to come over?* I gave her a second to apologize for even asking such a thing, to erase it with something acceptable like, *Oh my god I'm so sorry babe, are you okay I'll be right there*, but there was only thick silence, the hint of her deep, afflicted drag on a Camel Light. *Yes*, I said. *Now*.

She lived right down the street, an equally suffocating and filthy apartment I was constantly trying to wrestle her from. We hung up. I smiled a weak, sick smile, started packing my pipe with sticky green weed, poured cheap red wine from the gallon jug into my favorite coffee cup, all the way to the brim. I gulped compulsively, filled the room with my thick white clouds, sat empty and still as an ancient deity, staring blankly at the scuffed walls, sloppily painted in cheap landlord beige. I wondered how many cats had died in this apartment. How many hearts broken here, how many lives wasted.

6. your power is stillness & silence

Jenny shuffled through her college feminism book and looked disturbed. I didn't care anymore. I smoked and drank and started seeing Madeline's tiny dead body everywhere, in the pillow on my floor, Jenny's knee, my high school theater club sweatshirt draped over the kitchen chair. She was still lying in the hallway. What do you even do with a dead animal?

I would figure it out later. Right now, I just wanted Naomi to see her like that. To see what she had made me come home to alone. My sweet dead AIDS baby, adopted to prove to myself I could care for something, anything, to ensure that I was capable of love. I lit another cigarette, massaged my aching jaw. Waited for my girl's familiar knock on the door.

CLOWNS, DRAG, AND GENDER

Jones

It is a ritual. I transform with every stroke of color, pulling a bright blue line from the tip of my nose over the crest of my forehead before spearing downward and across, shading in dark navy curtains lined in pearlescent trim. The eyes are huge, ombré, a thick black line accentuating a heavy set of false wings. A curling mustache crusted in tiny, cheap diamonds. Sparkle, dust. The eyebrows have been penciled in anew, high and sharp over the ghosted outline of their daytime counterparts. Cheeks are cuts of pink glass. The lips have been enlarged. They sit like maroon spotlights and will command an entire room by their movement alone. The voice will not be needed.

Color hardens beneath a cloud of spray-on glue, and certain things are taped flat. Pulled taut. Padding fills out the fantasy. Leather comes next. Or silicone, or lace, or cotton, or tulle. Sometimes, something rubber. Rhinestones, glitter, paint. Platforms hooked on a dagger. Six inches gained here, there. Snap-in teeth, fistful of claws. Don a periwinkle suit stoned to the tits. There are trapdoors in the seamlines. Surprises hinge on an impatient spring. The belt is an old scarf. The props are papier-mâché, headlines gummed together in a stiff shell patiently drowned in buckets of green paint.

Layer by layer, the real is undone.

Layer by layer, the fantasy manifests, discarded curls left in its wake as I straddle the Uber seat and try not to crush my plastic balls. Absurdity catches my eye in the tinted glass. Drag is a nonsense, not a delusion. I will get there long after I have arrived.

The queering of my gender largely took place through drag. If gender is social construct solidified through daily acts of expression, drag is a performance of ungendering. Clowning erases it entirely. The playfulness and principles of fun promoted through both protest the strict, sometimes deadly, expectations of society, which are invariably bisected by gender. I've kinged, thinged, queened, and clowned plenty of times, too, and each experience of erasing or amplifying gender has had its hand in unleashing mine. It's the process of manifesting a fantasy that shifts the sense of self. When we step on stage and the crowd *fucking loves it*, that change starts to take root.

Clowns and drag artists craft works of ridicule anchored in a sense of play. Exaggeration is our essential tool. Oversized props and inflated makeup imbue the act with a sense of absurdity, priming the audience to assume all other pretexts of normalcy have been disbanded. Nothing here is to be taken too seriously. With drag, these features often point directly to the hallmarks of gender. Tits ballooning beyond the bra, nipples intimidatingly taught. Dicks that dangle by the knee and tinkle with a clutch of silver bells. Fake eyelashes and purple mustaches. The joke is on gender. But sometimes, as is the case with clowns, the joke is put on gender by eliminating it entirely. Drag performers and clowns relate through our ostentatious, purposeful departures from the binary. We meet when things get stupid.

Experimental, straight-up silly acts like ours welcome the creative springboard of error. Whether our idiocy is planned and practiced, or we are responding to a real mistake, clowns and drag artists both work from a state of play. We invariably extend this invitation to the audience, prompting interaction and adjusting the narrative as we negotiate the energetic peaks of the show, the whole room working in tandem to climax on the same comedic beats. Play necessitates a belief that we are all on the same side here, that success is marked not by flawless execution but a collective sense of joy. It embraces failure as another opportunity for fun. When I step on stage, I must release myself into the hands of my routine, moving in flux with the moments I've practiced and the sudden drop into a split I never planned, any misstep forcing me to lean into the mistake and make it funny, make it *work*. I tend to blossom in these moments, my consciousness squeezed to a horizon line between intuition and action, an ecstasy for someone as chronically anxious as I am. Practice is not what makes an act perfect. Performing requires an instinctual finger glued to the show's pulse, a trust that the body is in tune and the audience is onboard. It's a covenant with failure, an exorcism of shame. This makes us masters of fear, both yours and ours.

Over years of stuffing my crotch and redrawing my body, taking the stage each time in this costume of absurdity, of ridicule, I have stepped into a state of constant play. Gender clashes or disappears on my body. The fantasies run on a carousel. Even outside of drag, I have taken to this idea of clothes as costumes, of makeup as a mask—not because I want to disguise myself or be someone else, but because *it is fun*. Clowns, drag stars, and many queer folk actively step into this zone of play. We strip down to the meat sack and build it back up with the sole objective of joy. Why not have a butt as big as Mars? Why couldn't a bow tie double as a waterspout? What's to stop us, any of us, from wearing polka-dot pants? It. Does. Not. Matter. And damn, it really does.

When we cling to a particular version of our projected selves, carefully building a narrative of who we are through how we look—how we are *supposed* to look—unwilling to experiment and fail, to look stupid or unattractive, we negate the natural multiplicity of being. Nothing is stagnant. Nothing is certain. We are all performing all the time, moving through input and output, negotiating our place in this world, and adapting to the response. This is inescapable. But when we engage with nonsense, when we let our fantasies rip and pour into new, handcrafted forms, we expand our sense of self and become active participants. We remember how to play. Fuck a careful narrative. Let's get messy ourselves. Let's continually pivot into joy, pirouetting through riots of color, texture, sound, pressure; clashing, reacting, building, and bulldozing. Living is a profound absurdity. Realness is a slippery eel. It is enough to feel you have a hand in making it.

Eventually, though, we are all bound to take a shower. The costume must be painstakingly removed, suits unzipped and headpieces detangled. Shampoo methodically worked against the glue. Bobby pins *clink, clink* (*clinkclinkclinkclinkclinkclinkclinkclink*), *clinking* against the porcelain tub. Soap cuts through color. The mask slowly melts away, flooding down the neck, the torso, diluted to pale rivulets by the time it hits the feet, rhinestones like little pebbles caught in the torrential rush. The tape comes off. I stain everything. Beyond the plastic liner, my partner works the vacuum in precise, diligent lines up and down our apartment, lest the cat start shitting glitter.

The character comes undone.

Layer by layer, the real returns.

I imagine the clown honks that red nose one last time, a final, mournful squeak, the sound a little wet around the sides. I think of all us performers, color splotches and stubborn streaks, wigs in a heap, props stowed in broken trunks, brushes in the sink, makeup back in the overstuffed bag. Remains. Residuals. I'll step out of the shower steaming, pack on a luxury of creams, and pray my skin forgives me.

But, alas, I am absorbent.

THE FOOL AT THE DRAFT BOARD

Kate Bornstein

Michelle Tea asked me to submit a CLOWN story. She knows me all too well. I'm very old now, and over the course of my life I've lived a whole lot of CLOWN stories. This one is particularly fun, because this is a CLOWN story in which my clowning around got me out of active duty in the Vietnam war, and so probably saved my life.

*

I was still deep into my anorexia in 1969 when I arrived at graduate school at Brandeis, just outside Boston. It wasn't called anorexia then, not for boys. Anorexia was for girls. For me, the doctors kept calling it anemia, and it kept me in and out of the hospital. It also kept me out of the Army. I'd grown my hair long, and I wore sandalwood beads over flowered shirts, suede vests, and striped purple bell-bottoms over groovy Frye boots. I wore a flowered headband around my shoulder-length hair. Skinny as I was, when I looked into the mirror, I could almost see girl.

I'd just begun my postgraduate studies in acting when the draft notice arrived. I didn't know much about the politics of the Vietnam War. I was too busy rehearsing, fucking, or getting stoned. I knew it was fucked of the United States to be overseas, meddling in someone else's country, burning it to the ground. I was expecting my draft notice, and I wasn't scared when I got it. I had a plan: I was an actor. I knew I could lie my way out of it, and I knew I could get a lot of help doing that.

Theater people help each other out, and my acting teachers helped me devise a subtle act of madness. The night before my draft physical, some girlfriends of mine helped me shave off all my body hair—there was a lot, so it took a long time. We invited other theater people; we all got stoned and called it a happening. My skin was red and raw when we finished, and my lady friends rubbed me head to toe with a homemade patchouli-scented lotion. I couldn't stop touching myself, I was so soft.

The next morning, I brushed my shoulder-length hair all shiny. I pulled on my tight purple pinstripe bells and my brightest paisley shirt. I smelled like a girl. Skinny me, that's who I was at 8:00 AM, when I was standing in the boys' locker room of a local high school gym with about a hundred other young guys who'd been called in for their draft physical.

A sergeant ordered all of us to strip down to our skivvies, leave the locker room, and line up on the basketball court in alphabetical order. I took off my shirt and pants like everyone else and took my alphabetically correct place in line.

"You there, naked boy!"

I smiled dreamily at the red-faced sergeant, just the way I'd been coached. I wasn't wearing any underwear.

"Get your skivvies on, boy!"

"I don't wear underwear," I explained patiently in a soft voice. "It chafes."

The entire draft physical process ground to a halt for the five or six minutes it took for the US Army to decide what to do with me. They ordered me to walk through my physical wearing my low-slung unisex striped purple bells. All the soldiers and other draftees wore some version of white underpants or olive-drab Army uniforms. I alone was colorful. In this avatar, I strolled from station to station, where I was poked, prodded, quizzed, measured, and queried—every square inch of soft-skinned, sweet-smelling me.

At the last stop, I told the psychiatrist about the dream I'd had all my life—the one where I get turned into a girl against my wishes.

"In this dream," I told him truthfully, "I live in a country of all men." I told him that in my dream, there was a country of all women, and the two countries/genders had been at war with each other for an awfully long time—as long as anyone could remember. I wasn't lying. It was a recurring dream.

"For the first time in years," I told the psychiatrist, "a truce has been called. I'm being sent over to the women's side. They've tied me down to a roughly hewn wooden cart."

"And why is that, young man?"

"I'm a peace offering," I breathed. "They're gonna make me into a girl."

The doctor glanced down with what seemed to me to be a wistful look at the waistband of the girly jeans hugging my flat, hairless boy hips. A cloud of patchouli encircled us.

"I'm worried," I told the doctor.

"Why are you worried?"

"Am I going to be able to eat my macrobiotic diet while I'm in the Army?"

My medical records were filled with bouts of anemia, which would support my macrobiotic lifestyle claim if he were to ask for proof. But instead, this doctor looked me in the eye—like he was good daddy—and said,

"Son, the Army doesn't want you."

He gave me a psychiatric draft deferment, designation 1-Y.

I asked him for his name and address, and my father sent him a box of cigars.

From *A QUEER AND PLEASANT DANGER* by Kate Bornstein

MY SO-CALLED CLOWN LIFE

Deez Nutzian

I am one thousand percent natural clown. Not a professional by any means, but clown is who I am, and clown is the company I keep. I am a natural clown and a product of my environment. My clown origins: just a real fat weirdo hailing from Berkeley, California, where they used to have a parade, "How Berkeley Can You Be," which translated to weird and wacky and hippie. My parents were in the midst of financial ruin after trying their hand at a non-hippie life aimed towards capitalism but failing miserably. I emotionally ate myself through this transition and was staunchly THE fat kid at school. It was a challenge to dress myself because we had no money, and I tried my best to piece together anything that might fit my body in those pre-size-inclusion days, the "anything" coming from a free box or thrift store or my dad's closet. Unfortunately, my mom always hovered around ninety pounds, so of the closets it had to be Dad's to build these clown-fits from.

Entering public school during this time I was a strange, hand-me-down clown that could not hide, as I had experienced puberty early and was the biggest in the class. It was a fairly harsh entry after my brief stint in a hippie school we could not actually afford. On top of all of it, I am Armenian, and was around profoundly, overwhelmingly non-Armenians in the Bay Area. The Armenian thing adds another level to my clown look. I looked way different than anyone and definitely did not have a crew. Often, even the tiniest bit of makeup can quickly venture you into the realm of drag/clown. Really, being a clown was foretold in the stars. I was just drawn that way.

The era I grew up in was by far one of the most clown decades of them all, the 80s. Wacky would probably be about the best way to describe the vibe; surely you have experienced the movies and television. Some of my early, significant cultural clown inspirations were Rainbow Brite, Strawberry Shortcake, My Little Pony, Punky Brewster, Cyndi

Lauper, hair metal bands, and Prince. In Berkeley there was always a hippie influence to all the normal clown activities. There really was a famous Grateful Dead clown that, besides having a Ben and Jerry's ice cream flavor named after him, had a summer camp called Camp Winnarainbow, where the kids learned to walk on stilts in nature. My hometown was an alternate universe of art cars and children named after seasons who maybe only started wearing shoes to school when they entered the double digits. As I moved from weird kid to weird nerd, witnessing and experiencing grunge and 90s, alternative staples ended up being a bridge to the most ultimate clowns of all, who continue to shape me to this day: punk rockers.

Punks are the biggest, most profane clowns to ever exist. Who else besides clowns had hair that color, bursts of exaggerated emotion, loud weird shit, climbing in garbage cans, showing up with their trash treasures, decorating the house with them, decorating themselves with repurposed whatever-the-fuck?

Some clown moments I experienced deep in the teenage punk years were: a stick of vegan butter in the pit; the prank of a rigged, whiteout snowstorm of plastic spoons raining down, Carrie-style, upon a mosh pit at full thrash to a band dedicated to the pro-fork/anti-spoon movement; a pit at an East Bay suburban house show, a squat powered by the unsuspecting neighbor, where the entire pit ended up squirming on the floor like worms; a stabbing by butter knife over getting firsts at a freshly filled keg at another house show; and the man who swung on overhead pipes, in anticipation and excitement for a wildly feral Japanese band who, as they began to play, broke the pipe, sending a flood of water and sewage all over the venue and out to the street, effectively ending both the show and the venue, permanently.

I really want to mention THE GOTHS before I move on, as they, too, were with me in my teens. Goths and punks run side by side; they are siblings, they share a Venn diagram, they are clowns. Clowns of darkness, clowns of play, clowns of the cemetery showing up to have goth photoshoots on crypts and headstones. Raised in the same house so the foundation is similar, sometimes super annoyed with each other, weird ass nicknames, call me Slug vs. call me Raven, both be at the club, but they just be dancing different. I myself have never been an actual, card-carrying goth, but I look goth and act stoically without smiling or expression (it's an Armenian thing). I like goth things, a steady wardrobe of black clothing, deadpan af, listen to goth music, have a history of depression and malaise, have bat tattoos, enjoy the darkness, Halloween, and get that fucking overhead light out of here, please.

As I sauntered into the next stage of my clown life, I passed through some all black-wearing, white belt clowns of a different variety, finding myself staunchly in the midst of another Venn diagram, where punks and queers meet. This was the era when I would eventually earn my nickname, Deez Nutz. Olympia, Washington was a notable clown town in the late 90s, and it's no wonder I was drawn there, with music festivals handing out yo-yos with admission. For the duration of the festival—and a time after—you would see festival goers yo-yoing all over town. I lived there for a small but influential period of time, when I was nineteen and moved there on a whim after the dot com boom ruined my dreams of cheap rent in the Bay Area. This is where I came out as femme and began my life as a lipstick clown. The vibe was total clown antics. Everyone was always finding reasons to dress up or have a show at their house. It's a small college town with not that much to do, and you really had to make the fun happen—which is why it had such a legendary and one-of-kind creative scene (with some influence of Evergreen College, of course). The scene was lots of people just fucking around, secret cafes in people's apartments, and excuses to hang out either by band or by art.

There was a period of time when every Thursday a bunch of queers would meet up in the Safeway parking lot for "Hesh Night," where we all gathered in Hesher drag. Heshers—or Heshians—are rockers, in case this is a foreign concept. Think *Heavy Metal Parking Lo*t. There, in our heavy metal drag, we would be drinking Safeway Select sodas but pretending they were beer alongside our greatest Hesher accessory—a Radio's 70s van with the diamond-shaped pop out window. Inside her van was shag carpeting, the walls wood-paneled but wallpapered with vintage 70s nudie pin-up girls. The ceiling was all gold-speckled-mirror, and naturally she had a sick sound system and would roll up blasting AC/DC. We loudly mimicked rocker dudes and pretended to get wasted off of the soda. The police came and really couldn't do anything, because we were not actually drinking. Eventually we were evicted from the Safeway parking lot for loitering and had to relocate to the parking lot of a closed Les Schwab down the road. We popped the hoods of our cars, and the Hesher drag ultra-dudes would start talking about their hot rods, aka our sensible used cars that were not blinged out in any way, but for the sake of Hesh Night they were muscle cars as we roasted toxic masculine culture, laughing and clowning the entire time.

One of my most clown moments happened during this time, at a women's mud wrestling party at my friend's house. The house was called the swamp house. You would turn into what was essentially a hole on the side of a country road, and you would meet up with an unpaved driveway canopied with trees and wiggle your car up the rocky road to the land the house was on—essentially its front yard. The house's supporting beams had rotted, so it was held up with metal stilts over the swampy area, and those stilts looked rusty. It was crooked, and you could definitely see the outside through the inside, but it was cheap, shared by a bunch of people but set back and hidden from the road so no city officials came to check on. If they did, it would have been condemned. This party was highly anticipated by all the queers. I decided I wanted to wrestle, and I came up with a wrestling character for myself—Reefer Slut. Becoming Reefer Slut had me dying my hair bright red. I wore a red shirt with a big blue star on the back. I got some blue tighty-whities and ironed-on letters spelling my new wrestling name on the butt. I already loved smoking weed; this was my actual stoner era, and I was definitely going to be smoking a big fat joint when I would enter the pit. This was my vision.

The scene at the wrestling match was boisterous celebration. All week long, my friends had dug a hole in their yard for the wrestling pit, pulling out rocks and letting a hose run to make the mud. They also would pull out rocks from the mud, so it was smooth and no one would get cut up. When it was done, it was about the size of a kiddie pool and a half, and a bit deeper. They fashioned a stage and their band, The Need, played during the duels—not their own songs, but wrestling music they were improvising. Tons of watchers and wrestlers were assembled, there was a ref with a whistle, and a hose to clean yourself off after your time in the pit. I was matched with a friend who had a shaved head and purple bangs. They wore a catholic school skirt and white button-up top with lots of chains and studs, but stripped down to boxers before entering the pit. I made a big show of smoking my joint before joining. The thick, slimy mud squished around my feet as me and my opponent circled each other before grappling.

In retrospect, smoking the joint may have been my biggest downfall, as I was really feeling the mud. Pretty quickly we went down, and I discovered in that moment that I liked being pinned down and could not get out of the position I found myself in and ultimately was eliminated from the rest of the competition. I hosed off, and later showered many times, but for over a week mud came out of my pores.

The next clown era was in Portland, Oregon, at the tail end of the year 2000. This city was also pretty clowny. My friends in Portland were always throwing themed house parties, and everyone took the dress-up seriously. Examples of some themed parties were: monochromatic, your favorite pop star goes to Mardi Gras, business casual, and yacht rock. One time a friend of a friend was having a party at their house, and we were all bored and went and discovered that it was a crusty punk clown house. At some point, literal punk clowns became a very real thing, and punk circuses made the rounds. These crusty clowns made me remember the crusties I used to drink with as a teenager, only these crusties had red noses and a bit more color in their wardrobe. Plus, a pet rat.

In Portland, I worked with a fake wrestler (another community of clowns in their own right) at a porn store, at the height of the Suicide Girl era. This job was one of my most clown jobs, as the antics and folly were high from both co-workers and customers. One fellow and I would work an entire graveyard shift together, slinging smut and selling sex toys. After work I would come home and pass out immediately; after work he would come home to his roommate in the living room making squish porn of sexy, punk clown, girl-on-girl scenes in a Jell-O filled kiddie pool with whipped cream filled balloons and whatever else squished and looked good on camera. Lucky to get some sleep between takes, he would then wake up, practice his fake wrestling, and go and do it all over again.

After my porn clown days, I moved to San Francisco proper—different than the East Bay I grew up in—with an eclectic group of clowns, some being literal clowns, some figurative. The gays, the drag, the theater, the disco, the outfits, the attitude, the sparkle, all swirled up with the chaos and garbage of the punks and other city dwellers. I was home. A friend who was partially creeped out by clowns lived with an actual, real, literal working professional red-nose-wearing clown there. She got to live in a gorgeous rent control flat in a beautiful, desirable neighborhood, but the real price was being frozen in her doorway when she returned to her sanctuary only to find her roommate in full clown makeup and clothes, in a darkened room before a flickering television. She slid against the wall and kept the clown in her vision, repeating silently to herself, *don't look at me clown, don't look at me clown*, on repeat, until she reached the safety of her room. Eventually this situation got the better of her, but she stuck it out for years before moving to the east coast.

One of my best friends in San Francisco considered herself to be both a "downtown clown" and an ice cream cone. She was a makeup artist and worked for Mac at the Nordstrom downtown, with freelance jobs on the side. Her hair was fire engine red, her makeup incredible, she dressed in all black on workdays and clown colors and patterns on off days. She said her red hair was the cherry on top of her ice-cream-cone-shaped body, below the neck being the scoop of ice cream, below the waist being the cone, after which the hips tapered down to whatever little pointy shoes she was wearing at the time. Time with her was always high clown and high art (think John Waters). We all worked on our friends' passion projects, extra hands when the dirty, queer, punk, glamorous, gutter-trash community needed authentic selves for the sake of their vision. Once I was dressed in fashion tatters, my face painted hot pink with large feather eyelashes, and with a gang of everyone sporting some version of this, we all boarded the 14 Mission Muni and rode it to Daly City and back, taking over the entire back of the bus filming our friends' music video. We thrashed wildly from side to side as our friends looked bored and unaffected, fake-playing their instruments.

After years in the Bay Area the latest dot com boom pushed me to pioneer another part of California. I moved to Los Angeles, where I could live alone and meet up with some of my favorite clowns—including the ice cream cone herself—who had all relocated for the same reason. What I found was the most clown town of them all—a Mecca of Hollywood clowns, a completely different and unique variety, found only in that region. Again, both literal and figurative clowns were everywhere. Thick with self-importance, industry clowns threatened people that they will never work in this town again; clowns at the top of the trash heap, clowns claiming aspirational career positions with the hope that they can "Secret" and magical think them to reality. Actual clowns training other clowns and forming troupes. Botox and filler clowns, comedy clowns, exaggerated-wealth clowns, spiritual New Age clowns, fitness clowns, professional dancer-actor-musician clowns, influencer clowns, content clowns, fashion clowns, art world clowns, adult Disney clowns, comic book clowns, and psychic vampire entourage clowns trying to suck the energy of their symbiotic relationship's host. The desperation of trying to make it, the trapdoors, the booby traps of life, all in a cartoonish fashion.

I found work in different areas of the entertainment industry. I worked on big movie lots where people paid money to tour the artificial world within and also on dirty patches of dirt within the TMZ (thirty-mile zone), where the productions were not required to pay travel costs to the crew. I worked on game shows and reality competitions in the world of studio audiences, and also sound stages, custom little worlds lit up to be whatever it was—music videos, feature films, scripted projects, and commercials, all in a very blue-collar way. People were dressed in wild interpretations of the city, either down-on-your-luck or full-on goth clown in booty shorts. The artificial environment was intoxicating, the celebrity insider information intriguing, the most fun but also the most toxic place. I bloomed and played, observing camera people in fake bushes, a little girl who spoke to sea snails, the sea snails in the literal trash after the animal advocates were gone. Meditating with crystals, in studios riding bikes to nowhere in a club atmosphere, intense dark nights of the soul, the delight of the freedom of not giving a shit about the circus I lived, took part in. Eventually I took myself back home to the Bay, to lead a humble life as a Bay Area Clown once more—but with a little more sparkle after those years in the fun house, where the ground shifted constantly under my feet and palm trees lined the distorted mirrors I encountered along the way.

BUFFED FAG
Justin Chin

I want to be a buffed fag.

When I walk down the street, I want folks to do a double take, gawk in disbelief, mouths agape, and say, "Oh my god! That faggot is so buffed!"

I'll spend six hours in the gym every day, blasting my quads, doing leg lifts, squats and presses and curls so I will be The Buffed Fag Of Your Dreams. I will pose and flex my muscles while having sex because that's what turns the boys on. I will have them worship my muscles and tell me how good I look as they chow down on my glutes. I'll bend press until I look like the Tasmanian Devil of Bugs Bunny cartoons, as I walk down the street in all my big chest skinny waist top heavy neanderthal arm drag swagger, thinking I'm the hottest shit in the universe and I am . . .

Because I am a Buff Fag (at least I want to be). I will have sex with the towel boy at Muscle Systems, the guy who makes the protein shakes at Gold's, and the trainer at Market Street Gym; and I too will be able to pull off the bad fag attitude thing, previously reserved solely for store clerks at Tower Records and Video.

Oh, I do so want to be a Buffed Fag, hanging out in the locker rooms of gyms to pick up other buffed fags and score injectable steroids, remembering to wash my needles with bleach and never sharing them, because I don't want to be a diseased fag, just a buff fag with a dick shrunken to the size of a Vicks inhaler; but I won't care, because I am a buffed fag.

I will scan the L.L. Bean, J. Crew, and International Man catalogs and pick who I will marry; last week it was the one-piece perforated lycra jumpsuit, this week it's the low-cut easy-breathe fundoshi, next week it's the tan-thru bikini underwear, and folk will believe me as I partake of my fantasies because I'm a buffed fag and I have the god-given right to sail through the world being *just like everybody else*, to have the whole puny world owe me a living because everybody loves a Buffed Fag (even though they're assholes), and everybody listens to a Buffed Fag (even though they have the IQ and personality of a box of cat hair).

You know you too want to be a buffed fag, you can't help it as you watch them waddle down the street, sure that folks would move out of their way, downing their protein shakes, spirulina shakes, shaking their way down into the psyche of Ooo-Ooo-Baby-Hot-Baby, boogeying down to our little techno-trance dance clubs, breeding ground display cases for buffed fag bodies. So, c'mon, what's stopping you? Decency? Pride? (Forget it.) A sense of self-worth? (Ha.) Intelligence? A semblance of a life? (Forget that.) Let's all be Buffed Fags and the whole damn scrawny world will belong to us.

CLOWNING FOR CORPORATIONS

Noel Alumit

When I graduated with my ultra-expensive BFA in acting, I became a clown. Actually, I became a caterer, then a clown. A friend from college worked for Elite Parties, a high-end catering company who boasted Fortune 500 companies as their main clients. Elite Parties had large outdoor events, with their main money earning months from spring to early fall.

They served expensive food (think lobster and steak), and a DJ spun a variety of music. They offered carnival rides, a slew of games, from a potato sack race to a truly competitive session of Simon Says. They rented beautiful areas by the beach, in the mountains, in large, woodsy parks.

Most of us arrived a few hours early to set up. A majority of their staff looked like people I grew up with—I was an immigrant Filipino kid who grew up in parts of Los Angeles described as the "inner city." I felt completely comfortable with them. I spent my college years at a private college, and though most of the students were on some type of financial aid, I had met debutantes and kids with last names associated with big oil companies. Once a classmate accidentally found himself in my neighborhood and called it a "shitty place," not knowing I was from that shitty place. Another classmate once said to me, "You know what I like about you, Noel? You're poor but you don't make a big deal about it."

What I liked about working at Elite Parties is I worked with people who came from similar neighborhoods. Some said they'd been to my neighborhood to eat or party.

I joked with Teek, an aspiring singer and ex-con, about singers we liked. He asked me who my favorite singers were and my gay ass said, "Madonna and Whitney Houston."

"Whitney can sing!" Teek said. "You know her mama is Cissy Houston. She's a big-time gospel singer. I don't think Cissy likes Whitney singing better than her. They were singing together and Whitney be singing aerials. Cissy didn't look none too happy."

Miguel, a lithe, sinewy guy of nineteen, jumped around the grounds helping out where he could. He walked around shirtless to let everyone know he went to the gym. Elite Parties hired a lot of young men, like Miguel, Teek, and me. There was a lot of lifting and moving heavy equipment. Muscle was needed.

"Need help with that, Noel?" Miguel asked, as I tried lugging a table across a yard.

These guys were pros at Elite Parties and had no problem helping the new guy. Once everything was set up, the kitchen in working order, the rides in working order, it was pretty much easy street.

Luke, the clown they hired, ran around and made everyone laugh, just acting all foolish. He led the relay races and teased people, leading everyone in laughter. He sat down at tables and ate with families, and they welcomed him.

Jack, a burly supervisor, pulled me aside and said, "Noel, we're thinking about making you a manager."

I had only been working there for a few months. I knew there were men who'd worked there far longer.

"Why don't you promote one of the other guys?" I asked.

"Well, we want our managers to be college graduates—it would look bad if these big companies knew our managers were just high school graduates or people who didn't graduate at all."

I almost turned it down but began getting notices about my student loans payments. There would be a small bump in pay, and it looked pretty good to the debt I racked up.

When I was introduced as a new manager, I saw a few guys cross their arms and look away. Here I was, a new guy, and in a few months I was promoted. Miguel said under his breath, "I wish I could be a manager." Teek stopped talking to me.

Some of the staff congratulated me. They knew why I got promoted and why they didn't. The divide had begun. I wanted so badly to say, Hey, I got through on student loans and working three jobs. I wanted to tell them I was the poorest kid in my class, and my dad's a security guard and my mom's a nurse. I wanted to tell them I grew up in a neighborhood that had one of the highest crime rates in Los Angeles. My home was next to a crack house.

I was dejected. I felt more kinship with the people I worked with than the supervisors who ran the operation. I went around the grounds cleaning up trash from the tables. A woman from one of the tables looked at me and signaled her friend to watch her purse. She grabbed her purse and placed it far from me. Great. My co-workers think I'm some snooty college kid, and these women see me as the brown guy who might steal their purse. Let me be clear. The women who hid their purse were also Asian. I imagined them to be from some kind of Southeast Asian country, a place ruined by dictators and war. Places where there was atrocious rape and murder, and the people who did it looked like me.

Just as I was about to quit from all the animosity, Luke, our clown, didn't show up. He just went AWOL.

Jack said, "Noel, didn't you get your degree in acting? Do you want to be the clown? We need one."

I put on the costume and put on some face paint and voilà, I became the clown. I'd watched Luke clown around for weeks and followed his schtick. I laughed with the kids and did funny dances.

There was something freeing about it. I managed a little bit but clowned around a lot. The tension I had with the guys seemed to disappear. I mean, who would be threatened by a clown? I was comfortable with the crowd, and no one thought of me as being a potential thief. As a clown, I was free from class and race. I was the guy with wacky hair and bizarre face paint and big, baggy clothes. I stayed a clown for the rest of the season. Only one season. I was not meant to work as a clown to please Fortune 500 companies.

I would go on to do AIDS work for the next twenty years. AIDS was different from what I had experienced at Elite Parties. Due to the stigma of AIDS, anyone was welcomed to fight the disease. We needed bodies to help the dying bodies that seemed to be proliferating.

Somewhere in there, we had to laugh. In such an intense environment, one developed gallows humor, described as "grim and ironic humor in a desperate or hopeless situation." A little bit of clowning around got us through that horrible circus.

CIRCUS IMMIGRANT

Tania De Rozario

paint your face white
paint your body white
paint your words white

practice

be a ventriloquist
be the dummy
stick your hand up your ass

do as you're told

your hand is white your ass is white
your mouth is red but

your tongue is white

your clown suit is fancy
you must only wear fancy
walk on stilts but

don't stand too tall

make us laugh
trip over yourself
bringing us joy

perform

diplomacy — a joy buzzer
immigration juggles papers
balloons are hot air, deportation

a disappearing act

we love your antics we
love your bluster

these shoes will always be
too big for you.

I AM NOT A DRAG QUEEN I AM A TRANS WOMAN

féi iká shumarí

We both take our wigs off at the end of the night, but let me tell you something, I am still an estrogen pumped woman after stringing my 38DD sized bra on a lamp's neck and wiping the makeup off my face. I'm inherently a clown, I've even considered stand-up from all the comical atrocities that flavor my days, but *no*, I'm not a drag queen. I know trans people that are, and I clack my acrylics together in applause and support their job with deep admiration (Sasha and Kerri Colby, Peppermint, and Kylie Sonique Love, my homies from LA that tear the stage), but me? I'm just a regular girl—a commissioned graphic designer, graduate student, and writer—all feminine inertia, no performance that comes on and off. There is no stage for me, only a man's world.

Drag queens and trans women both doll up, both entertain in different capacities. The world is sweeter and brighter because we exist in our nuance. We have the experimental queens, and we have the trans nonbinary femmes. The Pageant queens and the dolls that serve fresh, fresh salmon. We have camp queens and sassy bricks. We have drag queens, bulky and muscular, but with flawless mugs. And then we have the high femmes, factory made. There is a shuffle of identities that *do* drag, including cis and non cis people, straight and queer people, and the endless spectrum of combinations of identities! Alike we are queer and therefore a resilient stain society can never erase. We are the secret desire people stuff into their pockets, the spiritual calling to be something close to divine (no pun intended). We are both essential contributors to preserving what is left of humanity, but the turn shifts are different.

Drag queens, in my argument, cis (straight/queer) men, take off the glam, the pageantry, the Bianca Del Rio, the weird, the hyper feminine Jorgeous, fulfill the work for their side coin, their Bob the Drag Queen "job," but trans women clock into the daytime shift and the negotiation of our livelihood begins. We are women in a man's world irrespective of being makeup, tuck, and wig *less*. We remain all of our woman parts in the glaring sun, no disco ball or gelled lights the color of a safer space to shield us wherever we go. There is only the morbid transphobic and bashing world, and yet we exist in our soundful strut and Colgate smiles. We remain a doll, even when we're dolled down. There is no collector's box we can revert into and be safer (unless passibility is factored into the equation).

We take the trash out as women. Grocery shop, walk three miles at a nearby park, go to a 9 to 5 or work remotely *as women*. Trans women who are also drag queens can be the only ones to attest to the differences (or not) of their experience on and off stage. The only question left to hold is: how do we negotiate the world perceiving trans women only as momentary glimpses of "entertainment" of those of us that are not drag queens? This is the power of the colonial imaginary. Trans women are *not* perceived as embodied women in *and out* of the "dolling up," (unless you're a learned ally or a decent human that has the dignity of giving others autonomy without questioning them). On nights out when I'm serving puss, I have been asked if I'm "one of the performers" or "what time are you going up?" Maybe it's precisely the fact I am serving c^nt that I'm assumed something beyond what I am, *a woman*. I can only make sense as a dolled up girlie or dolled down curvaceous rarity if I'm here to entertain, in every sense of the word. Honestly, this turns me into a flame emoji-eyed caricature of myself throwing a shaking fist in the air! I am turned into a stand-up comedian that will only ever be a red nosed clown and that doesn't suit my ferocious feminine prowess.

CLOWN ALLEY

Maz Murray

What follows is an oral history of the circumstances which led to a group of clowns and allied workers disrupting the University College London Women's Liberation talk: What does the Supreme Court judgment mean for lesbians? *on June 25, 2025 in London.*

Pag

I went to the doctor with an extreme case of malaise. I'd signed up for this particular GP because he was on an Excel spreadsheet of dubious origin which listed doctors who weren't as transphobic as they could be. Someone in 2018 had received a bridging prescription from him, and then perhaps no one since, or the spreadsheet was just old. Time moved differently in the Trans Masculine Support and Advice UK Facebook group. I didn't tell the doctor about the malaise, I read aloud a statement from a guide from the aforementioned Facebook group, in the hopes he would prescribe me HRT and not SSRIs. *It's actually safer*, I said. He pushed his computer monitor against the wall, shook his head, and looked at me.

Treatment is very simple. Great Gender Critical feminist Julie Bindel is at UCL tonight. Go and see her. That should cheer you up.

But doctor, I said, *I'm the Great Clown Pagliacci and I'm onstage at the Circus tonight!*

He said, *I'm sure you'll figure something out*, and went back to typing.

I rang up the other clowns and told them of my predicament. They told me news from our circles, for example Pierrot was back in town after a two-year stint with Clowns Sans Frontières. He didn't have a civilian phone, but I could contact him through his girlfriend, Emily.

Emily
When Pierrot first joined Clowns Sans Frontières, I was convinced he would die. There's no way clown school in France had prepared him for the things he'd experience out in the field. His commitment to clowning was one of the things that made me fall in love with him, but at that moment I felt like ripping the red nose from his face. He was the first trans clown to graduate from the École Philippe Gaulier, with a few caveats. His mentor was a ninety-two-year-old man from Normandy whose voice was indecipherable. It was fine, because they mainly communicated through mime. I found myself communicating with Pierrot this way, too. It was something he suggested during couples therapy. I felt on uneven ground, but I came to understand the beauty of mime as an international language, and why he'd want to use it in conflict zones.

He did two tours at refugee camps in the Mediterranean. I lit a candle next to a red nose every day. He returned for a while, and things were good between us. Then one morning I woke up, and his oversized shoes were no longer by the door. He'd left a note telling me it was safer if I didn't know where he was, along with a beautiful bouquet that squirted water in my face. I was terrified. I dreamed of being woken up to a knock on the door, a small white box with a battered red nose inside, and that would be it—he'd be taken from me. I received intermittent updates from his Instagram (@that_trans_clown). When I was scared, Pagliacci comforted me. Somehow, their oversized shoes beneath my bed made me feel closer to Pierrot. Their red nose, brushing my lips, brought back the joy of those early months in Bristol. Of course, Pierrot could never know. To be usurped, not just by another clown but another trans clown, and what Pierrot would call a *circus clown* with no righteous cause or direction to their clowning, would destroy him. Pagliacci left to do a stint with Zippos Circus, and for a while I was alone. Then Pierrot arrived at my door, shaking, haunted, bare-faced. He said he would never clown again. Told me to go back to calling him Eli. I started ignoring Pagliacci's calls, and gradually they stopped. Then, a few weeks later, I sensed he needed me. I looked down to see his name flash across my phone. I picked up.

Eli/Pierrot
Emily wanted me to have a sense of purpose again. It's like that sometimes with clown partners. They get too invested. Before you

know it, they're joining clown rights associations, doing fundraisers for clowning initiatives. She told me about this Julie Bindel event and how it was getting Pagliacci down, and I didn't wanna know. I'd been out of touch with what was going down in England, it all seemed small to me. Plus, I didn't care for Pagliacci's craft. She told me there was a meeting that afternoon and put out my shoes and nose, pointedly.

She didn't know that for security reasons, our group of clowns always meet in civilian clothing, and use non-clown names on Signal. At the meeting I was greeted like a hero, but I didn't do it for the glory.

Krusty

Some of the clowns at the meeting thought an event like this wasn't in our interest, us being a mostly clown liberation focused group. But Emily pointed out that both Pagliacci, Pierrot, and a few others were transgender and that this ruling would prevent them from using the appropriate facilities at national clowning events, for example the International Clown Festival in Bangalore. And I've always thought, underneath the paint and the britches, we're all just humans, aren't we? Clowns aren't about gender, you know; Pagliacci was telling me clowns are quite a lot like this thing they call nonbinary. I cancelled my 6:00 PM slot at Great Ormond Street and twelve of us bundled in my car down to UCL.

Kurly

We spent so long worrying about cops we hadn't thought of the other obvious threat until our comrade was pinned to the ground by a seventy-year-old woman in orthopedic shoes.

Bozo

I'd tried quite hard to dress in a manner befitting a TERF meeting. In fact, I was wearing bootcut jeans, a long linen shirt, and a shawl. At the entrance to UCL, in the foyer outside the meeting room and at the door, the organizers—a couple of white women in their sixties and seventies—were very smiley. But as soon as Julie Bindel set eyes on me, she seemed suspicious. It didn't help that we were the only people under fifty in the room. Also, when I sat down the bootcut jeans rode up a little and my clown shoes were much more visible. A butch woman next to me glared, turned to her presumed wife and typed out *lot of queers here* on her phone. When the first disruption took place, the TERF audience members started screaming and getting physical almost immediately. She was screaming, *YOU CUNTS FUCK YOU FUCK YOU*, and then she had to take out her inhaler and sit down for a bit. I started to feel scared. Once the first wave of my comrades had been grabbed and pushed out of the room by the TERFs, the crowd began to settle down and one of the speakers warned the attendees to not use physical violence against the agitators. The first speaker, a lawyer who was trying to explain why the court ruling was good, started up again. One of the scarier attendees—a tall butch woman with a gray mullet and quite an Australian vibe—stood up and proclaimed, *THERE'S MORE OF THEM IN HERE*. The attendees started to look around themselves. I craned my neck, shook my head demonstratively, crossed my arms as if in disdain. Another audience member shouted, *WHY DON'T WE ALL TURN TO THE PERSON NEXT TO US, ASK THEM THEIR NAME AND WHY THEY ARE HERE*. The panel started grumbling and someone said that was a stupid idea. My heart thudded against my chest and I tried to rehearse a believable alter ego. The speaker started again before anyone could ask me, but I felt eyes on me still. It would be impossible to retrieve my ruff in a subtle manner.

Emily

It was my idea to have two beautiful lesbian women caucuses beginning and ending the disruption of the meeting, with clowns in the middle. I thought the image of me, or someone like me, dragged out by my beautiful hair or arms by perhaps a big burly security guard, would be very impactful to the press we'd invited. Unfortunately, as soon as I unfurled my banner and began my chant, an old crone ran full speed at me and grabbed me about the waist. Not wishing to injure the old bitch, I let her drag me across the room. Another even older woman joined her and grabbed my forearm, leaving marks. And I'm not really one to bruise, just ask my shibari top!

Binky

I'm one of very few trans femme clowns in the community so I know people were quite worried about me going to this meeting, but it felt symbolically meaningful for me to attend. Some of my trans sisters were waiting at the pub afterwards, for post-protest support/clown car watch.

I had in my possession the airhorn to signal the second, and most clown heavy, wave of disruption. I'd have approximately five seconds to get the air horn out of my tote, sound it, put on my red nose and ruff, and get out of arm's length. I was particularly concerned about a woman sitting on my row, who'd shouted that she wanted to batter the previous wave of protestors and had waved her crutches at them threateningly. I made brief eye contact with Bozo, who I'd always considered a bit of a weak link within the trans clowning community. Given the violent reaction the audience had to the last wave, I couldn't account for my comrades not standing up when the time came.

Eli/Pierrot

It was hard to watch them attack Emily like that, but I had to keep my cool and wait for my wave. I adjusted my sweatshirt which had *Feminist* printed on it in pale pink letters (a regrettable pre-transition online purchase), shook my head and jeered like the other attendees. Before long, Binky sounded the air horn and we sprung to action, shouting *SHUT IT DOWN SHUT IT DOWN YOU'RE NOT FEMINISTS YOU'RE JUST CLOWNS*. I had objected to this chant during the earlier meeting, as it plays into anti-clown bias. However, I did concede that the general theme of the protest utilized anti-clown bias towards a just cause and therefore was an acceptable tactic aligning to the spirit of non-reformist reforms.

Kurly

After the first clown wave, the TERFs got really paranoid. Their eyeballs were vibrating. Everyone was looking around, trying to sniff out more clowns. The scary Australian seeming butch saw a few of us seated honestly a bit too close together, our mistake, and began to accuse us of being agitators. An older attendee stood up and pointed at us and said that we should be made to leave. A younger attendee argued with her on our behalf and said that she was age profiling. I said I was a student. The younger attendee was really going to bat for us and seemed quite upset that we were being singled out this way. After a bit more arguing the paranoia settled down and the speakers started again. I'm pretty sure they hadn't even got to Julie Bindel yet. Anyway, joke's on them because obviously then we got up and started chanting, put on our red noses, and unfurled a banner that this one very aggressive older woman tried to rip from our hands. They'd learned a little bit to restrain each other from violence so it was security who got us out in the end; they were much less bloodthirsty. As we were bundled out I shouted, *THERE'S FOUR MORE WAVES TO COME.*

Pag

Kurly had just been trying to mess with them, but after we unleashed what was supposed to be the final wave, a cavalcade of clown cars burst through the back wall of UCL and hundreds more clowns poured from the miniature cars into the meeting room. The sound of honking horns and screams filled the air. I watched as two clowns pulled Julie Bindel's chair out from under her, and she fell on to a gigantic whoopie cushion. Another clown swept the tablecloth from the panel table, leaving their water jugs and glasses intact with a magician's flair. Another clown then jumped up on the table and kicked all items to the floor with his big clown shoes. The mostly old white women, plus a few middle-aged white men, who made up the non-clown audience, were no match for these new mercenary clowns. A clown with a balloon pump was stringing long thin balloons together into a huge chain which he then wrapped around the cowed TERFs until they were bundled into a big pile on the floor. Wordlessly, unless you count mime which I personally don't because I'm not fluent yet, the clowns piled back into their miniature cars and sped back out of the holes they had made in the walls mere moments before. The rest of us walked out of the swiss cheesed wall onto the street in a daze. Pierrot and Emily were waiting for us. Usually, it hurt to see them together, but I was on such a high from what had just transpired that I marched right up to them and embraced them. *What was that—did you see—who were they?* I jumbled my words. Pierrot took me by the shoulders and looked deep into my eyes. *That was Clowns Sans Frontières. I called in some favors.* I felt tears prick my eyes. *You did that* . . . I said . . . *For me?* Pierrot looked away. He was a proud clown, always had been. *It wasn't just for you, Pagliacci. It was for all of us.*

DOT
Anya Ventura

What are you doing here? the old woman asks me.

I'm a ragpicker, I whisper in her ear, combing her hair back from her head. I'm here for stories.

I don't know if I want to give them away yet, she tells me.

In the window behind her, the hummingbird vibrates around a wooden birdhouse. Taped next to the window is a sign: *Please don't shut the blinds, I look at the birds.*

I can tell you the story of the woman who lives in the desert, I offer.

I don't know what's mine anymore, she tells me from her bed. She is always in bed.

Neither do I, I say, I don't know if I should be here.

I don't tell her that I have already looked at her file while she was sleeping: she was a nurse, she lived alone, she was never married. Her niece visits every Thursday.

Your name is Dot, I say, Here, eat, and held a spoonful of applesauce to her dry lips.

I'm the writer of this story, I tell her.

But not all stories, she shoots back.

We are silent, listening to the squeak of the nurses' shoes on the linoleum floor outside the room. Dot, like a dot on a line, I say.

Please leave me alone, she says.

I can't. I keep thinking of you.

You don't know me, she says, and fumbles for the remote control that is lost in the tangle of sheets.

I tell Dot that I spent the morning talking to a stinkbug and then at the end of the conversation, swallowed it. When quashed, she says, stinkbugs smell of all the sadness of love.

The sadness of love, I say.

She allows me to visit if I bring sweets: bars of chocolate and pale hard cookies. And the more often I visit, the more often we like to repeat each other.

When I come by in the evenings, Dot tells me her dreams, which I am surprised to find are the same as mine.

I tell her I am writing a story about a woman who escapes her life. She drives out to the desert in the middle of the night.

That's a good one, she says.

Deserts are easy to dream of, I say, but hard to live in. In my story, the woman lives in a trailer with a very old cat.

The old woman says nothing, but she knows, we both know, that she contains all the stories that everyone has ever told me, the multitude of them, and when she's silent she's saying all of them. She already knows the story of the woman in the desert.

There is another version, she says, where she stays in the cabin by the lake.

Or another where she stays in love, I venture, not wanting to mention O.

Possibly.

When I can't think of anything to tell her, I narrate the events of the outside. The patterns of the weather. I describe the look of the shadows on the cornfields. The crop dusters. The rows of failed flowers.

I see Dot more often now. Whereas before I saw her only once a month, now we have begun to meet weekly. Each time I walk in the room, she greets me with the same blank look, and I wonder if we will have to begin again, as we sometimes do, with the recitation of ordinary details, starting with my name. My name, and she makes me repeat it, but I like reciting the facts of my life, my age, the place where I live. I tell myself it is good to be reminded. I take up the habit of delivering long monologues, long senseless streams of talking with no clear beginning, middle, or end, but simply carry on with a succession of and *then's*. But other times she remembers and cuts right to the story.

Does anything ever happen to the woman in the desert? she asks one day. Or is she just there, collecting?

You might say I invented her to avoid the tedium of days, the dull record of only myself. To simply have someone to talk to when I grew tired of trying to speak to God. *Dear reader*, was where it began. I walked through the desert and picked up the rusted cans, thinking that stitched together they would make a beautiful armor, and took off all my clothes.

One day, to my surprise, as I'm saying one of my monologues, she wakes.

You don't have to go into all this, she says.

After she falls asleep that night, I rub small globs of cold cream into her skin. Slowly, I take out her tube of Midnight Pleasures, painting her lips bright red and then drawing two lines upwards to each cheek: a lurid clown face.

My notes, I tell her. At some point in the past year, I stopped sleeping well. I would get up in the middle of the night and not be able to fall back asleep. My disappointments ate at me. I needed to leave to heal, I tell her.

Tell me more about the woman in the desert, she says.

She can't sleep either.

The woman in the desert lives alone, I continue. She walks in the sand at sunrise. Listening to the howl of the coyotes in the dark, and then, once light, seeing their prints in the sand. The ghost tangle of creosote. The leftover tin cans rusted to black. These are just my notes, my little rags! I tell the old woman.

I wanted a story.

Let me go on.

What happens to her in the desert?

Her skin becomes red and creased, wind-bitten, coarse, like an old hide.

Does she become a tough woman?

I think so.

I have only a few notes, I say again. Against all that flat dryness she watched the moon move from one side of the house to the other. Even looking at the rocks in the yard made her feel holy. There are twelve nameless hours of love.

My first husband, Dot begins.

I thought you were never married.

I wasn't, I never was. But Bill.

What about him?

He loved flowers.

I had a child, I said, or thought, and the image in the small mirror of my mind curled up like smoke.

I tell her about the plums. How I'd eaten all of them.

I know that one, she says. None saved.

I say there is a plum tree by the cabin where I live.

Is the tree flowering?

It depends on the season.

And you don't know?

No.

If it's winter, the plums are gone.

When I die, Dot says, bury me by the plum tree and it will grow more fruit.

And what if the children steal them?

So let them.

This is my life, I tell her, and it is a little like death.

I tell Dot that creosote knows how to die well. They know how to conserve themselves. To seal themselves during the heat of the day and open only at night to drink. Their open mouths. Sometimes at night in the cabin I wake up hungry. I move toward the bowl of fruit in the dark. The persimmons and the plums. I cut the fruit in quarters and eat it from my hands. When I put the fruit to my lips, I think of him. The taste of it—how nice and sad. The plant knows how to die: how to prune a portion of itself so only the vital part remains. I came to the desert to fill it with my dreams but it has filled me instead.

I am hungry now, so hungry. The thin thread of the coyote song has stopped. What sounds like dripping. I can't hear it anymore.

Dot no longer eats. She has grown brittle and dry as a cocoon. When I read poetry to her, I don't know if she can hear me, though they say the hearing is the last to go. I read *Leaves of Grass* until the day grows dark and the dogs begin to howl.

We are not, she reminds me, at the edge of the world.

Now when I look into the mirror, I see Dot's face. She has begun to make visits to where I live in the cabin. Sometimes I see her standing in the kitchen, her hip against the milk-white shine of the stove, watching the blue flame of the burner.

It's easy to get lost here, she tells me, not taking her eyes off the flames.

Or sometimes she has managed to crawl outside near the woodshed, crouched near the stacks of cut logs, and she is talking to the spiders in a whisper. When I find her all she says is, "They know things I don't."

Or she is at Zumba class with a black cloth covering the hole in her throat. But she is there, slowly moving her body in accordance with the simple and ongoing beat. I tell her I would like to crawl into the hole in her throat.

Would I disappear into it? I ask her, but she does not respond.

If the hole is a vacuum of nothingness, and nothingness is the most alive thing there is, containing all possibilities in the scattered everywhere, then one possibility in this narrative is that I climb into the hole in the old woman's throat.

I notice yet again how severe her features. The intricate carving of her nose. Her eyes that travel far back in her head. The fat fallen away. I long to touch the edge of her cheekbone, the place where the flesh drops off. The body makes so little of itself as it prepares for death.

I'm ten pounds lighter, she tells me.

You're dying, I want to say.

There were years where I weighed everything that I ate. Can you imagine that? That I was the woman who tried to weigh everything?

When I see that she is sleeping, I try to pry the remote control from her hands. The Home Shopping Network is playing without the sound on.

I'm watching, she says with her eyes still closed.

I have written a story about this somewhere, I think, this is the sum of every story I've ever told, including the stories of my dreams.

But I am wide awake, thinks the woman who lives in the desert. I am wide awake, she tells herself as she walks toward the dark swell of the mountains. And that is just how I have written it: *dark swell.*

Dot tells me she is dreaming of fixing the fence again. In another recurring dream, she is washing dishes. Some nights she dreams so much that she is tired the next morning, as if the dreams were so heavy that her body is tired of carrying them on her back all night long. I can tell which nights she's dreamed heavily because the nurses have difficulty waking her in the morning. To wake her, they blast her favorite song, which is "Another Brick in the Wall" by Pink Floyd. When she fails to appear for breakfast, the other people ask, "Where's Dot?" wondering if she's died yet. They are always dying. Hardly one day goes by without one of them dying, and they feel their dying together. They have no use for us anymore, one man told me, holding a photograph of his dead wife in a blue feather boa, the picture placed carefully in a plastic sleeve.

Everything is practice, Dot tells me.

You can't tell all the stories at once, she complains. You have to pick one.

You have to settle on a time and place, she adds.

But, I say, I'm watching you sleep. You might not wake up again.

What if silence is not emptiness, the absence of sound, but the sound of all the stories in the world, being told altogether and all at once?

You think too much, she says. The question is big and I am tired.

Just a few rags today. And I was right about the moon. The light from the neighbor's window pressing through the wall.

The world is too much with us, I tell her.

Not enough, she says and turns the volume up on the television.

We fix our eyes on the television and watch the shows about houses: buying houses, fixing up houses and then tearing them down. It is the spectacle of the houses, going up and going down, that captivates us.

I tell her I have been reading the story of Orpheus and Eurydice and writing a series of letters that begin, "Dear Orpheus."

I can't tell you anything yet about crossing over, she says.

Maybe we've already crossed. You can tell me the names of birds.

The old romances of the face.

Picking rags again.

There is something I want you to know, Dot tells me, without moving her lips.

I had just told her about my newest dream about O, how in the dream he was the captain of a boat.

The best we can hope for is imperfect healing, she says, and scratches her armpits.

I know we're not in the desert now, she says. But sometimes we are.

In my story, I say, the woman lives in the desert and cleans up cat poop. But that can't be all there is, I complain, scraping shit and staring into the eyes of other animals.

Oh, can't it? she tells me, a glint in her eye.

Why do you keep coming here? she finally asks. The nurses have already made their evening rounds, drop by drop all the night's medicine has already been spooned out.

I don't know.

Maybe: I am learning how to live and die.

Don't shut the blinds just yet, she tells me. There is still a little bit of sun left.

When I was a child, I say, I tried to never close my eyes.

Even at night, I slept with just a thin crescent of sight, my eyelids lowered but not fully shut. Every time you shut your eyes, I reasoned, a piece of the world leaks out.

Climbing into Dot's throat was only one possibility among many. It was only one action that led to a particular configuration just as my choice of words, the arrangement of these letters, these words in a sentence, were one configuration in an infinite array of possible outcomes—why I chose to write "the tangle of sheets" instead of "tangled in the twisted sheets." The words are slightly different, but the meaning is the same. Only one possibility out of the many possibilities that includes the possibility of myself in the cabin, myself in the desert, myself at the bedside with Dot.

I'm a ghost, she says simply. Why don't we just admit it.

I'm leaking, I tell her, I am not myself. My underpants are red with blood.

So am I, and she looks down to the rise of her swollen belly.

While she has lost the face in her face, her jowls hanging loosely, her belly has begun to grow as if she were pregnant. Her legs too are sweating fluids. The loose outline of her. Her hands shake as she points.

Stupid women, I say.

When I die, she says, cover my belly up with my patchwork quilt and it will be a mountain to cry on.

Shoulder, I correct her.

Whatever, what have you, phrases.

Are there worlds inside that belly? I ask her, but she's already fallen asleep, or is maybe dead already. It can't just be another void, I say, when you said there is no such thing. When I'm sure she won't wake up, I tell her I want to crawl inside her belly and find whatever is hiding there, what the story tells itself when no one is around.

Life is difficult. It's strange to be here, I write.

I'm bored, Dot says. Start again.

SEND IN THE CLOWNS

Sophie Robinson

The origin of the sad clown story is in Ralph Waldo Emerson's 1876 essay, "The Comic." In Naples, a man is overcome with melancholy. He goes to see a physician, who prescribes him an easy cure: the clown Carlini is in town, and laughter will immediately dispel the patient's melancholia. *But doctor, I am Carlini*, the patient answers.

Earlier this year, a series of losses and changes led me to Los Angeles, and to the reopening of my heart after a long period of relative celibacy. I'll spare you the details, but what became evident to me faster than I'm willing to admit is that it meant a lot, and I became increasingly desperate to win a kind of love and affection from her that she had made it clear she did not have the capacity to offer. Over a sequence of days and weeks, I felt her pull away. A familiar sadness settled onto me, like slipping on a clown suit. A neural pathway. People like me until they know me. Honk honk.

Wild with grief already, and as a last resort, I decided to leave her a ten-minute voice note telling her exactly how I felt. In the preceding week, I had discussed it with my therapist, my sponsor, my best friend. I had given myself countless pep talks, I had comforted myself with self-help idioms: saying how you feel will never ruin a real connection. I remembered the ways in which we had shared intimacy with each other, the ways I had trusted her with my body and my heart, the ways I had doubted myself and felt anxious and been reassured. I felt, in the feral jangling of grief, I had nothing to lose. It was the biggest risk I had taken, outside of my writing, in an attempt towards vulnerability, boundaries, and self-expression.

It couldn't have gone worse. It was over. In truth it was already over and had been for some time, but the space of grief I had already been inhabiting—the trail of deep and painful losses I had been running from—had reduced my capacity for any form of dignity, politeness, or restraint. I refused the gentleman's agreement and named the strength and depth of my feeling, the deep sadness I felt at the mismatch of intensity, the failure of romance, of love, of desire. I spent the following week feeling increasingly clownish, embarrassed, foolish, selfish, invisible, pathetic. It was a familiar feeling—there is nothing more cringeworthy than the mismatch of emotion between two people. I slipped on my clown suit, laced up my clown shoes, painted my nose red.

The most clownish part of the experience was not the sudden, cavernous gap between my inconsolable heartbreak and humiliation and her apparent indifference, but rather my recognition of the ways in which I had ignored or misread the clues and cues, distrusted my own intuition, broken my own rules, freely given the most intimate, private and sacred parts of myself. Nobody had asked me to do that, least of all her, and yet I did. The burden of shame the sad clown carries is not what is done to us but what we allowed ourselves to do in the name of self-abandonment.

The same week I sobbed in my clown suit, I had my final session with my therapist. We'd been working together for a year, I'd seen her twice a week. The work we'd done together had changed my life—she'd seen me through a great deal of grief and heartbreak, and it wasn't my choice to terminate. I felt doubly heartbroken. Our last session was almost useless; I sobbed so much I could barely talk. She nodded patiently. *Hmm, yes, it is sad*, she said, mustering a kind of detached compassion. I wiped my nose on my sleeve, looked away from the Zoom screen and nodded. Our last exchange was an invoice, which I promptly paid. I texted her: *I'll miss you*. The number had already been disconnected. I felt like I was disappearing, invisible, powerless. There's an urge, in such moments, to show the ones who hurt us our sadness, but it does nothing but increase the feelings of humiliation that lead to the donning of the clown suit in the first place: it is humiliating to feel so strongly in the face of indifference or—worse—pity.

I put on Judy Collins in the bath and call a friend. She tries to console me: *what choice did you have? You said how you feel!* I laugh whilst crying. *I could have just shut the fuck up, written a poem about it and moved on. Nobody needed to know!* It's 4:00 PM and getting dark; the music hums on. *Isn't it queer . . . You're funny when you're sad*, my friend says. *Quicker somehow.*

Sondheim wrote "Send in the Clowns" for Act Two of *A Little Night Music*, and in the context of the musical the original meaning of the song is doubled: Desirée is humiliated after being rejected by a suitor who originally pursued her, but she is also humiliated because she deviated from her script, the script of her life. She has taken a miscalculated risk and suffered the consequences. She has forgotten her lines, slipped out of character, lost her way. Sondheim's inspiration for the song was the theater adage, when the show is going badly, send in the clowns. The final line of the song is the punchline: don't bother, they're here. Desirée's anger, her transformation into the clown, is not at the rejection of her proposal but at her own part in it. *But doctor, I am Carlini*, the patient answers.

Bernadette Mayer's poem, "The Way to Keep Going in Antarctica," has sustained me in times of melancholy and grief for two decades. A line that always sticks with me: *Nothing outside can cure you but everything's outside.* I hang up with my friend and dunk my head under the water for a long moment, steam rising in the dusk, a thick fog, drifting southwest from the North Sea, enveloping the city. We are our sickness and our cure. In moments of desperation and humiliation, I cannot help but be reminded of the banal cruelty I have inflicted on others; the ways I have failed them, made them question their sanity, their self-worth, responded less than graciously to their feelings about me or their gestures of attachment. I have hurt and I have been hurt, I have loved too hard and not enough.

The street lights flicker on outside my bathroom window. When I get out of the bath, my nose is red from the heat, I have rings of mascara around my eyes. The music stops and the house is silent, eerie. Why am I embarrassed? It's just me here, nude and barely visible in the steamed-up mirror. The final line of Mayer's poem: *If I suffered what else could I do.* I dry myself off and hang up my clown suit.

TWO POEMS

L Scully

clockwork

I'm not as moved by sound as I should be.
Music is predatory gelatin.
I like barking and I rather hate drag,
but if I were to participate . . . girl . . .
I'd be Helen Boytoy, the face that launch'd
a thousand dicks. Perform for an audience
of urchins. Dollar bill diarrhea.
Behind the curtain is my heart of hearts.
She wears a dinosaur costume made of
gold leaf. Protective as she milks my spine.
I met you when your breasts were full of glass,
no bra, no problem, love was penniless.
Now if you'd please stop that wretched music,
I'll remember how to end a poem.

if/then

Lest the universe bend toward goodness,
diving instructors might tape your ankles.
If you're right, and everything is content,
I'll stop giving you shit about novels.
But if I'm right, and your stomach turns an
emotional yellow, the ligament
of my grandfather's knee might end up
in your holiday turkey sausage. I'm right,
bitch. You know all my tongues. Gamblers
who don't own too much say, "sorry I lost
the basement." There was no house to start with.
If I sneak a toaster into the bath,
call it natural selection. Embalm me
with gazpacho, the color of my thirst.

AMERICAN DENIM

Alex Freeman Hischier

Remember when you used to feel like a fucking god under these lights? That's what I ask myself right as the crowd roars, erupting in laughter. *What the fuck happened to that guy.*

Tonight I taste coins, warm and primal. Pennies. I suck back the little pool of blood forming right behind my teeth and shove both hands down deep into my pockets. I know I need to be pressed back into this moment. What I'm looking for is the straitjacket grip of my Wranglers to squeeze me tight, but all I find is a gaping abyss, loose denim.

It doesn't usually faze me, at all, what I'm wearing. This costume has function. It has to, peoples' lives depend upon it. Out here, it's life and death. I know this. But for whatever reason, tonight it feels like alls I am is a guy in a skirt. There are a thousand eyes on me. Probing and perceiving. They're entertained. Hell, they're captivated because I'm good at what I do. I can tell they don't see me as a man and right now maybe I'm not, cuz honestly I don't really even feel human. Everything goes dark for a flash until my eyes open back up like coin slots. I tip my hat and keep moving. Maybe this is how women feel.

"Nice work out there, Biggs." One of the other barrel men shouts this as we jog past each other. It's my name, not the compliment, that jolts me out of my brain. *Biggs.* He's looking at me sideways like either I'm some sort of legend or a god or a goddamned ghost. He's all baby-faced, young—shit, maybe even younger than me, and I nod but don't say anything. No reason to take a dump all over his bright eyes, his hope.

I'm glad it's my turn to go on break cuz honestly, I'm feeling a little out of sorts. This arena might just be bigger than all the football fields back home put together. I keep jogging towards the edge where some of the contestants are gathered, and I turn to look out at the grandstands. It's one big frenzy, a chaotic sea of flesh, and alls I can see is the whites of people's eyes as they shovel more food into their mouths and slurp their drinks.

A hot wind blasts my face as I step through the fence and saunter up to the coffee pot. I push past the familiar tangle of people. Most of us have been on the circuit for a while now. I'm looking around, still all starry-eyed. This mythical place. I keep half-expecting to turn around and see someone famous, but I don't. There's a thin veil of dust floating in the night air, kicked up from all that nervous livestock. I continue to sweat, even in the sun's absence, and the makeup drips down into my mouth which instantly gives me this sort of weird boner. I picture an icicle.

It's been less than twenty-four hours since I crossed the state line. I got half a tank of gas and twenty-eight bucks to my name, give or take. The year is 1983. I'm twenty-two years old.

At a certain point you just learn to live with it. The overwhelming desire to jerk the steering wheel into oncoming traffic or the compulsion to stick your hand in the garbage disposal. You push it down. Tolerate it. Know it will pass. Pray you don't act on it. Until it all becomes a sort of atmospheric soundtrack that echoes along in the background of your actual life. And maybe you find a job where it sort of doesn't matter or at the very least, no one will notice. It's like I have this bad taste in my mouth that I've just gotten used to over time.

My tongue traces the edge of the Styrofoam and I'm smiling, looking around like a crazed tourist. I can't help it. I know this is inland, but I swear I can taste the salt just sailing in on the bathtub-warm breeze. The ocean's that close. Everything here's hot but not unpleasant, and it feels like I'm in a goddamn commercial or something because it's dark out and the stadium lights are on but the faint colors of the sunset still paint the sky if you look for it. I blow into my coffee like an idiot.

Chopper shots. My mind always defaults to the hovering bird's eye view. I see fat clusters of grapes hanging heavy on their vines that spread out in all directions like arteries. The leaves, rusted gold, starting to change. On the east side of the arena there's an abandoned orchard where persimmons the color of unblemished basketballs cling to the branches and all around the event center, dotting the perimeter, there's these sporadic bursts of palm trees reaching into the sky like fingers. They're whipping back and forth in this crazy hot wind and I'm staring out at them wondering how they haven't already just snapped right in half, hearts in my eyes. Nothing about this place feels real to me.

"This your first time in the golden state, son?"

"Yessir," I say, spinning around obediently like a dog on command. There's this beige flash with a butt-white sparkle at its center, and I instantly know it's Russell Owens, one of the announcers. He's wearing a brand-new-black Stetson, leaning against the fence holding his coffee in one hand and a half-ate donut in the other. He looks more like a lizard than a man and he's smiling at me with those unbelievable Hollywood choppers like he thinks he knows me or something.

"Been hearing about you on the circuit awhile now, Biggs. And much to my surprise, you're just as good as they say you are. But what I can't decide on is whether you're fearless or just have a plain ol' hope-to-die death wish." He sips his coffee thoughtfully.

I sort of half-smile. It feels like he's eyeballing me but when I really look at him, I can tell he's spacing out, staring right through me. His eyes are glowing, neon pink. I'm watching his pupils drift past the palm trees, violent and swaying. Little circles of Ferris wheel reflecting back at me.

"I'll bet this all just seems like some sort of paradise compared to where you come from."

"Pretty much." I shrug. "Like another world."

"Wait till these devil winds really get going, puts everyone on edge." He pauses, glancing over at the holding pen. "Animals included."

Right then a blood-curdling scream slices the night, instantly dwarfing all other sounds. It only lasts a few seconds, but we turn anyways looking up like we can't help it. A lone baseball cap rips through the sky so fast you can barely make out what it is exactly, a red blur riding on the wind. At the tippy-top of the Ferris wheel a frantic woman searches the air, engulfed completely in her own hair.

"That's my cue." Russell stuffs the last of the donut in his mouth, quickly sucks the powdered sugar off a finger. "Better head back up to the booth. Get a clear view of all the action. I can't wait to see what you do with these Santa Ana's, son."

He flicks his eyebrows lazily a few times, up and down, like he's trying to really make sure I know he's serious. I'm nodding politely, looking over at the press box. It's partially enclosed so I can't really see into it or anything, but I know there's a few other announcers up there, probably also dressed to the nines, seated in front of their microphones and their monitors. I feel keenly aware of the face I'm making because I know it's only gonna be amplified tenfold in all this makeup. Doesn't matter though cuz he's gone already.

I can feel the commotion coming from the bullpen; it's adrenaline-laced and feels like thunder against my chest. I refill my coffee even though I know my break's nearly over. There's a bull thrashing about the chute, the metal groans beneath its weight. Seventeen hundred pounds of pure muscle. That's my guess, anyways.

In my mind's eye I see a whale in a cup. The picture materializes then vanishes just as quickly. I take a quick sip and swallow it down even though the coffee's a little too hot. I gotta get back in the arena. I notice all the typical fair odors floating around on the breeze, especially the ones I'm accustomed to like funnel cakes and manure and fear and refined sugar. But here, beneath all of that, the air smells of oranges. It's faint and mystical and for a split second I feel giddy like a teenager, all lovey-dovey on California.

A Roughie walks by, spurs jingling, and he stops abruptly a couple feet away from me to stare at the chutes. The draw number on his back is flapping wildly like a white flag of surrender in this hot wind, #86. Its sound reminds me of speeding down the highway getting flanked by a desperate-to-pass semi, and I can't seem to look away. That's when he turns around and his face lights up. For me, what happens is that time slows down, because I instantly doubt what it is that's actually happening. *This isn't supposed to happen.*

"—Biggs! You old bastard, look at you. Christ, I haven't seen you since you were about yay high."

He says this as he's walking towards me, a hand hovering above his waist. It's him. It's Tony. I recognize the voice almost instantly and I feel like I'm gonna throw up. The way the sound raised the hairs on the back on my neck. Swore to myself if I ever did see him again that I'd confront him, but I don't of course. Everything inside me feels like Jell-O, and all the things I wanted to say just sort of evaporate right into that moment. It's do–or die and I don't *do* anything. I'm just standing there and I feel like a goddamn clown, which is pretty poetic, isn't it.

I sort of go on autopilot. I'm working so I just smile like it's all part of the performance, waiting on the words to come. I'm glad my face is already covered in white makeup cuz I'm sure as shit sheet-white right now, looking at him. I have to compose myself. Pretend this is normal. Pretend this is no big deal. Here we are in California of all places, land of the golden dream, where anything's possible.

"Oh, come on now!" I say after a few seconds pass. "I think I was a little taller than that, coach." It's 1977 all over again and he's shutting the office door behind me. He always seemed so much older back then, but now that I'm standing here and it feels like a whole entire lifetime has passed, ten years doesn't feel like that big an age difference.

Tony laughs and it makes my skin crawl.

"Aw, I know. Just messin' with you, Biggs. But man oh man, has it been a long time."

"It sure has." I nod, running a finger slowly over my eyebrow and down the side of my face like I'm drawing a line in the sand of my flesh. There's a hint of baby blue smeared across the upper part of my palm, and I force myself to breathe.

He was the assistant football coach that year. Just for one season, but everything changed after that. He looks the same to me. His thick neck. His crooked smile. The chipped tooth. He took a special interest in me when no one else did.

His chaps are flashy even though they're faded, the color of melted orange sherbet. He's holding his bull rope in the curl of his fist, looking me up and down like he's amused or something.

"I never really paid much thought either way to the world of rodeo clowns before, you know? But you've changed the game, Biggs. You got reputation. You're one helluva bullfighter, I'm glad it's you out there watching my back." He winks before turning his head back towards the chutes. "Speaking of, I gotta git."

"See you out there," I say, and it feels stupid coming out of my mouth. Tony's already walking away and I'm just standing there holding an empty cup. I'm pretty sure the Santa Ana's are starting to blow again and I'm back to watching the violent flicker of that same draw number waving at me, #86. The wind knocks a half-full Coke can off a nearby table, and that's pretty much how I feel after seeing Tony. I'm a piece of garbage blowing around by some unseen force.

I'm sixteen again and I feel helpless. So vulnerable.

So impressionable. So fat with need.

The announcers are working their special brand of magic, cuz the crowd's all fired up and the energy in the arena is electric. We're in the short go now, so it's only the best riders, the cream of the crop. I'm back in the ring but still so far outside myself, it's like I got locked out.

Trying my hardest to shake it off, to suck it up, be unfazed, and instead I'm suddenly back to feeling like I'm not actually human but now for reasons other than how I'm dressed. I feel like a doll or a scarecrow, sort of impotent and empty. I kick the dirt and bend my knees in preparation for the next bull to charge out. This rider makes the eight seconds no problem and is tossed clear of the bull like a big pad of melting butter, so there's nothing much for me to do there. He throws his cowboy hat into the air and the crowd goes wild as the wind carries it right towards all those open hands in the bleachers.

The sky's as dark as an oil seep and there's no trace of sunset left behind anymore, all the colors gone back to black. This wind is relentless, heat filled. My eyeballs feel like bones. The line of palm trees in the distance bend impossibly from side to side, in unison, and I swear it feels like if these vicious blasts don't stop soon, they're gonna knock something loose.

The loudspeaker crackles above me and I tune back in to the announcer's chatter booming across the arena; they're hyping up this next matchup. Widow Maker is what they call the bull. I hear Russell's voice say, "This beast isn't just a bull; it's a force of nature, feared and respected in equal measure." The air's thick with tension and applause and that's when I hear it. Rider #86. My body goes limp and I feel all my cells recoiling at the sound of his name, his full fucking name, as it ricochets around the arena and people are cheering their heads off. What I want to do is disappear but I can't cuz I'm on display and on the clock, so instead I do a cartwheel and launch myself into a nearby barrel the minute Widow Maker's name is mentioned again and the crowd goes wild. I come back out and take a bow before dragging the barrel off to the side.

When the chute finally flies open, Widow Maker explodes into the arena like a grenade, and the stands erupt with excitement. He's twisting and kicking and spinning ferociously in this crazy wind. Rider #86 hangs on, his body moving fluidly in sync with the erratic animal. The crowd roars as the seconds tick past, and after eight seconds the buzzer sounds, but the ride isn't over, he keeps going. The bull makes a hard twist and

Tony loses his balance. He tries to dismount, but his hand is caught in the bull rope, trapping him against the bull's side. I see the beast sense this and start to buck even harder, dragging Tony mercilessly across the arena's dirt floor. Gasps and screams ripple through the stands as the reality of the situation sets in. "We need help in the arena—NOW! Get him out of there!" The announcer's voice falters calling for us bullfighters, but we're already on it.

We clowns spring to action. One waves his arms and jumps in front of the bull to draw its attention, while another dives for the rope. Widow Maker thrashes violently around the arena, refusing to be distracted. We try everything but can't seem to get close enough. Dust fills the air and the cheers have turned to horrified silence. That's when I see a window and instinctively move in.

Tony's flailing right in front of me, caught on the bull like a rag doll. I'm so close I can smell the stale nicotine on his shirt. I'm reaching out to get his hand free and I freeze, my fingers turning into spaghetti. It's like my body won't let me help him. My other hand pushes up against the bull's flank, its hide is hot with rage. I'm looking into Tony's face and there's blood streaming down in all directions, crusted in dirt. His eyes are fixed right on mine, he's watching me, and I can't tell if he's pleading with me or daring me as his lips curl into a smile. He looks just like a monster and I remember everything. I'm right there practically touching the bull rope, but my body revolts.

The Widow Maker bolts away towards the other end of the arena and I watch Tony's limp form flailing against its side. He's helpless as the bull drags him, his body slamming against the ground with each violent buck, and I feel nothing. Eventually, some of the other bullfighters are able to loosen the rope, freeing his hand. Tony is lying there motionless in the dirt as the bull runs off, and the arena is eerily silent.

The squawking of seagulls comes down in a light drizzle. It's daybreak and I'm lying on the beach. Their language is gibberish but they remind me of feral children, fighting over this brittle piece of pizza crust. The sky's lit up with light pinks, peaches, violets, and I'm surrounded by the constant chorus of waves crashing on the shore. I push the soles of my boots down into the sand as far as I can. My face is still covered in makeup but I'm wearing my Wranglers and I feel calm, peaceful. Sort of like everything's gonna be okay.

Dead leaves look like deflated brown footballs scattered across the beach. I take my shirt off and start walking towards the water. It's hypnotic, and the waves don't look that big, I keep my boots on. The ocean's ice-cold and there's something about it that feels different somehow; it's not like regular water. I feel lighter than I have in a long time. I'm on my back, floating away, and I can feel the denim getting tighter against my flesh.

WHIM REAPER

Dia Felix

Slowly but on the other hand surely I was flown from sky to earth in the talons of a giant bird: it didn't hurt. She was holding onto my jacket maybe, not my flesh? We drifted over water and then shore and then soft sand, closer and closer. When I was firmly on the earth, I was delivered from the dream back into waking life. How special, and I was refreshed. A sweet smell entered into my room, oranges and lemons and dark dirt after rain. Cheerful sounds entered from the window area, which glowed brightly. I learned that you cannot actually hold your own hand but—it's ok. I heard chimes, and the low bellowing honk of the faraway train. Like many, I like trains, liked being on them, liked hearing the sound of the train, a notification that travel was afoot, even as I lay in my bed, which felt like a sort of loaf cake of limitless self-love. A simmer. Love is in the pots, in the blankets, in the rashes, in the moist undergarments, in the drunken bedbugs, in the excrement, in the frayed wires, in the plastic, in the rot, in the fissures, in the pipes, in the sheetrock, in the limousines, in the cheese, in the cabinets, in the holy water, in the dirty water, in the snot that covers the baby, in the baby, in the box of chocolates, in the abandoned heart, in the beloved heart, in the subway smell, in the digital images—

When I heard a knock. Too close. Hello? I said, my rough morning voice. Mostly air. Hi, said a voice, neither calm nor fretful, neither morose nor exuberant, neither cruel nor kind, neither rushed nor languorous. Um, hi, I said, knowing that the person was inches away, on the other side of my nearly-closed bedroom door. Can I help you? I said, ridiculously. The window glowed still brighter. I heard some Cello notes in the back of my knees. I was naked, too. The Cello which was one of Bach's cello suites resonated up and down my legs and through my system. I felt flooded with bliss even as I knew there was an intruder and I could not vanquish them—I just knew this, and I accepted it peacefully. The delicate taste of yellow cake blossomed sourceless on my tongue, very subtly. Then, the very gentle taste of coffee ice cream. The room became a box of light. The door creaked open. A clown entered the suite, walking sideways, a touch jig-like. Billowy orange pants, funny little black hat. He sat on the side of the bed and held out his hand. I could smell his wax. The cello suite felt a little generic and the music shifted to the creamed waterfall of a human voice. It was the clown himself singing to me, hand outstretched. Oh, here we go, I thought. Such private extravagance. Such tiny fishes swimming through our hands, met. All those things I didn't do but—it's ok. The clown smiled his oversized smile. A daisy grew out of his hat. Death had come.

FLIES ON THE WINDSCREEN

Danny LeVesque

He had a little table in front of him, one of those hospital bed tables on wheels. It dangled over his chest and belly from the side of the bed until I would roll it out of the way so I could pull him up on the sheet below him. Readjusting his body every few hours helped him to not go crazy. A week ago, he went paralyzed from the chest down, and everything above that was scalding pain. Pulling him up in the bed helped to keep the blood flowing and made him feel like something could be done.

I never looked at the bedsore on his tailbone. I would proudly clean his shit, monitor his catheter output, keep him perfectly medicated, but I could not look at the bedsore. The hospice nurse would keep me posted, that was her job.

When I rolled him over so she could check it, I held his arms, told him it would be quick, she just has to look at it. I was running on cortisol and brain-protecting chemicals, those shock chemicals, where I could have lifted a car off him if I had to.

That horror strength that people get in emergencies, I had that for eight weeks. "The sore is getting big," she stage-whispered to me across his body.

"I bet," I said.

She talked about him like he wasn't there, wasn't listening.

"It feels like someone has claws, claws ripping my chest apart," he said. He made the motion of hooked fingers, pulling outwards from the center of his sternum.

"This sucks," he said. "Sucks, huh?"

"Yeah. Yup. This fuckin' sucks," he said.

There were a bunch of items on his table for a while, maybe for the first three weeks. It was a landing pad for the things he was clinging to, things he could control. He would move the objects around every half hour, making sure they were just right and everything was in its place, clean lines. A bell. A golf marker. His phone, glasses, water glass, plastic containers of lip balm, a full cup of applesauce, his dentures, a small plastic hobo figurine I had given him for his birthday when I was in fourth grade.

The figurine sat on his table in the far corner, right side. It was a hobo clown with holes in his shoes and a walking stick. Its resin face wore minimal makeup, a lot of the white had rubbed off over time. It was painted sad with small brushstrokes, rounded edges on the frown and around the eyes. Pointy make up is only for sociopathic clowns. Not all clowns are happy.

We need the sad clown, hopeless and free, not a nickel to his name and all the power of The Fool. I'd be happy as a hobo. It's all I ever hoped to be. Some tell me that's a low bar, but don't think for a minute that hobo clowns are lazy. They chose this. Survival is a hustle. Sure, they look sad in their downcurved mouth paint but underneath all the sad, they're still clowns. There's always a glimmer of "oh well, I'm sad, doo dee doo." Sad clowns are not clinically depressed, they're just poor and comfortable in their sadness. The only time they're happy is when they're sad.

"Look at my arms," he said. "I know."

"They're getting so skinny."

The visiting nurse wrapped a measuring tape around his upper arm twice a week, noting the dropping centimeters.

"He's losing a lot of weight," she said.

"Yeah, he is," I said, "he can hear you, ya know. You can talk right to him."

"Yeah, I'm not dead yet," he said, rolling his eyes behind her back for me to see.

We laughed, laughed a lot during the slow death.

As the days passed, he began to eliminate items from the table one by one. The construction paper lace heart: give it to my great granddaughter. The bell: get it away from me. For a week, the table whittled down to his glasses, phone, notebook, a cup of crushed ice, a watch, the hobo, and a child's juice box with a sad straw he struggled to find his lips with. I would guide the wet straw to his lips, tell him go slow.

"Never mind me. You need to eat something, Francis," he said. "Have you eaten today, anything?"

"No, I'm not hungry." I wasn't. All adrenaline breath and stiff muscles, I was balled up in the actions of one slow second at a time.

"Eh, you never ate much anyways," he said.

I dreaded dinnertime, always hoping for some food-pill breakthrough to come down the pike. All the nutrition in one pill, taken once or twice daily, I would have been licking my fingers. Since birth I have never been a foodie, resisting the bottle of Similac with a screech. Even now I find it boring, some vestigial human need that I can somehow ignore to death. There has to be a simpler way than all that chewing, digesting, plate cleaning. Give me the pill.

"Have something, Francis."

"Ok I'll have some cereal. And maybe one of your protein shakes you're supposed to be drinking. You're not drinking them, right?"

"Noooo, thank you. Drink them all," he said. He hadn't eaten anything in six days. Hadn't had a bowel movement in a week, intestinal blockage.

From the kitchen I could still see him, still talk to him. "What're ya having?" He craned his neck to look at me. "Uhhh, I'm gonna have some Mini Wheats I guess."

"The sugar kind?"

"Yeah."

"Ah I loved those," he said. Past tense.

I flipped the small wheat squares to be all frosted-sides-up, then dumped a geriatric protein shake over them. This protein shake is the closest I've been able to find to a food-pill so far. Shotgun it and bloat, in ten minutes I feel like I had a ribeye. I took my seat by his bed with my clumpy bowl of nutrients and took a bite. He laughed at me.

"What?" I had pea protein curdling at the corners of my mouth.

"You're funny," he said.

"Why?" I laughed.

"You just are, always have been." He looked at my cereal bowl.

"Are they stale?"

"Huh?"

"The wheat things. Are they stale?" He squished his face up. "I hate when they're stale."

"Me too." I took another big bite, making quick work of the food requirement. "No, not really stale," I said, downplayed it. They were stale.

He was still making the stale face.

"Gross," he said, "maybe next time just have the shake part."

"Agreed. The liquid format suits my constitution better anyways."

He laughed.

"What, it doesn't?" I said. "Why not?"

(This is how New England Canucks talk to one another, statements followed immediately by a defensive question—an automatic defense in the face of no offense. It's a useful tool of conversational aggression and it runs in my blood.)

He was looking up at the ceiling, smiling. He had stopped wearing a shirt, making it easier for me to change his fentanyl patches. He often would look up, smile at the ceiling, thinking. Laugh to himself, stretch his arms a bit, say, "ah, oui."

Rita had done similar things three years ago, while I laid with her on her deathbed in a beige facility designed only for the dying.

She would look up at the ceiling, outside of her body, already leaving. "Wow," she said, "Oh my God."

"What?" I said. "What are you looking at?" "It's so big."

"What's so big?"

"Love, Francis. Love is so big. I wish you could see what I'm seeing. Wowwww." "Tell me everything," I said.

"I can't. Can't explain it. My God."

She went in and out of consciousness a few times an hour, nipping at

the veil. When not in the holy place, she would return to the room, to the cursed body, to me lying next to her. Upon rejoining me she'd keep her eyes open, their small veins

rising and pumping, amber fountains adrenal. She'd scan the room, the flowers, my face. When she was floating, the room smelled like DMT.

"I wish you could see it. So big. Someday, someday you'll see it," she said, assessing the other side before she let go and dropped her body, ready to join The Bigness of it all.

When I was a kid we lived in the same tenement, her and my grandparents on the second floor and me with my family on the first. She had stayed with my grandparents since she returned from the convent in Oklahoma with a broken back. The nuns, they broke her back. Mother Superior made her dive into the pool, her switchblade lips twitching as Rita jumped. In a fabulous belly flop, her spine broke into pieces and that was that. She never really recovered.

When she got home, she was bedridden, living in my grandparents' apartment.

As soon as I woke up, I would run to her. I'd race down the dangerous steps of the cellar in twos and threes, across the lair of whistling water heaters, fuse boxes and ghosts, using the stairs on the other side to make my way up to the second floor. This was the way to navigate the tenement without having to go outside: use the cellar or the attic to access different staircases to get to different floors.

I would dash past my grandparents with a quick hello, and head right to Rita's room, my vibration bringing her around from a Demerol nod. She'd open her eyes and smile, connected, patting the bed until I crawled into it with her. For hours we could lay in silence together, usually falling asleep. She taught me the ways of the day sleeper, and I'd still rather sleep while the sun is beaming, with washing machines and screeching cars as my sound bath. Sunrises are overrated.

From her bed, Rita taught me how to read. She never complained to me about her pain. It was visible, it filled the world, there was no need to discuss it. When she was able to walk again, we'd head up the hill by the stoplight, up to the cemetery where the angels sat, spinning concrete ribbons over dusty bones. She'd have me pick out my ABCs from the names etched at their sacred feet.

Rita always looked out for me, making sure I had a doll, some fashion sandals, and anything else I required as a child fag. One time we took a bus to the mall so I could go to Spencer's and she bought me a tube of Clown White. The best gift I have ever received, that single tube set the trajectory for the rest of my life. "For your clown shows," she said.

I think I used it up in a week, tearing through it, absorbing it through my skin, solidifying a pattern that would follow me forever. Never saved a wake-up, I don't care what the plan was.

I looked at Rita from my place next to her on the bed. I was cuddled up with her just like when I was little, only now she was tiny and my feet hung off the edge. The tenement was gone, and here she was in this place, dying.

"Am I?" she said.

"Are you what, ma tante?" "Am I dying?"

"Yes." I said.

"Ok, I guess. I guess it takes a long time to die," she said. "But I'm not scared." A few days later I got the call that she was gone, and then the world locked up.

I wiped the glob of protein shake out of my nose and brought my bowl into the kitchen. He had his eyes closed now, maybe he was asleep. I sat back down at my station by his side, wearing my black sweatshirt with the hood up. I kept my hood up the whole time, its peripheral edges giving me a cave to retreat to without moving from my post.

"Hey . . . last night when you woke me up for meds I thought it was the Angel of Death, all I saw was the black hood and the shadow," he said, "I though ah marde, this is it. He's here."

"I'm sorry, Dad," I said.

"It's ok. Just a matter of time." "Yeah."

We would become silent and look at each other. He'd hold the edge of his blanket and wring it in his hands, his long skinny fingers pulling it in opposite directions. His oxygen machine would break any silence with its loud *pssssht* every forty-five seconds.

"Ya know, everybody keeps saying that oxygen thing sounds like waves crashing, but I dunno," he said. "To me it sounds like cannons firing,"

"Yeah, me too," I said, "it sounds like explosions."

He moved the items around on his table, seeing what he would eliminate next. The method fascinated me. He'd slide the objects forward and back until they landed in the exact spot, while he reassessed the purpose of each one.

"Hey, see this old watch?"

"Yeah, I like that watch," I said.

"Well, great, you can have it. Take it." He just wanted it off his table.

"It's ok, I don't wear a watch. Remember ma tante Rita used to buy me a watch every Christmas even though I never wore them?"

"Oh yeah," he laughed. "You had a drawer full of watches. She just bought 'em because she loved you, though. That's why."

"I know," I said, "I never knew how to break it to her that I couldn't stand a watch, I just let her keep buying them."

"Well, if you don't want this one, can you at least put it over there?" He picked it up and gestured in no particular direction as he handed it to me. "Yeah, put it over there for later, maybe your cousin Marc will want it. Yeah, send it to Marc."

One more thing off the table, everything in order. He took the hobo clown in his hands and brought it to his chest. "Remember when you were a kid, we did our clown show at the church?"

"Of course," I said. It was a fuzzy memory to me, but he saw every frame clearly, remembered the whole skit.

"We both came in from opposite ends of the stage, we didn't have shoes on, remember?" He smiled, ocean eyes swirling memories.

I did remember. He had created our outfits, putting shadow beards and dirt smudges on our faces by burning the end of a wine cork and rubbing the ash onto our skin. He painted frowns over our lips with one of my mom's old lipsticks. We wore

overalls with the legs rolled up and lumberjack shirts with holes in them. Each of us carried a stick with a bandana pouch on the end, cementing the total look.

Performing for the assembled church families, we entered from the wings and met each other center stage, two strangers, aimless tramps just happy to find each other. We did a glorious double pratfall when we bumped into each other, both falling over backwards with silent open mouths. He was a master of pratfalls, as am I. Those people should have clapped. We were that good.

When we got up off the floor, we shook our heads in circles like dizzy cartoon characters, dusted ourselves off and then brushed each other's shoulders off with the back of our smudged hands. He took a hidden feather duster loaded with talcum powder out of his pocket and smacked it across my face a few times, creating a dust cloud. We brought props, operating way above the level of any of the other performers that night. This church did not deserve us.

We took a beat—the entire performance was silent—and then began to look around the set, which was comprised of old crates, cardboard boxes, and a stop sign that my sister's derelict boyfriend had stolen. I think he's a cop now, the boyfriend, officious and miserable in that same disappointing town we lived in. Maybe he's dead.

When our hobo eyes connected, we looked each other up and down, both of us observing that neither one of us had shoes on. We mimed concern verging on sorrow over our shoeless feet, with sweeping arm movements and back-of-the-room facial expressions. Here we are together, our feet bare. He started rummaging through one of the cardboard boxes, diving in and pulling out the contents one at a time.

First, he pulled out bits of trash, cans and balled up newspapers that he tossed blindly over his shoulder onto the stage. Then he pulled out a flattened diaper, holding it up for the crowd's examination before doing a hot-potato and throwing it into the air. When the diaper landed on the stage with a plop, I feigned horror by placing my hands at my jaw and slapping on an exaggerated scream face. Classic. Then both of us went deep, pinching our nostrils and waving our hands around to indicate smelliness. The miming was getting serious and the crowd was eating it up. You can't lose with a diaper gag. We were hitting our stride.

Next, he went into the box and pulled out our family dog, a worn-out poodle named Mimi, who had been in there for ten minutes. We imagined her doing a hind-legged pirouette or some other poodle trick, but she proved untrainable for serious clown shows. She was shooed off without ceremony, exiting stage left, to my clapping sister. Mimi wasn't as effective as the diaper, and it seemed we were teetering on a magic show. We had to pull it back.

Our attention landed on a pair of shoes sitting by the foot of the box, previously hidden from the audience by a bucket that held up the stop sign. They were bright blue pleather with tassel embellishments in the same blue, tone on tone. We looked at the shoes, then down at our dirty bare feet. The scramble began, who would get the shoes first. We dove onto them, our elbows thumping on the stage. Comical mock fisticuffs erupted. He had been a boxer, so he made it look realistic while still reading comedy.

We danced around the shoes in frenzied circles until we both tried to grab them at the same time. We rolled around on the floor for a few seconds, then pulled our arms up from the fray to reveal each of us holding a single shoe.

He put his arm around me, and we sauntered over to a busted crate that we sat on, a single blue shoe in each of our hands. He gestured at my left foot and then got down on one knee by my side, putting his shoe onto my foot, then sat back down on the crate. His thumbs twiddled, and he made his mouth into a whistle as he peeked at the other shoe in my hand. I looked down at his feet and then back up at the shoe, repeating the back and forth three times.

I sunk my head for effect, slumped over a bit. I took a look at my feet, and then at his feet. I mimed that he should have both shoes, that he could have his back, and I would give him mine. In return he shook his head in a wide no, wagging his finger.

I gave the Oh, Well shrug and motioned to his right foot. He smiled as he lifted it off the stage. I presented the shoe to him, holding it in front of his eyes, and then slipped it onto his foot. We threw our arms around each other's shoulders, grabbed our bandana pouches, and made our exit, both of us skipping away wearing one bare foot and one blue shoe. The audience clapped.

He was still clutching the hobo figurine, wrapping it in the edge of his blanket. "Remember those blue shoes?" he asked.

"I do," I said.

"Where the hell did I get those shoes?" "I don't know," I laughed.

"They were so ugly. Blue shoes. Who wears blue shoes, I mean I never bought blue shoes, so it's not like I just had 'em laying around. God, they were ugly. Where the hell did I get those stupid things?"

He was going back in his mind, mining for questions he had never asked, and he really wanted to know where the shoes came from. He had wanted to know all the answers for a solid week, and then the script changed. I don't know what order everything went in for that last chunk of time. It wasn't a blur, it was a hyperfocus. Too crisp at the edges, rapid fire bits of information blending together, his hands turning colder, shakier, with veins bulging. With his blue eyes getting icier and more clear, he looked like an angel, like a little boy.

Going back and moving forward were meshing, he was starting to evaporate, his bones disintegrating. Everything became accelerated and charged, the house vibrating with visiting ancestors. He would speak in French to them, the figures in mist, ghosts on the ceiling. He'd answer their questions and ask some of his own.

"This is a hard step to take," he said. "Dying?"

"Yep. It's like there's a hole I could step into, it's just taking that step, my god, it's scary. It's a lot to commit to, ya know?" He was focused on the spinning fan on the ceiling. "Hey...hey, can you turn that thing off?"

"Sure." I got up and turned the round switch, then returned to my place by his bed. "It was bugging you, the fan?"

"Yes," he said, "things are starting to bug me. I'm even tired of people." He made his fingers do a little walk on the tabletop. "Tired of people. Except for you. I'm glad you're here, Francis."

I gave him a bunch of oxycodone and some morphine, some liquid benzos under his tongue. I kept him pretty loaded as the pain increased every minute, every day.

"What's happening?" he would say, "why is it hurting more now?"

"That's just another shitty thing, Dad. As this progresses, the pain gets worse. As you get closer, I mean."

"I'm getting closer, huh?" "Yes."

"Hold my hand," he said.

He made a circle with his other finger, tracing the edges of the planet. "Ya know, everything we've been taught to think is important is actually

opposite," he said. His voice got small, barely audible, tears cracking in the voice box. "Is that becoming more clear now?" I asked.

"Oh, yeah," he said, "for sure. All we do is give ourselves shit about stuff that doesn't matter in the end. God, we're so hard on ourselves. Listen, son, don't ever give yourself shit. Ever. There's enough of that to go around already."

He drifted off to sleep as dusk settled to dark, his thin hand still in mine. I dozed off in my chair to nightmare sleep, instant R.E.M. upon closing my eyes. When I woke up it was dark in the room and he was talking.

"I dunno . . . I dunno," he was saying to the air.

"What don't you know?" I asked, my eyes leaking fire. He looked at me and smiled, glad I was awake.

"I dunno, Francis. I can't pin it down but I'm seeing it."

"What is it? What're you seeing?"

"Whelp, look, there's a panorama of beauty like you've never seen, never seen in your life." He pointed at the ceiling fan. "Behind that fan, you know. There's stripes.

And they're moving this way." He held his hands up and pulled them slowly away from each other. "This way."

"They're opening up like that? Like gates?" I said.

"Nope, not like that. Like that probably but nope. They open up and then they come, drop down, then they close again." He was making all of the motions with his hands. "Nope, they close and they stay closed . . . but then they shine like the sun. I don't get it. They're supposed to be pastel. Ah, I don't know."

"There were pastel stripes? "Pastel what?" he said.

"Stripes, pastel stripes," I said, "you were talking about pastel stripes."

"Ah, oui." He looked up, his hands still held high to the ceiling. "Well, I dunno, everything's disappeared now, see, they have it. My story is gone now, my story disappeared. Oh, but it's gonna come back. It's gonna come back, what I saw on the other side of that fan, it's gotta come back. Yeah. There's something behind all of that."

"Is it another world, what you're seeing?" I was swirling in a mirror of ghosts, no separation. He wasn't visiting them; they were here in the room, and I was part of it. I could see them too, could hear their whispers. The lights flicked on and off in Morse code patterns, a solid minute of them going on and off by themselves, nobody near the switch.

"I don't understand it," he said, "see, I am an understander. I like to think. I like to be able to figure things out."

"I know."

"But I can't figure that out. I've never seen anything like that in my life," he said. "It just happened tonight?" I asked.

"Yessir," he said, "Wow. Yessir. It was something, it was something that almost...ityour eyes can penetrate through...does that sound funny?"

"No."

"It's like I can look, I can look through everything right now," he said, pointing at the ceiling, "and see . . . I can see . . . the beauty that's on the other side. That is such gift, to be able to say 'I know what that's like. And I wanna go there.' And eh, maybe I don't but I do. You understand?"

"I do."

"I don't know . . . I'm gonna . . . look, I'm gonna say something here, and it might rock this boat a little, but I don't know . . . I don't know if it's the medicines that are causing . . . these hallucinations . . . that I'm having . . . but the medication, I'm sure has something to do with it." He was reaching for explanations, wanted a concrete answer. Then he looked at me and said, "Hey I still get two more pain pills and a sleeping one tonight, right?"

"Yes," I said, "you can have as many as you want. I'm not gonna let you suffer." "Nope I won't suffer. I'm not gonna suffer," he said. He looked around and then

into my eyes. "Hey Francis, is what I'm seeing real? All that stuff behind the fan, ya know, when everything goes away? Is it real?"

"Yes, it's real," I said, "if you are seeing it, it's real." "Well, that's the only thing that matters."

"You got that right," I said. "Huh?"

"I said you got that right."

"You better believe it I got that right," he said, "you better believe it. And . . . ah . . . well . . . I guess . . . que será, será . . ."

I started humming it, choking on mucous and the salt of tears. He joined in, singing in his dying voice.

Que será, será
Whatever will be, will be
The future's not ours to see
Que será, será
What will be, will be.

He put the figurine back onto the table, slid it around on the surface till it reached its place in the right back corner. He looked at it and smiled, patted its head.

"Can you hold my hand again?" he said. "I love you, you know that right?"

"What I don't?" I said, "what I don't know that?"

He closed his eyes. The hobo sat there holding court, proud and strong, overlooking a tray of pennies.

It would not be moved by him again. The hobo would still be there when they took his body away, when they wheeled him out to a van to transport him to cremation. I forgot to take it from the table, I don't know what became of it. I dream that it will show itself someday, in my version of heaven, and he will be there, whole, surrounded by all the hobo saints and beautiful clowns that come tumbling in, tumbling in to call us all home.

GAZELLE

Riley Yaxley

His car smelled like hand sanitizer and used condoms. He asked for the randomly-generated pin to confirm my identity, and I read the number from my phone, waving goodbye to my friend through the tinted window. He thanked me for flagging him from the intersection to prevent him from turning left on 18th Street and needing to make an immediate U-turn. I primly placed my purse on my lap and fumbled with the zipper, intending to remove *The Topeka School* and continue reading: I wanted to know whether the father, a psychologist, would cheat on his wife with her closest friend and colleague, and cement his prior infidelity into a pattern, signaling an incontrovertible attitude toward monogamy, his wife, or marriage generally. But the driver interrupted before I could open the book.

How is your day going? the driver asked. He looked at me through the rearview mirror. He was middle-aged and stocky. He had a misshapen nose that looked like it had been broken multiple times and vaguely resembled the colorful, organic-shaped holds of a rock-climbing wall. I thought he was attractive for an older man.

Pretty good. I was seeing a friend before they move to Mexico later this month, I explained and slid my thumb in between the pages of my book before closing it.

Out of courtesy, I asked how long he had been driving that day, which I thought was less generic than asking about his experience driving for Uber since the answer always seemed to be the same: inconsistent pay, flexible hours, good if they enjoyed socializing, bad if they were precious about their car's cleanliness and longevity.

Eight hours, he answered. Though, I'm on vacation.

What do you mean? You're working on your vacation?

I was supposed to visit my father in Texas, but he called last week and told me he would visit me later this month in Chicago instead. So, I have the week off from my day job. I'm a full-time building engineer for an investment firm downtown, he interjected, noticing the inquisitive look on my face.

Oh, interesting. Do you see your dad often?

Twice a year, usually.

Are you from Texas?

No, I was born and raised in Chicago. My dad and I were both in the Navy. He moved to Texas because there's no state income tax, so your money goes farther.

I was uncertain how their military service related to our conversation, but I assumed it was a clumsy interjection, a detail he wanted to share with me but couldn't find a clear transition to introduce, like an amateur filmmaker alluding to some extraneous detail, disrupting the tone of a scene. Where in Texas does he live? I asked.

He's north of Dallas, in Sherman, a small city near the border of Texas and Oklahoma. Unremarkable place, honestly, but Eisenhower's birthplace is nearby if you're interested in presidential history.

Not particularly, I remarked. My friends and I visited Lincoln's home last spring during a trip to Springfield when we had an afternoon to kill. We watched like twenty minutes of a reenactment film in a room that smelled like mildew and reminded me of a courtroom before my friend grew bored and insisted we visit a dying local shopping mall, which my friend thought was a much more "American" monument.

My friend wanted us to meet the mall security guard she befriended during her residency in the university town, an older man who often told my friend he would have married her if they met when he was younger and still virile. I thought he was unremarkable—flaking knuckles, narrow shoulders—and I was disgusted when he placed his hand on my friend's shoulder and rubbed his palm in wide circles.

The driver watched me closely through the rearview mirror as if trying to read a weathered poster glued to a lamppost. I wondered if my voice betrayed that I was transgender. I decided to ask him another question to minimize my speaking role: Are you close with your dad? What is he like? I asked.

He's kind of the silent type, you know, doesn't really enjoy making conversation. A bit of a womanizer. That's why he and my mom are separated. But he has a pontoon boat we take out on Lake Texoma in the early mornings to fish together. Last November he caught this massive blue catfish. It must have been three or four feet long. I had to help him pull it into the boat because it was so heavy. We fried it that night with some potatoes. Real Southern shit, he reminisced.

Nice, were you looking forward to visiting him?

He dodged the question or didn't understand it. He brought up his job again and explained he worked long hours during the week and drove for a few hours on the weekends for extra cash. It's good to have multiple forms of income, especially in this economy.

I considered telling him my boyfriend said something similar whenever I considered quitting one of my freelance jobs, but asked a simpler question instead: Do you like driving for Uber? A pointless question. I didn't care to hear his response.

He was quiet for a minute and adjusted his phone so he could see the map better. And then he made a confession: I've dated three of my passengers.

Was he trying to add a fourth, I wondered, and balked. I replied drily: I'm sure it's a great way to meet people.

They were both younger, he added, smiling, as if he was a winning athlete posing with a medal.

How much younger? I asked.

Can I tell you the story?

Sure, I said and looked at his phone screen to check how much longer I would be in his car—forty-three minutes.

He continued: This one girl insisted on giving me her number at the end of her ride. I'm not that kind of guy, you know. I have boundaries. This a professional setting, and she looked young. I'm forty-eight, almost fifty. But I don't think it's unusual. Most older guys prefer younger women. We want something pure. Nobody wants someone who's ran through, who has all these other experiences with men. They get an attitude, and their shit isn't as tight, he said, taking his hand off the steering wheel to gesture toward his groin.

I nodded, removed my thumb from between the pages of my book, and returned it to my purse before folding my hands in my lap. I briefly attempted to tally the number of men I had slept with, but lost interest and considered ending the conversation, feigning a headache or fatigue like generations of women before me and disappearing into my phone. But I was intrigued by his pompous declarations, as if his view of women and sex was self-evident or universal. I rarely talked to men at length.

B was the last I could recall. He was a recent UChicago law student working for a federal judge in Indiana before he would relocate to Los Angeles for a year and then to New York City to assume the comfortable life of a corporate lawyer. We were the same age. His lips were pretty, like small tropical fish. The first time I invited him to my apartment, he admired my bookshelves and confessed he was a slow reader—he made little progress, usually reading a few pages in bed before falling asleep. During our three-month tryst, he never finished *A Confederacy of Dunces*.

B was careful when he talked about women, self-correcting often, and told me he was obsessed with making women orgasm, that he was single handedly trying to rectify the "orgasm gap." Whenever we finished having sex, he requested feedback, and I obliged.

I was the first trans woman he had slept with, so his repertoire was limited. The first time we had sex he told me I didn't have to shave unless I wanted to. He explained he was exceptionally hairy and could not expect me to make such an effort if he would never reciprocate. I often had to fish around in my mouth to remove one of his pubic hairs from between my teeth. I liked his self-serious expression while he freed me from this unspoken feminine duty, mostly because I could tell he wanted to prove he was exceptional, like a husband who reports to his wife whenever he's finished a simple domestic task, such as vacuuming or washing dishes. I smiled and told him I was hairless from the waist down—omitting that I accomplished this through months of laser hair removal, rather than some preternatural womanhood.

Despite my detailed post-coital feedback, our sex mostly remained the same—a vigorous handjob preceding and following penetration, while I repeatedly told him to be more gentle. He attempted, but I was usually raw for days afterward, experiencing a dull ache like a sunburn. I eventually ended our short-lived relationship, but I sometimes asked if he would translate a confusing text or interaction I had with another man, requests he obliged with gentlemanly thoughtfulness.

Out of a similar mixture of boredom and curiosity, I encouraged the driver to continue talking. I nodded my head and occasionally punctuated his declarations about women with simple sounds: Mmmm, Uh-huh, Tsk, as if I was an anthropologist observing the rites of some foreign culture, careful to avoid disruption or transference. The driver resumed his story about his rider:

She insisted that she wanted my number and called herself from my phone. She texted me nonstop for a week, so I caved and offered to take her on a date. I told her to arrive at my place around 6, 6:30 PM at the latest. She came hours early, around 3:00, so I suggested we could run some errands together. She said she didn't mind. I like that in a woman, easygoing. But she totally switched attitude when she found out what I have.

My house isn't extraordinary, four bedrooms, two baths. But I own two apartment buildings, and I had to collect rent that day. I have this leather envelope—he pointed toward the glovebox. Most of my tenants pay with checks, but one of the girls is a stripper, so she pays mostly with singles. That's a lot of cash. He chuckled, and I wondered if he merely enjoyed seeing a large amount of cash, or if he found it pleasurable to possess this money other men used to pay for her body and time. Anyway, when I got back in the car, she noticed the envelope was much thicker. She asked if I was a drug dealer. He scoffed to demonstrate he found her question offensive and added—I make my money the honest way.

The next time we saw each other, she asked if I could drive her to the beauty supply store. I said yes. They rang her up at the cash register and then she looked at me. I realized she expected me to pay. It was like $600 for everything. That seemed like a lot for hair, but I'm not Black, so I don't know, and I don't have hair. He gestured to his head and paused. I'm mostly attracted to Black women. And Latinas. I'm Mexican-Italian, he added, as if this was a relevant detail.

What did you do? I asked.

I walked out and ghosted her. If she mentioned beforehand, she might be a little short, I would've paid for it because that's the kind of man I am. But the expectation I would pay for it pissed me off. I'm nobody's sugar daddy or trick.

His voice rose on this last word, like the wet sound of a knife being unsheathed, and I momentarily felt guilty, as if I had solicited him like a street fundraiser. I softened my voice and asked: How old was she?

Twenty-two.

Oh, that's really young. Most twenty-two-year-olds are a little self-absorbed, I suggested, and recalled the middle-aged man who gave me his number and invited me to an expensive seafood restaurant when I was the same age. He lived in a high-rise across the street from the art museum where I worked odd hours as a coat check attendant and shared my grandmother's married name. We shared an order of fried calamari and an oily swordfish steak. After he paid, I insisted I had to head home, rebuffing his offer for post-dinner cocktails in his condo. He walked me to the train stop, kissing me outside the McDonald's and biting my neck in quick bursts like a cloud of persistent mosquitos. I never returned his phone calls but occasionally saw him walking his Maltese outside the entrance of his building when I left work.

The driver dodged my observation about her age and changed the conversation. Yeah, she was a track runner. She had a nice body. I like women who are fit, thin. He looked at me through the rearview window and asked—Do you mind me asking about your race?

I'm white. I replied.

Really? You kind of look like you could be Latina.

No, I laughed and suggested he thought so because he picked me up from a popular Mexican restaurant in Pilsen. I wondered if he was hopeful I might fall within his racial preferences, or if this question was his subtle attempt to signal his attraction. We continued to make eye contact through the rearview window, which drew my attention to his eyes and created a heightened sense of intimacy, as if I was gazing through the narrow lens of a peep show before the shutter closed.

I broke eye contact and inspected the back of his head. He was wearing a Sox baseball cap. He was bald or balding, I guessed. His beard was gray and coarse, like a wire-haired terrier. His fingernails were surprisingly short and clean. I caught his eye again and momentarily imagined holding his gaze while he forced his hand inside me, as if neatly turning the sleeve of a sweater inside out.

Our prolonged silence appeared to unnerve him. He asked another question. Do you want to hear the story about my ex-wife who cheated on me after a decade of marriage?

Yes, of course, I replied eagerly. Stories about cheating thrilled me. I had devoured every Rachel Cusk novel that summer for that reason. His question reminded me of a few paragraphs I wrote two years earlier, after a friend playfully suggested I cheat on my boyfriend. She thought it might positively impact my understanding of myself and therefore my writing. A few weeks later this same friend confessed she had a crush on me. I did not take her advice. But I wrote the title "My Infidelity" on a purple sticky note and fixed it to the wall above my desk. When my boyfriend noticed the note one morning, he asked: What does this mean? His face fluttered like a flag at half-mast.

Oh nothing, I responded, plucked the note from the wall, and tossed it into the trash. It was just an idea for a story, but I never made any progress. I decided I had no insight into the topic and little desire to imagine the scenario unfolding in our relationship. My boyfriend's expression soured, but we did not discuss the unwritten story further. I thought about this attempted story again, in the backseat of the Uber. A few weeks before, I spent a weekend in Michigan on a writer's retreat. I shared a cabin with a lesbian from New Mexico who taught me the names of her favorite WNBA players and asked about the novel I was writing. I had considered her question carefully before declaring: infidelity.

I listened attentively as the driver described his wife. She was Puerto Rican and thin. I slid my tongue along my upper teeth when he repeated the word thin and narrowed my eyes. He continued: I made her a housewife because I didn't want her to work. I needed her to keep the machine oiled, he chuckled, and comically slapped his right bicep twice. You know, cooking, cleaning, blowjobs. She could get her nails done once a week, and her hair done every two weeks. As long as I had a say before she made any big changes, he added thoughtfully, while I imagined his wife—waifish, waist-length, platinum-blonde hair, and hands that perpetually cracked and bled. He appeared to consider the controlling nature of this dynamic and justified their arrangement: She had access to my credit card. She had whatever she wanted. She loved clothes, he said, elongating the first vowel of "loved."

Maybe I'm oversharing, he warned, but I want my women to wear booty shorts all the time at home, you know? I nodded quietly and remembered my boyfriend shared a similar desire with me once after I found photos of other women on his phone. They were shorter, looked barely legal, and mostly wore pleated schoolgirl skirts with thigh-high socks. He insisted that I should wear microscopic skirts that could be lifted at any moment whenever I was at his apartment, and grinned after pinching my ass playfully; the driver made a similar lustful expression while he made a gesture with his hands to mimic grabbing the waist of some imagined woman.

But she has to be classy when I take her out to dinner, he warned. And I'm not going to compliment you if you wear the same thing all the time. If you wear something new and look fine as fuck, I'll shower you with them, but I'm not that kind of guy. You have to earn the compliment.

I noted the sudden introduction of the second person pronoun passively, as if realizing I was about to miss my train stop and ambivalently surrendering to the inconvenience of reboarding at the next stop.

The driver returned to his description of his wife. She had two daughters. One thing I learned: bras are fucking expensive. I took them to that store, Victoria's Secret, all the time. Do you know how many bras I bought? And matching panties? Why do the panties have to fucking match? he asked indignantly. Every shopping trip was like $900 each time. And these weren't even my own daughters. I treated them right though.

He paused pensively and turned down the radio. Anyway, one day my boss told me to go home early. I was supposed to work until 11:00 PM like usual, but I was a union worker and would've gone into overtime. I made like $52 an hour at the time, so I would've been making almost $80 an hour, so they had to cut me. Whatever. I understood, so I agreed and went home early.

I remember I was driving my sports car that night. Hold on, let me show you. He fumbled with his phone and removed it from the mount. As he reached for his phone, he absentmindedly turned the steering wheel and drifted toward the car in the neighboring lane, correcting abruptly when the driver honked their horn and made an aggressive gesture with their hand. Relax, he shouted back, I was in control the whole time. These drivers are ridiculous, right? He placed his phone in his lap, opened his camera roll, and slid his finger across the stream of images until he found it: a vintage red Italian sports car with a prancing horse on the hood. I didn't recognize the make or model, and I didn't ask.

Pretty women should never be driven around in a four-door car, he said and winked. He found another photo of the car's dashboard. This is the stereo system I had installed. That night I was blasting my music as I drove through our neighborhood. I remember the exact song. "Bedrock" by Young Money. She would've heard me pull up to our house, he said and grimaced. He was watching the road more closely than before. When I parked, I saw a man climbing the fence in our backyard and thought someone was breaking into the house. So, I found my gun and went to confront this dude.

At the mention of his gun, I tensed and looked about the car, wondering if he had a gun in the car. But I would not ask. I preferred to remain ignorant, as if confirmation of its existence would sour our conversation, like a misplaced comma in an otherwise well-constructed sentence.

He continued: A man is supposed to be a defender. I wasn't going to allow someone to threaten my home. But my wife convinced me to call the police instead of shooting the guy as he fled. And then a year later I caught her in bed with the same man. A younger guy. He worked around the corner at a cell phone store. Fucking whore, the driver spat.

Woah, I offered in sympathy. I wondered about this confrontation, whether the gun made another appearance, but allowed the silence to continue. His expression was stony and distant, ensnared in unpleasant memories.

We both flinched when a car pulled onto the shoulder of I-290 beside his car, a grinding sound coming from underneath it. We both turned to look, worried the sound belonged to a collision. The driver, a younger guy, slowed to a stop, reversed quickly, and then swerved his car sharply to dislodge a tire from underneath it before rejoining the flow of traffic. My driver gripped his steering wheel tightly, nodded his head, and expressed admiration: Smart man. He said these words proudly, as if the younger driver's actions reflected a shared competence.

What happened to your wife? I asked

We were separated a year before the divorce. He explained. Luckily, I made her sign a prenup. She still got $45,000 though, and one of my cars. I thought she should've invested it in a building like I taught her, but she blew it on a vacation with that guy—and designer purses. You know, she called me on my birthday this year. It's been almost ten years. I asked what she wanted, and she wanted to know if I missed her. Guess what I told her, he prompted, and I shrugged my shoulders.

Fuck no! I told her and hung up. And I haven't heard from her since.

Wow, that's crazy, I said.

The driver pulled off the highway and onto California Ave. At the stoplight, he turned around to look at me directly for the first time and said: Enough about me. Tell me about yourself.

I'm a writer, I offered.

What kind of books?

Oh no, I corrected him. I haven't written any books. Not yet. I write about art.

His eyes glazed over.

I stared out the window. We passed the Fred Hampton mural, a grayscale portrait with the slogan "Free Em All" beside a restaurant distributor and an abandoned lot.

Do you mind me asking how tall you are? He asked.

Of course not. I'm 6'2," I answered.

Does that make it difficult to date?

I'm not sure, I replied thoughtfully. Most of my boyfriends have been shorter than me. If they found it intimidating or emasculating, they never told me.

That just means they're not secure, he insisted. I'm 5'11" and I wouldn't mind. Do you ever wear heels?

No. Not often. I don't like being that tall. I can never hear the people I'm with because there's like a six-inch difference between us.

You should, he urged. Men love it. They make your calves look so nice. I don't know how, but they lift and shape the muscles in a certain way. He paused. His eyes were glassy again. You're a beautiful woman, you know, the driver said. You have legs like a gazelle. That was the first thing I noticed when I saw you standing at the corner. And you're in shape, thin. That's good. He continued to appraise me as if reading the reverse label of a nice bottle of wine and then added: You look young. How old are you?

Thank you, I replied drily and ignored the question about my age.

He asked me to describe my ideal date and then asked if I thought it was impolite to invite a woman to the Cheesecake Factory. I evaded the question by insisting it depended on the woman. He explained, I like the food and ambiance, and I'm the one who's paying anyway. I think women these days are so snobbish. I have six sisters, and they all used to hang out at this bar on Armitage with all their friends because I was a bouncer there. I'm a big dude, he said and pointed at his arms again. His arms were unremarkable. Cylindrical, sure. Like a sleeve of ground sausage. He lifted his arm and flexed even though he was wearing a long sleeve shirt: I can bench like 250lbs, and squat 300. Neither of these numbers meant anything to me.

I'm one of seven children, too, I remarked, returning the conversation to his sisters.

He ignored this fact about myself and continued his earlier point. Whenever I was working, I noticed my sisters and their friends never paid for their drinks. None of the women did. Yeah, they're all pretty and wore slutty outfits, but it's so unfair. Men are expected to pay for everything.

Mmm. I nodded.

We arrived at my apartment. Thank you for the ride, I said. He turned around again and thanked me for the conversation. I can tell you're a special woman, he insisted. For a moment, I wondered if he was going to ask for my phone number, whether I would enter my real number or a fake one. He did not ask. I exited the car. In the stairwell of my apartment building, I gave him a five-star rating and a 20% tip.

Later that night I searched the online employee directory of the investment firm he claimed to work for while lying in bed, briefly imagining messaging him. Why? I wondered. To ask more questions about his wife's affair, maybe, or if he knew I was a trans woman and whether he wanted to ask me out. But his name, photo, or contact information was not listed.

HARLEY QUINN, MY FAVORITE CLOWN

Sunny Lu

Every Halloween, straight couples take it upon themselves to dress up as the Joker and Harley Quinn—everyone's favorite (hetero) villainous DC power couple. Iconic though this pair may be, I always found it curious that couples choose to take on these characters as their one-night alter egos. In nearly every rendition of Harley Quinn in film, television, and graphic novel form, the narrative clearly identifies the Joker as Harley's abuser. At the very least, their relationship is one that is deeply toxic and destructive. Between the two of them, it is Harley Quinn who suffers most, often both within the narrative and through the structure of the narrative itself—most people conceive of Harley Quinn exclusively through her identity as the Joker's girlfriend. The Joker is valorized by a certain type of guy, ridiculed by YouTuber Jenny Nicholson in her hilarious and searing review of Todd Phillips's 2019 *Joker* film; how many of those guys care about Harley's canonically harrowing childhood trauma and clear neurodivergence that parallels the Joker? While the Joker's harrowing childhood trauma and neurodivergence are the bedrock of his character, for many people, only Harley's relationship to the Joker is the bedrock of hers.

"Dark romance" has been getting its moment in the genre fiction universe; I think people think there's something sexy about unhinged, fictional people in toxic relationships. Yet, despite this moment toxic romance is having in pop culture, recent adaptations and interpretations of the Harley Quinn character have steered quite clear of romanticizing—or even centering!—her relationship with the Joker. In fact, both *Birds of Prey (and the Fantabulous Emancipation of One Harley Quinn)* (2020) directed by Cathy Yan, and the HBO Max animated *Harley Quinn* (2019) television show start off with a breakup with the Joker. In addition to these recent adaptations, a young adult novel series of the Harley Quinn narrative hit bookstore shelves in 2022. A trilogy by Rachael Allen within the DC Icons adaptation series, *Harley Quinn: Reckoning*, takes Harley's adolescent identity in a fully *STEMinist* direction. It's delightful, full of queer, feminist girl-gang power that more teen readers should get their hands on. But, unlike the film and TV show, it doesn't portray Harley's relationship with the Joker as a personal one, and so I'll get to discussing that book later.

The animated introduction that *Birds of Prey* begins with features Harley, played by the extremely talented Margot Robbie, delivering a voiceover of her origin story: her childhood of abuse ("When I was a kid, my dad traded me for a six-pack of beer"), her personality ("I was never an establishment kinda gal"), her academic and career success ("All things considered, I did good. I even got a PhD!"), and ultimately, her relationship with the Joker. She tells us, "I lost all sense of who I was. I only had eyes for Puddin. We all know the saying, 'Behind every successful man, there's a badass broad.' Well, that was me. I was the brains behind some of Mr. J's greatest stunts. Not that he let anyone know it." In *Birds of Prey*, Harley begins to tell her own story and rewrite the narrative of the Joker as the genius maniac brain behind all their villainy, Harley merely a sidekick. It's a gloriously flashy, animated introduction, suitable to Harley's personality and aesthetic. The introduction also works as a genius framing device for the rest of the movie, allowing Harley's voiceover narrative to carry us through the overlapping perspectives across the same timeline. *Birds of Prey* never over-relies on voiceover narration as a weak substitute for actual storytelling; it's a crucial aspect of how and why the narrative is being delivered to us, the viewers. The end of Harley's full introductory sequence tells us one final thing: "This is our story. And I'm telling it, so I'll start where I fucking want." Title drop! With the text colored in the bisexual flag colors, no less.

Just as both HBO's *Harley Quinn* and *Birds of Prey* rip Harley away from her role as merely the sidekick-girlfriend-companion to a more 'serious' male villain lead, both the movie and the show work to characterize Harley as an "imperfect victim." As law professor Leigh Goodmark articulates in her book, *Imperfect Victims: Criminalized Survivors and the Promise of Abolition Feminism*, an "imperfect victim" of gender violence is often a criminalized one. Imperfect victims often end up embedded in the prison industrial complex. For Harley, who hops in and out of Arkham Asylum over the course of the HBO show and attempts to avoid institutionalization by running from Detective

Montoya in *Birds of Prey*, prison is also where she met the Joker and began their relationship. Goodmark's powerful and enraging *Imperfect Victims* is full of stories of real-life women struggling through incarceration and the brutality of the prison industrial complex; I don't mean to demean their real-life experiences by drawing on this framework of imperfect victimhood to analyze a fictional supervillain character. However, I do find it a meaningful lens to look at Harley, since she is so culturally misunderstood. I argue that recently, through the work of women writers and directors, her identity as a survivor of trauma, gendered violence, and the love she has for the other women in her life has come through in sharp relief against the backdrop of her sexualization (often coinciding with her mental illness and instability), which plays fully into pop culture's fetishization of her terrible relationship with the Joker.

In both the show and the movie, Harley is undoubtedly a victim of the Joker's intimate partner violence. In fact, the very first live action scene we get in *Birds of Prey* is of her getting physically thrown out of the Joker's abode by one of his goons, and a shot of Harley's mascara-tear-streaked face as she bangs on the window to be let back in. After moving into "an amazing new place that was all mine"—a second-story walk-up over a Chinese restaurant—we see Harley throwing knives at a dart board with a drawing she made of the Joker's face. We also see her tattooing her thigh with "PUDDINg cup," and it's adjacent to a heart with an arrow in it that says "P + H." (Personally, I think this tattoo also nods towards the iconic Poison Ivy x Harley Quinn-ship that becomes canon in the animated television series.) The camera moves quickly between Harley's other post-breakup activities, from cutting her iconic dyed hair into the pigtailed-bisexual bob she rocks for the rest of the movie, to adopting a pet hyena from a sleazy guy. In his attempt to sexually coerce her—"I take payment-in-kind . . ."—she unleashes her new pet onto him; in the next shot, Harley shoots canned cheese directly into her mouth while sobbing on her couch, the hyena chewing on the sleazy pet-seller's detached leg. From the very beginning of the film all the way through to the end, we see how Harley believes in violence, as both self-defense and self-expression. Every scene in the first fifteen minutes of the movie makes this clear, from the way she ruthlessly elbows her roller derby opponent in the face to her aforementioned acquisition of a new pet hyena.

Following the public announcement of her breakup with Joker, Harley's voiceover narrates to us: "Every person I ever wronged now felt free to come and take their pound of flesh." On screen, she sprints through the streets of Gotham with her just-purchased bacon, egg, and cheese sandwich. (Side note: I like the nod to Shakespeare in this line, with "pound of flesh" referring to the Jewish Shylock in *The Merchant of Venice*. Harley Quinn is canonically Jewish, and the animated show especially takes humor and joy with that aspect of her identity. One example: the shot of Harley holding a Menorah announcing "Mazel!" right before the title drop on season 2 episode 2, "Riddler U.") In *Birds of Prey*, her breakup with Joker launches her into new heights of danger, and for Harley, it's not the fun kind. Before she can even take a single bite of her sandwich, Harley starts getting chased by Detective Montoya, an antagonist who ultimately gains a begrudging respect towards Harley in the young adult novel *Reckoning*; her storyline in *Birds of Prey* helps bring the disparate perspectives of all these Harleys together.

The attention to detail in *Birds of Prey* reveals itself from Harley's perspective, from the slow and sensual shot of her breakfast sandwich being made, to the paintball sequence in the Gotham Police Department raid. (My second favorite line in the movie is when Harley gleefully reloads her gun in the lobby and shouts: "Run, piggy, run!") There is simply no way that Harley went in there with a paintball gun and knocked out half the force. She definitely had a machine gun on her and we, as the viewers, get to see the magic of her insane and colorful view of the world; instead of the blood, guts, and gore that masculinist action movies revel in, colorful powder, confetti, and glitter explodes all around her. These fight scenes are masterfully creative. Harley's jailbreak mission sets off the sprinklers in the jail; amidst a shower of water in a dingy corridor of jail cells, she manages to fight off half a dozen men with only the butt of her gun and gymnastics stunts. The fight choreography utilizes the setting and props without relying on the lazy cop out (ha!) of firearms featured in most action movies.

As seen in both the cops' pursuit of Harley and the way the end of an abusive relationship instigates a terrifying vulnerability for her, Harley's imperfect victimhood is what makes her such a compelling character to follow. Though she is not exactly a criminalized survivor (no media portray her as facing criminalization as a result of self-defense against her abuser), she is still an imperfect victim who utilizes violence to her own ends. Like the vast majority of incarcerated women in prisons across the United States, she has survived relentless traumatization and abuse since early childhood. Her continued survival in the face of male/state violence resists every misogynistic impulse to shrink Harley's sense of self and her beautiful, colorful, glittery chaos.

The directorial vision of *Birds of Prey* centers her clownish wildness as much as it prioritizes a feminist filmmaking ethic. Even after her shitty boyfriend ends things with her, Harley still has to deal with shitty dudes trying to take advantage of her. Womanhood! Harley reacts to the whole breakup with violence, because she herself is a violent person—we see her on a roller derby team, absolutely smashing her opponents and then getting absolutely smashed afterwards. She blows up an ACE Chemical plant, where Joker first baptized Harley in a vat of chemicals, "making" her into Harley Quinn. She tells us, "Some people have the Eiffel Tower, or Olive Garden. The Joker and I? Our love bloomed in a highly toxic industrial processing plant." In the animated show, Harley realizes that the narrative she has always told herself of her origin story—that Joker pushed her into the vat of chemicals—is not the truth. The Joker tells Harley, "If you love me, then jump." Harley responds, "A dream come true, Puddin.'" Harley's recollection of being forced against her will becomes corrected by the reality of the past. Like in *Birds of Prey,* the narrative that Harley tells herself and the audience is one deeply seated within her own perspective, regardless of whether it reflects literal reality or not.

Harley is not a palatable victim. Even her own recollection of her abusive relationship is not consistent with reality. The expectations of victims of gendered violence often require both a perfectly consistent, provable, and documented history of abuse, and likability in order to be believed. Of course, many people do not like Harley, and often for completely justifiable reasons. Harley remains unbothered by it, until the consequences of her actions start catching up with her—which *Birds of Prey*'s plot follows relentlessly. Crucially, for the Gotham Police, Harley is a wanted criminal; she practices what Kali Nicole Gross names as "vengeance feminism." In *Vengeance Feminism: The Power of Black Women's Fury in Lawless Times*, Gross describes "vengeance feminism" as a feminism where women break the law for their own means, their own self-defense and dignity, and because the law itself is an unjust measure set against their survival.

While Gross's focus as a historian is on poor Black women in 19th century Philadelphia, I want to apply Gross's understanding of women working outside the bounds of law to enact, receive, and apply justice in their lives to Harley's character in the HBO show, *Birds of Prey*, and in *Reckoning*. It is second nature for Harley to enact vengeance feminism. In *Reckoning*, Harley literally starts a girl gang with other women on campus to attack, expose, and terrorize the rapists and predators at the university. (This a novel written for and marketed to teenagers! The kids might be alright . . . ?!) One of my favorite scenes in *Birds of Prey* occurs three minutes into the film: while Harley celebrates a win with her roller derby team at the club, she spills her drink on someone while she dances on a pole. "Goddammit it. Sit the fuck down," a man in a suit tells her. As he puts his feet on the table in front of him, stretching out his legs, he says: "I said sit your skinny ass down, you dumb slut." Harley shrugs, smiles, says, "Ok!" She promptly jumps on top of his legs, breaking them in half. "Call me dumb. I have a PhD, motherfucker," Harley says.

Harley is not one to take disrespect kindly. Her vengeance feminism works hand in hand with her imperfect victimhood. She is not afraid to inconvenience, harm, and break the legs of the people around her to get the justice she pursues. In the DC show, Harley's reaction towards Joker's abuse of her is not one of perfect acquiescence where she never defends herself or uses violence. Harley never simply turns him into the Gotham police—the expectation that all victims are subjected to in the American prison industrial complex, as Goodmark details in her book. Firstly, because Harley herself is a criminal, and secondly, like many of the real-life women in both Goodmark and Gross's books, because she doesn't fuck with pigs.

Birds of Prey clearly depicts Harley as a wanted criminal who has done horrible things to other people in Gotham, and those people will not let her forget it. In the film, show, and book, Harley is a complex, traumatized, and flawed woman—an imperfect victim. As Goodmark articulates in *Imperfect Victims*, an "imperfect victim" is often a criminalized one. In *Birds of Prey* and the DC show, Harley already lives in Gotham as a renowned criminal, and her experience in an abusive relationship with the Joker often draws her into crime, both at the beginning of their relationship and throughout the course of it. In real life, and as Goodmark thoroughly documents in *Imperfect Victims*, many of the women locked up for felonies were arrested and charged with their male partner, who often coerced or forced them into committing crimes with them. For Harley's storyline in *Birds of Prey*, what drives her to action is how both other criminals in Gotham and the Gotham police seek vengeance on Harley for her crimes, now that she no longer has the "protection" of being in a relationship with the Joker. Like Goodmark writes, many victims of gender violence understand that they have a choice between the abusive relationship of getting victimized by the carceral state and the prison of an abusive male partner who coerces and violates them. In fact, the very first episode of the animated show on HBO follows Harley as she gets locked away in Arkham during a crime she and the Joker commit together—but only she experiences carceral consequences, while the Joker gets away scot-free. This parallels Goodmark's documentation of real-life imperfect victims, who are routinely sentenced more severely than their male partners who also committed the crime or forced their female partners into committing it in the first place.

For cartoon-show-Harley Quinn, what adds insult to injury is the fact that the Joker promised to break her out of Arkham as soon as possible, after not letting her on his getaway ride after they got busted by the Batman. Being the Joker—and being the abusive, piece-of-shit boyfriend that he is—Harley spends over six months languishing in prison, waiting. As an imperfect victim, and also as a realistic victim, Harley clings to the notion that the Joker will save her eventually, which never happens. Less than five minutes into season 1 episode 1, Harley boldly tells Batman and Gordon, the police chief of Gotham, "I know my man'll break me out of Arkham before I spend a single night." Immediately after, screen text over a shot of Arkham reads: "SIX MONTHS LATER." In a scene of the Arkham Asylum visiting room that immediately follows this hilariously depressing shot, one of the visitors refers to Harley as "Porn Clown," summing up what most people think of her. "He's not coming!" A chorus of her fellow prisoners shouts at Harley. Still delusional and devoted to the Joker, Harley does not face the reality that her evil boyfriend does not give a fuck about her until her best friend (and, later in the series, girlfriend) orchestrates an elaborate stunt to prove this.

As the pilot episode to an HBO adult animated show within a massive superhero franchise, the dialogue is remarkably explicit in its feminist and progressive principles. The very first lines of the whole show, "Gentlemen! My fellow whites! Let's raise a glass to this pyramid of money. The foundation of which was built upon our favorite pastime. Fucking the poor!" Similarly, season 1, episode 11: "Insurance would never pay for this. I think we can all agree they're the real villains, yeah?" The framing device of season 2, episode 5 features two archetypical dude-bros sitting on a couch with a bong and beers around them, considering what show to watch. Their T-shirts say, "RELEASE THE SNYDER CUT" and "THE LAST JEDI IS NOT CANON." Snyder cut T-shirt guy says of the *Harley Quinn* show, "It's just another heavy-handed female empowerment story, where the true villain is the quote unquote 'patriarchy.'" Clearly, the show is quite self-aware of all that the Harley Quinn character must combat before being understood as an interesting enough main character of her own. Most strikingly to me, however, is the show's depiction of Harley's unrelenting attachment to Joker, even when she is imprisoned because of him, when he fails to deliver on all of his promises to her, and when every single person around her tells her that Joker is not coming to save her.

According to RESPOND, an organization working to end domestic violence, on average, it takes victims of domestic violence seven attempts to leave their abuser for good. Additionally, it is the very moment when a victim is attempting to leave when they are most likely to be murdered by their abuser. In the aptly titled pilot episode "'Til Death Do Us Part," we see commentary pointing towards the devastating and terrifying reality that, for many victims, their death precedes the end of the abusive relationship. Not reacting "appropriately" to intimate partner violence constitutes imperfect victimhood. In courtrooms across the United States, criminalized survivors get interrogated by legal officers about why they did not simply leave, instead of acting out against their abuser with violence. "Prosecutors regularly counter victimization claims by arguing that the defendant was angry or jealous rather than afraid, that the violence they describe is minor, was mutual, or did not occur, that the defendant could have left the situation rather than committing a crime, and that 'strong' women (i.e. women who can 'hold their own' against their partners) couldn't possibly be abused," Goodmark writes. The fact that Harley struggles to gather the chutzpah to leave the Joker throughout the entirety of the pilot episode, faces prison time for her criminal activity with said partner, and does not hesitate to enact physical violence against the Joker for the rest of the show, all speak to her imperfect—and realistic—victimhood.

I argue that Harley and Joker's relationship arc in the HBO show represents some key themes of abolition feminism. Despite being the man-hating lesbian I am, season 3 episode 6's "Joker: The Killing Vote" still managed to capture my heart in its portrayal of Joker's redemption. He becomes a suburban dad who becomes the socialist major of Gotham, and tells the self-proclaimed "damn good cop" Gordon, "My first act as mayor is dismantling the police department. You're out of a job." Joker does not evade justice. Harley seeks her retribution, but meanwhile, the Joker no longer abuses the women in his life. As Goodmark told us during our Lesbian Feminist Book Club meeting discussing her book, the survivors she works with don't want to be incarcerated and they don't want their partners incarcerated either. They just want the violence to stop.

We see the manifold ways Harley's character stops gendered violence across these adaptations, all without utilizing the prison industrial complex that also works to cage her and her friends. From the vigilante feminist gang in *Reckoning* to Harley's vengeful feminist dog-walking of a collared Joker in the show (season 4, episode 10), I don't think it's possible to tell Harley's story without having an abolitionist feminist ethic. Harley is herself a criminal character, and the way she has been subjected to gendered violence is inextricably linked with the prison industrial complex. She can't use the tools that oppress her to liberate herself and her friends, and she doesn't try to.

Not to say that the more recent renditions of Harley Quinn haven't had their problematic aspects. It's unfortunate that in *Birds of Prey*, the little Asian girl sidekick suffers from serious blaccent. It's partially the script, and partially the young actress. Ella Jay Basco in the role of Cassandra Cain, a pickpocket in foster care, does a passable job at portraying the young Gothamite. For being a child actor, Basco is convincing enough in the role. But Cassandra Cain's character embodies an unfortunate instance of East Asians speaking in African American Vernacular English. Meanwhile, in the adult Harley Quinn animated TV show, the only significant Black characters voiced by Black actors are Frank, a talking plant side character; King Shark, who is literally a talking shark; Lex Luthor, an oligarchic villain; Catwoman, who plays a minor role in a few episodes, and Queen of Fables, another villain. This baked-in anti-Blackness in superhero and supervillain adaptations is not new, of course, yet, it is still deeply disappointing, to say the least.

Harley Quinn has yet to be directed or written by a Black woman, despite all of the ways her characterization and storylines directly reflect the experiences of Black women in America. As Goodmark delineates, Black women are vastly more likely to experience survivor criminalization and get identified as imperfect victims than any other population in the United States. Bisexual and lesbian women are also far more likely to be incarcerated than straight women. Harley's iconic canonical bisexuality paired with the facts of her Americanness, unabashed practice of vengeance feminism, and her consistent imperfect victimhood all point to her character desperately needing a Black woman's creative vision.

When it comes to race and creative visions, however, I find it interesting that Harley as a character has been repeatedly tackled by Asian American women writers and directors. Being the Chinese American daughter of immigrants myself, I was elated to discover that the writer and director *Birds of Prey* were both Asian American women. I remember first watching *Birds of Prey* in theaters with my friend. This was just before the pandemic, before we even knew there was a pandemic looming in our future. My initial draw to the movie was the soundtrack. Big into our female rap phase—which has never went away, by the way—we were excited primarily to hear the new Megan Thee Stallion, Doja Cat, and Saweetie songs on the tracklist. *Birds of Prey: The Album* is masterfully woven into the worldbuilding of Gotham, and it's stacked with an all-female lineup that appeals to everyone from the queer indie girls (Charlotte Lawrence, Maisie Peters, K.Flay) to avid listeners of standout women in pop (Halsey and Lauren Jauregui). I didn't know it at the time, but this movie, that I was not that interested in—I didn't really give a fuck about the DC/Marvel superhero/supervillain world—would become my favorite movie of all time. A movie I would watch time and time again, post-breakup, when I was feeling depressed and alone in the world, or to show to skeptical and unconvinced friends. I remember going to class the week after I saw *Birds of Prey* in theaters for the first time (I would go again with another friend a few days later) and telling my teacher that she absolutely *had* to go see the new Harley Quinn movie—even though we both agreed, of course, that *Suicide Squad* (2016) was ass.

From the costume design all the way down to the fight choreography, *Birds of Prey* creates a boldly feminist vision that tells Harley's story with her own voice. *Reckoning* constructs a teenage Harley with ADHD, a knack for science and gymnastics, and a group of kickass female friends. HBO Max's *Harley Quinn* portrays her as beautifully and hilariously flawed, but nonetheless deeply lovable and loved. She's a messy Jewish bisexual psychiatrist badass, and she's a survivor of Joker's abuse. She's the fictional feminist icon we need in the era of "clean girl" girlbosses and the relentless drive of carceral feminism. As my best friend and *The Lavender Menace* podcast co-host Renaissance told me when they re-watched *Birds of Prey*, "Harley Quinn should have gotten the hype that Margot Robbie's Barbie performance did, and the fact that Harley was hated and Barbie praised [shows] that we haven't evolved in cultural feminism at all." Despite decades of misrepresentation and misinterpretation, Harley exists in a league of her own: the most fantabulous clown in Gotham, and probably the universe.

ON COMEDIC TIMING

Dorothy Santos

I remember a time when I got an Amazon Alexa (you know, as a part of my research. That's the primary excuse for getting anything in my life). I asked Alexa to tell me a joke that I can barely remember. It was about Dwayne "The Rock" Johnson and cooking. The pre-programmed jokes might all be considered Dad jokes; they were corny and based on word play, which can be funny at times. But I'm reminded of the two Filipino brothers that created a different version of Alexa, called Tita, which loosely translated means "auntie" in Tagalog. Not sure if these men knew that they were engaging in queering the voice.

Full transparency: I have no desire to be a stand-up comic. The biggest reason why I wanted to study joke structure was due to Cathy Park Hong studying Richard Pryor. These days, I study Sheng Wang, Ali Wong, Marie Faustin, Tony Baker, Irene Tu, and Alok Vaid-Menon. There is something sharp and witty about the way they deliver. From their prosody, what silence affords them. Tone also comes to mind. Stuff might sound funny when it's written down, but nobody really knows until it's spoken. I can get loud and curse a lot, but that doesn't mean I'm funny.

I wonder what would happen if straight comics started to queer and strange their own sense of humor. I mean, Mladen Dolar talks about the voice of God as a way of understanding one's interiority and self-talk, but it's also a way of grounding and embodying some form of consciousness. That's the thing about the comic—I have wondered what allows for the bypassing of decorum. What is the boundary and the contour of what is funny versus gratuitous?

After reading Cathy Park Hong's book *Minor Feelings*, I was inspired to study stand-up comedy. From doing open mics and studying Richard Pryor's joke structure, Hong attempted to understand race in America in a way that made it much more palatable to the general public. Growing up, I wasn't allowed to watch Pryor, but as soon as I was in my late teens

I became fascinated by comedy and what it takes to make someone laugh. Similar to Hong's attempt, I made an earnest effort at consuming as much stand-up over the pandemic, while finishing my PhD, because I needed something other than True Crime as a form of escapism. I came to understand stand-up comedy as equal parts self-deprecation, catharsis, and philosophizing.

I signed up for a multi-week intensive on writing stand-up comedy. It was my chance to craft stories through the lens of joke writing. The funniest part of the entire thing was that the class was being taught by one of my ex's best friends. (Yes, I briefly dated a stand-up comic.) Maybe, I was trying to heal old wounds or pathologize my ex or find a way to make the mundane humorous, because I've watched so many people do this work. Yet, like pole dancing, the easier the dancer makes it look, the harder I know the dancer worked to achieve optimal core stability. Joke writing is the same way. From the exposition, trackback, element of surprise or twist, to the ultimate punch line, it is difficult to write a great joke. Even more so to write a joke that is extraordinary and perennial.

Many jokes from the 1970s and 1980s have not aged well. Yet how does any joke stay perennial without cultural context or familiarity? I am certain that jokes from 2025 will sound archaic and crude fifty years from now (2075!). I assumed that taking a writing workshop would help me, but I was wrong. Trying to write jokes about maxi pad design and Animal Crossing as cultural criticism didn't exactly go over all that well with a digital room filled predominantly with straight, Filipino, cisgender men. Very few of the participants were women or femmes. Why did I think it was a good idea to do a stand-up comedy writing workshop *online*? I mean, it's called "stand-up" for a reason. I remember thinking to myself that I would learn a lot, but I only attended two classes.

A lot of men signed up for the course trying to be the next Jo Koy. I wondered if men strived to be as funny as a woman or queer comic. Usually, when people think of humor and stand up, there is something about irreverence, but not an association with women. When women or QTBIPOC comics do comedy, it almost seems like they are misfits. Yet Hong was right! There is something about studying the structure of earlier comics that says a lot about the cultural and political climate of when the comic was joke writing, what they were responding to outside of themselves.

As someone who writes and makes artwork, you would think I don't mind the masochistic nature of writing something clever about the moment, yet perennial (so the joke doesn't age poorly), AND making people laugh. Comedy, and being a clown or a jester of culture to the public courts of social media and the general population, is no joke. It's grueling work to make people laugh. Also, as I was thinking about this archetype of the "clown," I couldn't help but think about the comic's voice. I've been listening to all types of voices over the past few years, for academic and creative purposes. Isn't that another aspect of comedy, the voice of the comic? It's not about gaining trust necessarily, it's about making people laugh. The most terrifying part of comedy for me is that people will take what I say or write in such a way that it starts to craft a mythology or create some urban legend that I never intended. I mean, we saw what happened with the woman who is credited for the "gender reveal party." She regrets it! If I was her, I would, too. She's probably not benefitting from any profit that the baby industry has put into gender profiling and in the hopes of selling its latest products. I'm digressing.

After two classes, I was chicken and told the instructor that I would be focusing on other things. Yet I haven't given up my dream of taking another stand-up comedy writing class. I thought about the one-person show that I want to do, telling stories about how I found my gender expression—fantastic stories and also an ongoing narrative about what it means to be queer and grow up in an immigrant Filipino family. Joyful and sad in equal measure. Funny, humorous, but also dark, because everyone has a shadow that follows them around, and we have got to give love to that part of us that keeps us sensitive to the light.

What does it mean to have a comedic voice? There are some comics I can't listen to and I won't list them here. There are parts of my own voice that sound a lot like Lewis Black. The much more family-friendly side of me probably sounds a lot like Jim Gaffigan. The languid yet sharp and cutting nature of Andrew Orolfo. But I have also been listening to Nori Reed, Alok Vaid-Menon and how some of the most insightful (funny) social and cultural commentary comes from QTBIPOC folks.

Why did I care to even write jokes? Something I notice in comics such as Leslie Liao with her deep, nearly baritone voice, is her fast and sharp cultural criticisms and word play. She does the trackback really well. She also displaces her gender in multiple ways that are clever.

"Who is this useless man I'm supposed to marry? I haven't even met this man yet and I'm mad at him. It's never going to work." "I can't believe I'm straight."

Also loving Irene Tu. I have loved Tu's work for a long time. "Big They Energy," "I'm a lesbian who skateboards." Even when Irene Tu jokes about having they/them energy, she relates it back to her immigrant family coming to America with nothing. Tu states that what it means to have no gender is not the same as the sacrifice of a parent. Reminds me of the quote from Ocean Vuong:

The great crisis of the first and second generation is the first generation made it here, and to live at all is such a privilege that they're happy, and even encourage you to put your head down: work, fade away, get your meals, and live a quiet life. And I think the second generation, the great conundrum there, the great paradox, is that they want to be seen. They want to make something. And what better way to make something and feel yourself with agency than to be an artist? So, so many of us immigrant children end up betraying our parents in order to subversively achieve our parents' dreams.

There was so much in Tu's set that resonates deeply when I think about my own journey. The complexity and nuance realized through QTBIPOC comedy allows for a richness that is unparalleled in other comic forms. Tu showed complexity by writing a joke about protecting their (racist) grandmother or going to the BLM protests of 2020. There is a deep commentary and cleverness in telling the stories (whether real or not).

I watched and re-watched sets by Leslie Liao and Irene Tu. Irene Tu was just as funny; maybe it was because I anticipated what they were going to say. I knew the punchline. I had a feeling of where it was going. I think Tu's set was just as funny because there were moments of astute observational comedy at play, but also word play and funny interjections. I read a little bit about Tu; they grew up watching Ellen DeGeneres. I can see it.

I started to think about the ways I am funny and the ways I'm not, but try to be. The clown, the jester, the one that makes people laugh before I can be found out. Does every comedian feel that way? Maybe not someone like Andrew Dice Clay. Reading about joke writing is laborious. It's not funny by any means, and it makes the craft feel even further away from what I actually want to do in life.

If I'm funny, it's because I'm loud, curse a lot, and can imitate popular phrases but use them like a dad trying to embarrass their child. Yup, that's me, that's all I got. I was reading Jerry Corley's post on his site, "How to Write a Joke," and he gave a really great example of a joke about his wife and giving her a present. The breakdown of a joke is as follows: Charter, setting, plot, conflict, theme, and narrative arc. Simple, yeah? But not so easy, because there are SO many things to write about in the world. Also, hecklers.

Watching Irene Tu, I wrote an incredibly funny joke about DivaCups. Not only was it clever, it made me want to revisit my maxi pad joke from the workshop that I refused to return to. Stand-up comedy makes me feel like I have the perfect best friend, or that hot crush that you're not sure if they have a crush on you, but the joking is a form of flirtation. It makes me laugh when I feel pessimistic and depressed about the state of the world. Tu's jokes are not only razor sharp, but they often have unexpected twists or turns that induce laughter and epiphany simultaneously. After all the reading, and binging YouTube videos of my favorite comics, I know there is, without question, differences between joke writing and joke telling. The comedic voice also feels different when jokes are told online, or when people write jokes that are meant to be read.

What does it mean to be a clown, a jester? Where does this history come from, and why is it important? Why does the absurd sometimes become funny, versus when it doesn't? What did I hope to learn from the experience? Why does understanding what makes people laugh feel vital and important to me? How did people make fun of me, and how did I work to prevent being laughed at?

I am trying to muster the energy to continue writing about comedic voice, but my brain and energy are waning. Voice over work and impressions are another form of comedic voice. What does it mean to voice a non-human character, or to be a truly acousmatic voice? I love thinking about Maxxie LaWow as a full-length animated feature comedy that is voiced by a wide array of actors, but is utterly queer. Speaking of a voice without a visual source (acousmatic), I am also exploring how comedy has changed through streaming, digital, and social media. Between social media and "television" evolving (maybe, devolving) into ninety seconds, or "lives" becoming their own sets, how does comedic timing even work when you don't have the laughter of a crowd? Instead, performers read in realtime comments and become the affirmation. You do vignettes that are meant to be funny and entertaining, but the only "laughter" you get are emojis and brief snippets of running commentary.

In my research, I found the Toastmasters International's "The Anatomy of a Joke," which was comical to me. Comedy is not something you can easily teach; to summon belly-aching laughter is much more difficult. While Toastmasters isn't *The Moth*, from the formulaic to the experimental, confidence and bravado is not something that is attainable through a workshop or class. You build it over time, through not-so-funny moments of humiliation and rejection.

THE BOY WITH THE DISNEY VILLAINS

Devon Divine

As a young adult, I didn't know what a "Disney Gay" was. I was a late bloomer, and my parents were not hip to anything beyond Selena and *Sábado Gigante*. When I suggested I wanted a Disney-themed fourteenth birthday party, no one batted an eye. I was just on the cusp of being too old for this—but I wasn't raised on Disney like my white neighbors. My parents were hella fresh off the boat; it wasn't until my Tio Carlos married Aunt Debbie that she introduced me to the classics: *Bambi, Dumbo, Snow White, Sleeping Beauty*. I immediately became obsessed, and as a sheltered nerd living in the midwestern suburbs, I was still catching up. My mom easily transferred all the energy she had from my non-existent quinceañera into turning my Disney-themed birthday into the Latin extravaganza she always wanted to host.

The landlines were buzzing as my friends—many of whom would grow up to be queer themselves—started choosing what Disney character they wanted to embody. I was a sensitive young gay grappling with the identity politics of it all. I was too brown to be Prince Eric from *The Little Mermaid*. I was too fat to be Aladdin. I was too insecure to pull off the ultimate drag queen—Ursula. I was left with a sinking feeling after every conversation, as hints of my friends' Ariel, Gaston, and Princess Jasmine costumes started coming through. What did I get myself into?

I made my weekly trek to the Disney mall store with high hopes of being inspired to embody the perfect character. As I stood there admiring all the possibilities of the disposable Disney trademarked party supplies—flying carpet napkins, thingamabob cutlery, Mickey Mouse cups—my eyes spotted a little plastic cobra staff with glowing red eyes that made a robotic snake sound. *That's it!* I was going to be Jafar, the evil sorcerer from Aladdin, and build an outfit around this plastic, hissing snake accessory! Although he wasn't as glamorous or famous as the other Disney villains, I did feel a kinship with his feminine gestures and the disillusionment of being an outcast.

With that important decision finalized, I needed a stylist and fashion designer. I let my drag queen mother make an outfit for me. And no, I don't mean drag mother like an actual drag queen. I mean my Costa Rican mother whose fascination with makeup, clothes, and jewelry soared beyond a purely femme identity to the drag queen level of all Latin mothers. This was a sore spot for a kid who wanted nothing more than to be a wallflower—no matter what I did, I'd always have my broken-English-speaking, tropical-outfit-themed mother shocking and educating the white First Ladies of the neighborhood. My friends were always asking, *Why is your mom yelling?* To which I replied, *She's not, she's just gossiping with her sister on the phone.*

For my mother, going out to eat meant spending hours choosing from her wall of matching neon cowboy hats and purses. Upon arrival at the Olive Garden, I became the reluctant translator. *What did she say? I don't speak Spanish*, a confused and overly fake-polite waiter would ask. Instead of pointing out that she was speaking English, I'd just translate her accent into white and respond: *She wants the Tour of Italy and a piña colada.* If Charo and RuPaul had a baby, it would be my mom. Of course she jumped at the opportunity to make me a couture Jafar garment for the Disney-themed faux-quinceañera of her dreams.

My mom knew just enough about sewing to hem pants, make a few curtains, and design a pattern for the gaudy tissue box holders which were displayed proudly in every Costa Rican home through the early 90s. Jafar's outfit was easy for my mom to sew, and on the plus side for me—it would cover my ever-growing chubby body that I was still very much uncomfortable with. My mom created an oversized black frock, complete with a fuzzy red belt and matching red collar. With my cheap, imitation, store-bought cobra staff, I wasn't sure if anyone would recognize who I was, but I had my mother to distract them. She took the opportunity of this party and my Aladdin-inspired outfit to wear one of the many saris she'd been gifted over the years from my Indian dad's family. This really fucked with all the white parents dropping off their kids—what Latin woman had a sari, and how do they even work? Who is this woman with a foreign accent, and where is she from? And what Disney character was this chubby, femme, bi, ethnic queen supposed to be?

The party was wholesome and nerdy—lots of singing Madonna in my parents' basement and overeating my mom's international cuisine. I'm not sure when my Disney obsession started to fade away—it may have been later that summer, during one of the most traumatic moments of my young adult life. The single-screen movie theater in my town played Disney movies as matinees throughout the summer, mostly so suburban moms could drop off their kids and go drink wine in peace for a few hours. This was super awesome for me, as I could rewatch all my favorites on the big screen, with a big tub of buttered popcorn in my lap, alongside a way too large Cherry Coke—both with free refills. This one particular day I was headed to a 2:00 PM screening of *The Little Mermaid*, and was just a few minutes late. The theater was pitch black as the movie started, and I quickly scrambled to find a seat. As I slowly sat down into what I thought was an empty chair, I heard a woman's voice behind me: *EXCUSE me—you are sitting on my little girl.* It was stated matter of fact, a whisper through gritted teeth full of restrained rage. It took me a second to register, and right at that moment I *did* feel something—*someone*—under me. I was mortified! I was the gay, fat, teenage boy at a Disney matinee that sat on a child!! I've never been late to a movie since. It took that level of embarrassment to start detaching from Disney onto regular teenage stuff, like smoking pot and meeting men off AOL chat rooms. Suddenly, the gay part of being a Disney Gay was more interesting than the Disney part, and my life went on.

Years later, at forty years old, I found myself standing in front of Sleeping Beauty's castle, with a grin ear to ear, drinking a spiked lemonade in a Donald Duck souvenir mug and questioning my internalized Disneyphobia. For my birthday, my friends and I all got matching bootleg Mickey Mouse tattoos—Mickey juggling three paletas on my inner arm—now here I was enjoying anthropomorphic mouse capitalism at its finest. My college education at a hippie school in the Northwest had exposed the consumerist machine that used to suck me in at the suburban mall Disney Store, and soon after graduation I moved to San Francisco and found my outcasts within the nightlife scene—though even then, Disney adoration had infiltrated my new community. One of my first dates was with a handsome Latin DJ who frequented the local bear bar. I arrived to his place, and as we listened to music and got stoned he asked if I wanted to see photos from his gay Disney days. I was slightly intrigued—I mean I *did* have an iconic Aladdin costume in my past. He gestured to a bookshelf next to his record player shelved with matching photo albums, each labeled "Gay Days," and a date. He pulled out the most recent one and showed me photos of him and three bear friends wearing rainbow Mickey Mouse ears posing throughout the park—with Mickey and Minnie, on Pirates of the Caribbean, with other (mostly white) bears in front of space mountain. T-shirts printed with the slogan "I'm his Beast" while eating corn dogs, more white bears hanging with Goofy—it was too much too soon. I lost my boner, made up an excuse to leave, and stopped going to that bar. Forever. No more bears or Disney Gays for me.

But walking around the park that day I saw so many brown families, tough tattooed cholos waiting in line alongside butch lesbians covered in collectable pins. I had researched the parks thoroughly before we purchased tickets, mostly so we could figure out how to eat mushroom chocolates and maximize our roller coaster experience. We discovered Disneyland had some secrets as well—an underground network of pin collectors, and there were rumors of Disney Jail which really piqued my curiosity. As we were waiting in line for Guardians of the Galaxy—a ride where you sit in a large freight elevator that continues to rise, then drop, rise higher, then drop lower—I looked over at my arm, and my bootleg paleta-juggling Mickey Mouse tattoo winked at me. I winked back, and we got strapped into our seats as Pat Benatar started blaring through the speakers to begin the ride. I wanted to ask my bootleg Mickey so many questions—Is *Beauty and the Beast* an allegory for AIDS? Was Ursula modeled after Divine? The mushrooms had fully kicked in, and as the elevator ride rose to the top level, the walls collapsed around me and suddenly I was on Pride Rock being lifted to the sky, just like Simba. I looked around with wide open eyes and I saw Neverland, San Francisco, home of the lost boys who never had to grow up. I was the ruler of my world, and I handpicked every Ursula, Scar, and Cruella I could find for adventures and rock 'n' roll dreams that Disney's hype could never live up to. All while dressed as Jafar, with a Latin mom in a sari.

CLASS CLOWN GF

Marisa Crawford

When I moved to Connecticut in 1990, we still had a backyard, but it was different. Bigger than the one in New York, much bigger and with a pool even—and surrounded by dense woods. However, in spite of these surface-level improvements, the new yard lacked in soul. In New York, my house was located on a series of streets that was a loop—a perfect circle, or an oblong oval. And all along the loop were families that were our friends; a constellation of soul connections. In Connecticut the air was quiet. The sound of friends playing was replaced with a light dust of bugs that flew into your mouth every time you opened it to speak, all summer long. My mom was quieter there, too. And meaner.

Other things that were different: my sense of humor, which was unremarkable in New York, became cutting-edge in Connecticut. I remember watching *Bill and Ted's Excellent Adventure* at the first sleepover party I hosted in my new house. It was a movie I'd seen many times before, blessed as I was to be shepherded into the cultural milieu of the late 80s and early 90s by my older sister and her excessively cool middle school friends. It was normal, for example, to like the New Kids on the Block as a third grader in 1990–but we hated them. We liked hair metal and also *Bill & Ted's*.

At the sleepover, all the girls laughed at the movie. But they laughed at the wrong parts, for the wrong reasons. Not at the jokes, but just at how Bill and Ted spoke, like they had never before heard valley speak exaggerated to humorous effect. I was disgusted by these small-town simpletons that I now had to accept as my new friends. In my body, the disgust and the existential loneliness combined to create a performative personality I had never needed before—if I felt sad, I could just make my classmates laugh! Perhaps I was simply coming into my own as a self-deprecating jokester; maybe it would have happened this year anyway, regardless of my geographical challenges. I was nine now, after all.

*

Flash forward a decade to 2001. It was fall, my second year of college in Amherst, Massachusetts; I was nineteen. In the midst of everything else that was happening that year, there was a yellow jacket nest in me and my roommate Shira's dorm room window. Don't ask why we never got someone to get rid of it. Too busy getting wasted on shots of Bacardi chased with Nestea from the vending machine, or kissing boys, or cramming overnight with Adderall for finals. Sometimes I would wake up in the top bunk to a yellow jacket flying over my head. Once, when I returned from the bathroom in the middle of the night, there was a yellow jacket on the door knob. I ran across the lawn to Van Meter, and slept in my ex-boyfriend Dan's dorm room instead.

The college town buzzed with record stores and hacky sacks and tours of Emily Dickinson's home just down the road. I was listening regularly to a burned CD of the Descendents's *Milo Goes to College* that had appeared almost by magic in my dorm room CD player, as CDs from the college radio station where my roommate worked so often did. We blasted music and I swiped powder onto my face from a Cover Girl compact, heading to class as a yellow jacket breezed by me.

*

Proximity to boys and men was long ago set in my brain as proximity to power, safety, coolness, calm. Proximity as in, climbing into their beds at 4:00 AM after finding a yellow jacket on the doorknob to my room. Hanging out with them in middle school, high school, and now college as they played video games, discussed punk bands, cracked dumb jokes, played the guitar, watched skate videos, and pounded Colt 45s. I sat there in silence, the audience to their performance, exalted just to be in their presence.

*

Dan and I had broken up the previous summer. Or was it in the fall, I can't remember. We kept breaking up again and again, and losing track of whose decision it was, who was being dumped and who was doing the dumping, or was it mutual? Then arguing over that and ending up back together, but only sort of. We were nineteen years old, very drunk very often, had the same group of friends at college and the same group of high school friends back home, so we were always, constantly together, even when we wanted desperately to be apart. It was not exactly a recipe for a clean breakup.

*

We broke up. I got furious at him for kissing someone else. Unlike in a normal situation, I was there while he kissed her, at the same party where he had driven me, pounding Malibu coconut rum straight from the bottle like it was a goddamned smoothie. The girl Dan kissed was a friend of our mutual best friend; I was enraged with her for bringing this friend there. As if she could control gravity or inertia or whatever force of nature brings people to make out with someone new, post-breakup, in the dead heat of summer in the backyard at Anthony's parents' house while his parents are at the casino. I watched them both with a rageful side-eye as Anthony kept picking up all the girls and throwing us one by one into the pool. I drank and I drank and I drank, puked out the door of Dan's car as he drunk-drove me home, wanted him back purely out of hangover and jealousy, and I think I probably prevailed, I can't remember. We broke up. He was furious with me for not being the shoulder on which he could cry, the one to help him process all his feelings about our breakup, since that is what best friends do and we, of course, were best friends first and foremost. That was our formal title for the years in middle school and high school, before we kissed and I became his "girlfriend."

*

Dan and I met in sixth grade homeroom. He came from a different elementary school. He wasn't a popular kid; far from it. He was a short, skinny, pre-pubescent nerd, but he stood out because he was the funniest kid in our class by miles, and everyone loved him for it—at least anyone with a modicum of taste. He ran for class president, and during his speech in the school auditorium he fake-cried while whimpering, "I promised myself I wouldn't pretend to cry," it was the most advanced joke I had ever heard a peer make. He was voted class clown in the yearbook. We became best friends. I was technically above him in terms of social standing, but I still liked him the best.

*

Perhaps it was the extreme overlap in our friends post-breakup that led me to seek out a new friend group, any new friend group, that did not include him. I didn't go to the hardcore kids first. First, I went with my roommate Shira to her college radio station meetings and became friends with Andy—a weird, sulking dude with sort of hot icy-blue eyes who wore a jean jacket with a Gary Numan back patch. Andy took me on a non-date to see some punk band at the Flywheel where he introduced me to Jenny, a cute lesbian with a deep well of *Saved by the Bell* trivia that rivaled my own. I loved both of them desperately. I beamed with pride at my new friends—the future is bright! I told myself—and it's springtime and everyone is breaking up and finding new love and the daffodils are starting to bud on the lawn outside Van Meter. Until Dan swooped in and made them his new friends, too. Andy was suddenly IMing me, not about how we loved the same bands but about how ignoring Dan wouldn't make him stop loving me. Jenny and Dan bought matching T-shirts with parrots on them from Goodwill and developed a secret handshake. He backed me into a corner where there was no one to go to but the hardcore kids.

*

Why did he always do that? Had he ever in his whole life, I wondered, made a single friend who was not mine first? And the worst part is I think they all liked Dan better. Of course they did. His exaggerated dance moves and his big laugh, perfect jokes, the stupid endearing nicknames he made up for everyone he met. The complex blend of slapstick and irony he was expertly performing even in the sixth grade. Dan was always getting praised or subtly rewarded for all his outlandish behaviors. Like that time when we stayed up all night writing papers for our English class, and his made psychotic, sleep-deprived leaps between Goethe and *Rocky IV* while I tried painstakingly to write a smart, normal college paper. I got a B- and he got an A+. He always got an A+. For shit he did in his sleep. While I got punished. I didn't feel confident making weird leaps in logic based on my life's authentic experiences in my school papers, just like I didn't feel comfortable making loud, embodied jokes like I did as a kid. While it's true that I was voted Best Sense of Humor in my high school yearbook, I could never really be the class clown; I could only be the class clown gf.

*

The hardcore kids rolled deep. They were a crew of 15+ boys, at least, that always seemed to be actively multiplying, popping up anew and somersaulting into the basement hardcore show mosh pit as if emerging from a clown car. Each one was clad in a uniform of skinny jeans and black punk band tee, black hoodie and/or Dickies jacket with punk band buttons pinned to the pocket. They were loud and drunk and immature and obnoxious, burly and skinny and handsome, tall and short and tattooed and pierced and clean-shaven and scruffy and cologned and unshowered and slapstick and funny and performative and charming and awkward and quiet and shy. Most of them had imported to the university directly from a private all-boys high school in Central Massachusetts. They were sexy and gorgeous and perfect; an untapped sea of potential boyfriends that Shira and I had happened upon as if a secret garden, both of us fresh off a breakup.

*

The hardcore kids let us into their group because we were girls of a certain sensibility. We had the right haircuts and the right skinny jeans and studded belts and facial piercings and the right taste in music, or at least—on my part—a willingness to fake it. They let us sit on their beds in their dorm rooms while they pounded forties and made dumb jokes, blasted music and flailed around the room, opining loudly on their favorite bands, movies, documentary filmmakers, and video games, while we giggled at them from our perch in exalted silence. They liked Le Tigre but only the song that was a NOFX diss track; the other songs about feminist art and sex work and misogyny weren't tangential enough to their worlds to hold their attention. And weirdly enough, I didn't care. My requirements for a hookup partner most certainly did not include *feminism*—it was the early 2000s, for God's sake, and I liked boys; I wasn't delusional.

If this essay were a movie, it wouldn't pass the Bechdel Test. I'm not sure my dorm room did, either. Well, that's not true; it couldn't be. We talked in my dorm room about Sleater-Kinney and Blondie and Easy Mac and our periods and our outfits and our homework for the linguistics class we took to satisfy the level 2 math requirement we were too dumb to test out of from high school.

*

To be fair: who did you want me to date? To make out with? To explore my nascent early twenties sexuality with? I will not apologize for making out with eight different members of this friend group in three years, for dating three of them, for making one of them my official boyfriend, for falling half in love with maybe two of them. For breaking the heart of at least one of them. The friend group seemed to stretch to pull all the boys I might be interested in into it, like a black hole. Even if I didn't know that the hot boy with tattoos in my writing workshop was part of the group, it always turned out that he was. The cute quiet emo boy with two silver spikes in his lip that I chatted with on AIM all night seemed separate, but he wasn't. The boy from Boston with curly hair and a black baseball cap who was visiting one weekend was friends with them, too. It was almost like there was no way for me to date or even to be kissed without being perennially laughed at by my male friends for perennially hooking up with the hardcore kids; as if anyone who I kissed was made one of them by virtue of my kiss. As if my entire dating life was one giant joke.

*

The hardcore kids once leaned a recycling bin full of pee against the door of one of their friend's dorm rooms, then knocked on the door and ran away laughing. They once stole a live lobster from the dining hall where one of them worked, put the lobster on a call box outside their dorm building, then called their room from the call box and started shouting "I'm a lobster on the call box!" into the dead of night. The hardcore kids once peed in their friend's gas tank, once peed in the punch at a party, once set off firecrackers outside the window where I was making out with one of them in his bed the morning after the party. Occasionally one of them would pull their dick out as a joke.

*

I don't remember what my jokes were when I was nine, just that they slapped. How at birthday parties and on the playground other girls would laugh uproariously at me; in jovial appreciation of me. In class, too; even boys laughed sometimes. It felt kind of like I was juggling, but I wasn't. At a school dance thing in gym class I busted out these 60s dance moves I had learned from my dad, one where you pantomime jumping into the ocean, holding your nose while waving your free hand, all the while bending your knees up and down to the beat. Everyone loved it! My peers took in my dance moves laughing, some of them joining in—until the gym teacher yelled at me to knock it off.

Why did she yell at me? Too much fun? Too much creativity while dancing? Maybe she felt attacked by all us youngsters united in laughter at the dance moves of her youth. Maybe she was mad at my desire for attention. Maybe she just found us all annoying or was having a bad day. But the message was clear either way: my jokes were not appreciated. They messed with some delicate social balance that I could feel slowly forming, buzzing around our dancing bodies.

TEARS OF A CLASS CLOWN

Chris E. Vargas

Despite being an acclaimed a jokester at the start of middle school, I was also profoundly miserable—in the exact way anyone who's gone through puberty in public school can imagine. The kind of misery where I pictured my every action, at all times, being scrutinized by a vast and cruel audience of my peers. Nothing original. Junior high lasted only two years, a transitional moment in time when the sixth grade had not yet been absorbed into Los Angeles Unified Public School System's newly branded "Middle School" timeframe, making ninth grade part of high school. The year was 1990, and I had entered grade seven as a popular girl. I was riding high, having graduated elementary school with two boys crushing on me. They were former best friends, and their friend breakup, I assumed, happened because Joey Becerra invited me to his twelve-year-old miniature golf birthday party, which ended in an after party at his house. He hadn't invited his best friend, John Mallach—my actual boyfriend, with whom I'd soon share my first sloppy French kiss with at an under-supervised pool party.

All the kids that had attended Van Gogh Elementary were tracked to nearby Robert Frost Jr. High, both in Granada Hills. The artist and poet school names betray their boring environments. They were both firmly on the Road Traveled. Van Gogh and Frost were in a "nice," very suburban part of the northern San Fernando Valley, in the foothills of the Santa Susana Mountains. My mom and I had experienced a fleeting affluence when we lived here, during her short-lived marriage to one Steve Friedman, a personal injury lawyer who my mom thought could give us a stable life. After a Jewish wedding which included a slow dance to Elvis Presley's "I Can't Help Falling in Love with You," some fun Christmas and Hanukkah seasons, and many mornings watching *Pee-wee's Playhouse* in the plush comfort of the second, not-just-for-decoration living room, the marriage ended. We were back out on the streets with our hobo bindles and our refrigerator, which people in LA were once expected to move from apartment to apartment.

Before and after this stint in Granada Hills, which occurred during my second and third grade years, my mom and I moved around a lot. We didn't move to far flung parts of the state, country, or even world—where I might make new friends and be cool and from Los Angeles, California (albeit The Valley). We moved to various apartments around the middle to northeast part of the San Fernando Valley, and in and out of my grandparents' house in Pacoima. Stints at my grandparents' occurred between leases, during rougher periods, and one time after the 1994 Northridge earthquake, when our condo was condemned and my prized The Cure's "Boys Don't Cry" poster was looted before we had a chance to move all our stuff out.

My white, country, West Virginia-born grandparents lived in the same house in Pacoima since 1962, bought for $10,000. The neighborhood was briefly white, but by the time my mom and dad met at San Fernando High School it had turned primarily Black and Latino. In my mom's 1970s yearbooks, she and my aunt were the only white girls in a sea of chola eyebrows and afros. My dad, a US-born Mexican, called my grandparents "the last white people in Pacoima." That house in Pacoima is still my home base, even though I made no lasting friends in the neighborhood because I had always gone to school elsewhere. From the start of second, grade we used Steve Friedman's address in Granada Hills so I could maintain stability during our shallowly nomadic existence. By the time I was in seventh grade, at age twelve, I had moved thirteen times.

Once I got to Frost, John Mallach was nowhere to be found and Joey Becerra wouldn't give me the time of day. But all was not lost—I met my best friend Fernando that year. We were boyfriend and girlfriend for all of two weeks. One day during lunch time, Fernando asked me out in a circle of our peers egging him. As he nervously approached me to pop the question, a jerk in the crowd yelled, "Don't do it! He's gay!" The girls, in that fag hag girl style, cheered and showered me with their blessings. He was after all a cutie and a very sharp dresser. I said yes and Fernando and I enjoyed a chaste, Victorian-style two-week affair, writing notes to each other and passing them between classes. He called me "sugar plum" and regaled me with fantasies of our future lives and babies together. We shared one quick, significant kiss at a temple that hosted Garret Naiman's clown-themed bar mitzvah party. The coveted clown head piggy bank centerpiece that I took home as a souvenir was just as memorable. Fernando and I talked on the phone just a couple times. When I thought I heard someone, his young aunt, in the background, saying he was going to break up with me, I quickly broke it off with him. It was hasty, but I couldn't risk the humiliation of getting dumped. We would find our way back to each other in eighth grade, when we became best friends forever. Fernando and I bonded over our many shared experiences—we are both Chicano, we both had at least one set of non-English-speaking grandparents, but we never formally learned to speak Spanish ourselves. I am half-Mexican, and he is full but passes as white. Most importantly, he was also being driven to school from a far-flung, poorer part of the Valley, Sylmar.

Save for the few busloads of brown kids being transported in, Robert Frost was pretty white. This was a moment in public school history when lower income and racialized students would be bussed into white neighborhoods in order to integrate schools and deal with racial segregation. This very awkward practice was ultimately deemed ineffective and was discontinued later that decade.

Still riding high on that vaguely popular moment that originated in elementary school, I was self-expressive in my junior high classes, or at least in my science class with Ms. Sinofsky. I was quite the entertainer. She even talked about me to other class periods—my first and last taste of fame. My main bit was to raise my hand and moan, like I really wanted—no, needed—to be called upon, and also kinda like I was taking a shit. The class loved it. I was too high on my own supply to be embarrassed, and really worked it. Me and Ms. Sinofsky had a rapport, and I approached class like we were a comedy team entertaining the other students. In actuality, I was a heckler, and she probably despised me when she was just trying to do her job. I suppose this made me popular, even if it was at the expense of my own self-respect. I had even managed to get elected, through popularity, of course, to a student government title: Class Historian. No one knew what this was, and I don't think I did much besides take photos on a disposable camera, a piece of technology that, like me peaked in popularity at this time. Did these photos end up in a yearbook? I have no idea. In the pedo files of some school administrator? Probably.

By the end of seventh grade I was gunning for the yearbook superlative, Class Clown. I embarked on a whisper campaign, planting seeds in the brains of my friends and classmates, of anyone who would give me the time of day in the snack bar line to buy candy during brunch (yes, it was called that) and lunch periods. I kissed hands, I shook babies. I amped up the clownery by doing impressions of my teachers who pronounced words funny. Impressions, the pinnacle of middle school humor. Finally, when the ballots for superlative voting were released in homeroom, the category had been violently and without notice changed to Funniest Laugh—but everyone knew what to do. It was a landslide. Not only did my winning come with an important title, but I was given permission to leave class to take a wacky photo for the yearbook. Luckily, I do also have a funny, sort of suppressed and nasally, Pee-wee Herman laugh. But after all that effort, what a letdown. I had been robbed of the distinguished title of Class Clown!

Perhaps as a result of this, a shift in the final year of junior high set me on the path to the rebellious teenager that lives in my heart to this day. It was October 1991; I momentously had attended my first concert. I was taken to the outdoor Pacific Amphitheatre in Costa Mesa, by my mom and aunt, to see the glam rock band Warrant, of "Cherry Pie" fame, along with FireHouse and Trixter, two lesser bands in the genre. All three bands were blonde, beautiful, and done up in full face beats. My mom, only thirty-three at the time, was at the start of her second adolescence, reprising a hairband groupie identity that she never got to experience having been saddled with me at age twenty. She would've been on the Sunset Strip being a 'ho for the likes of Guns N' Roses or Mötley Crüe. Instead, she was a single mom, working a full time job, saddled with my ass. When I finally hit an age where I was allowed to be unsupervised, she and my aunt were running the streets, seeing local longhair bands at a rock club on Lankershim called FM Station.

Warrant was technically my first concert, and I briefly felt pretty cool for it. A rite of passage had been obtained. My new friend Leland, who was to become instrumental in introducing our burgeoning friend group to cool new bands, had also gone to a concert over the weekend. Probably not her first. For a split second I naively believed Leland and I were at the same place at the same time. When, from under our pullovers, we ceremonially revealed the concert shirts we had each scored from our respective concerts that weekend, I was embarrassed to realize this was not the case. She had gone to see an obscure new band who was quickly gaining in popularity, Nirvana. Their breakout (Gen

X translation: sellout) album *Nevermind* came out in September and rendered hairbands like Warrant immediately passé, thus changing the landscape of rock and what signified (or smelled like) rebellious teen spirit. A couple years later, Fernando and I would have an important star sighting—Kurt Cobain at the Ralphs in Studio City. We stalked him around the grocery store, conveniently ending up in line just after him. We paid as quickly as we could and exited only to see him jumping over the short wall at the edge of the parking lot. Disappearing into the night.

In eighth grade our friend group was solidifying, and we were becoming bad. It was Fernando and I, Leland of course, and my best friend Angie from elementary school. One night, during a sleepover at Leland's, we snuck over to the school armed with spray paint. We wrote phrases like the Nirvana-inspired "This place smells like school," or "I am the Chees," a reference to a YA novel spelled wrong by Fernando. Also, "My Ass Is on Fire," and song lyrics, "Where Is My Mind." The next school day the principal announced on the intercom an incident of vandalism and ridiculed our misspellings and lack of artistry. A low blow. The student body was assured that the crime scene had been dusted and fingerprinted, and that the perps would get exactly what was coming to them. They (we) did not. It remains a cold case.

Over the course of that year, we each assembled a constellation of countercultural identifications with bands and popular culture—Nirvana, The Cure, The Smiths & Pixies, Sonic Youth. David Lynch's *Twin Peaks* and *Blue Velvet*, The Doors (including the new biopic starring a really sexy Val Kilmer as Jim Morrison), and *Cape Fear* (with an inappropriately sexy seduction scene between 90s icon Juliette Lewis and hot daddy Robert De Niro). We started carrying metal and plastic kid's lunchboxes adorned with signifying badges like my Good Humor's Vampire's Deadly Secret popsicle sticker that I got at an ice cream wholesale warehouse in Sun Valley. At the time my dad had an ice cream truck, and I would sometimes accompany him on inventory purchases, where I got stickers that one could affix to the outside of the truck to show kids what was for sale. We'd also go on neighborhood runs. I loved driving around with him in the truck, but I was horrified when he would occasionally pick me up in it; this filled me with such class shame. Given my tender age and my cross-class and race educational experiences, it didn't take much.

One morning a thing happened that Afterschool Specials warned both kids and parents about. We were in the hallway before class, and a kid named Neri gathered us all together. Neri opened their palm to reveal tiny squares of paper with a faint smiley face print on it. The four of us, Leland, Angie, Fernando and I all split one tab. That's a quarter tab each of LSD. A tiny dose, but for someone who had yet to feel the effects of even a sip of alcohol, I did not know what I was in for. I felt nothing for the first three periods, but by lunch we were all tripping our asses off. The whole world changed—the wind became supernatural, the sounds of the opening and closing of hallway doors reverberated through my whole body and brought with it angry spirits. It was surreal and terrifying. We decided to ditch the last two classes of the day because sitting through them would've given us all away. But ditching was equally improbable. With nowhere to go we wandered the hallways, crouched in bushes, killed time in bathrooms until the final bell. But what should've been a relief presented us with yet another problem. Where were we to go now? I was supposed to get picked up by my dad. I walked out of the gates of campus and there down the block was my dad's El Camino, brown with a white stripe down the side, another automobile of his that I was embarrassed to be seen in. I immediately turned around and walked in the opposite direction. Fernando was with me, and together we decided it best to walk to Leland's house. Her mom Jerri would understand. The couple of blocks were harrowing, hordes of cheerleaders were following us, old couples driving by were craning their necks, falling over each other to point and stare at us. When we finally arrived, her mother Jerri didn't so much as wince at our confession. She was cool. She also must've sensed we were doing bad. Leland and Angie showed up just after, and as Jerri comforted Fernando and I, Leland and Angie were having a good ol' time rolling around the backyard laughing at plants. As the woodgrain on her kitchen cabinets swirled and threatened to suck Fernando and I into their evil vortex, Jerri called Poison Control to see if there was anything she could do to lessen the effects of the drugs.

I would eventually try acid three more times before I finally had a good trip. I was determined to experience the fun everyone else seemed to be having. After I finally had a good time, I gave it up and went on to less risky drugs, like mushrooms and ecstasy.

Along with experimenting with drugs and listening to alternative bands, we were also discovering hair dye. At first, we played it safe with regular boxed dye from Sally's Beauty Supply—colors like Black Cherry, which was mostly just dark brown but caught red glints in the sun. This was a gateway drug, leading us toward the standout stuff: vegetable-based Manic Panic dyes. We bought them on trips to Retail Slut on Melrose, and at head shops like the hippie-ish Captain Ed's on Reseda Boulevard, which primarily sold Grateful Dead merch and "water pipes," but also carried punk patches and band shirts. All of counterculture was lumped together in the 90s, hence at any concert, there was always someone wearing a Bauhaus T-shirt.

A Manic Panic dye job was a much more involved process than the box dye days. First, I had to bleach my thick, black, Mexican hair down to a brassy yellow. Then came the toner—meant to calm or lighten the yellow, but it never quite worked. I was no doubt half-assing these professional procedures. This period ushered in perpetually stained bathrooms, pillowcases and T-shirt collars, not just upsetting parents with our rebellious statements, but with the messiness of it in their homes.

We began making our school debuts in our new hair colors and the school administration immediately expressed their disapproval. One by one we were taken out of class, summoned to the principal's office and sent home early with notes telling our parents we were to un-dye our hair because we were distracting other students. Tensions ran high between us and the administration for the rest of the year as our blue hair faded into sea moss green, our bright fuchsia to a dull, sad pink.

On graduation day we decided to make one grand, final statement. We arrived at the ceremony and were seated in alphabetical order according to our last names. As the MC began to call names, we waited patiently with our hair tucked underneath our mortar boards. First it was Fernando, then Angie. Leland and I, with V last names, were at the end. As the ceremony unfolded, we each walked across the stage, took our diploma, and yanked off our caps, revealing our brightly dyed hair—mine a hot pink, Fernando a bright blue, Leland a vampire red. We each pranced down the middle aisles waving to our friends and family. The crowd was shocked and awed, the exact response we were hoping for. When the ceremony concluded, we all gathered together with our families and took every configuration of solo and group photo. In mid group-pose, crowds parted, and the principal stormed up and angrily demanded our diplomas.

“Your diploma level will be now be changed from a class A to a lesser class B.” She stormed away.

I never bothered to retrieve this lesser document.

Later that month, as a graduation celebration, we all got dropped off at the Pasadena Rose Bowl to see The Cure. It was the 1992 *Wish* tour. Dressed in a trench coat, with teased Robert Smith hair and black lipstick, my self-effacing class clown had evolved into something different, something that pointed to the absurdity of being normal and, in that annoying teenage way, began to question everything. This shift would set me on a path of lifelong countercultural identification. I could now see the foolishness of institutions, the emptiness of their diplomas, the way an important and highly sought after title like Class Clown could be renamed Funniest Laugh. This was only the beginning of my growing cynicism. I was about to enter high school.

THE GOD-SHAPED HOLE

Grace Byron

I woke up with a God-shaped hole, so I asked it what it wanted.

Fire, the hole said. *Twenty dollars. A shotgun. Running in a field toward a train. Gummy worms and Hot Cheetos.*

I was in a bed that was not my own but it felt exactly like mine. The sheets were pale blue, similar to the kind I wrapped around myself as a kid. As I looked around. I realized I was in a child's bedroom. A girl's in fact. *Get out. You'll be the predator before they have any chance to ask why you're here. The transsexual vampire everyone has been waiting to rally around.* The smell of garlic and spices wafted under the door, just like the early dinners my mother used to serve. A TV downstairs was blasting the same show I remembered my sisters watching when I got home from school about a talking dog.

The mirror gave it away. I was a child—a little girl—somehow back in my family house at age twelve or so—with all my adult trauma trans woman memories intact.

My body was a melting Peep. I was wearing an awful little yellow dress like it was Easter Sunday. The God-shaped hole laughed. *We're not going to church.* If it was Easter Sunday, my mother wouldn't allow that. She would make sure we were all out the door in our little pastel dresses with our hair tied back in matching ribbons. I guess we were four sisters now, no awkward older gangly brother who hid a Taylor Swift T-shirt in the back of the closet.

"June!

Lucy!

Lily!

Abigail!"

The other doors on the second door flew open and a flurry of feet hammered down the stairs. My sisters made even carpet sound loud. June. My name was June. Well, that made sense, it was the name I had chosen for myself.

It wasn't dinner, it was breakfast. My mom was cooking eggs, using too much pepper and roasting garlic. A bag of shredded Kraft cheese was spilling on the counter. I wanted to pour myself a cup of coffee but I was twelve. What did a twelve-year-old girl drink? Only water with breakfast seemed insane. Milk even worse. No one was anti-dairy yet and while perhaps my twelve-year-old girl stomach could take it, I had no intention of finding out.

"How did you sleep girls?"

Everyone mumbled as they grabbed plates and gathered eggs and toast. My dad was on the phone in his office speaking in his faux-excited voice. He was wishing his parents a happy Easter. We were going to go over there for dinner. Ham, I assumed. From the grocery store my grandma liked before she developed Alzheimer's and stopped talking to me.

"June, can you take out the trash?"

I nodded, afraid to croak. My mom didn't see me though, so she said it again with a slower cadence.

"Yes," I said.

She eyed me for a second with an empty frustration I could never place. I got up and took the big black bag full of paper plates and water bottles to the garage, setting it dutifully on top of the overflowing trash can.

When I came back in everyone was looking out past the deck.

"There's a veery," my mom said. She spent so much time feeding the birds she'd named some of the ones she could identify by sight. The tense of past and present were rubbing against each other like two oarless virgins. I didn't know how to think about her. She was right in front of me, acting out another typical holiday. I wanted her to say my name again so I could taste it.

Lucy and Lily were scraping cheesy eggs around their plates as Abigail went back for more. She forked more eggs onto her plate and went upstairs to change out of her pajama tee.

My mom and I were the only ones staring at the veery. It looked so precious with its plump silver belly and terrifying black eye. The loud trill was annoying Lucy and Lily who rolled their eyes at us as they went upstairs.

Dad walked in on us and said, "Hey," in the way a suburban white dad interrupts his family to say something important in a casual way.

"Grandma's in the hospital," he said.

The day my grandma went to the hospital on Easter did not immediately come back to me. Either this feminine redux was different or my dad hadn't told me the full story the day it happened. I did vaguely remember we didn't see my Grandma one Easter we had planned to. I'd mostly been disappointed not to eat the Stouffer's microwave macaroni she made in huge batches and placed on the dining room table in nice stoneware.

My mom didn't say anything. She looked at my dad, wincing in his pain.

"Well, let's get going," Dad said softly. Lucy and Lily peered over the staircase, letting their red hair sway wild in the air.

"Brush your hair girls," my mom said.

I shuffled back up the stairs, trying to catch a hint of my parents' whispers behind me. They closed the door to the office and sat in the leather spinny chairs.

"Do you think everything will be ok?" Abigail asked with a toothbrush in her mouth.

"I don't know," I said.

"So serious June, come on. I'm sure it will be fine," she said.

Lucy and Lily were screeching in their room, deknotting and detangling.

The God-shaped hole turned over in my stomach. I grimaced and clutched my tummy against my childhood bedroom door. There were no locks in my childhood home. We were free to go and they were free to come.

*

At church I learned obedience and duality. The preacher was talking about resurrection. I liked to quote my favorite poet, "I had trouble with the Resurrection. So I would not join the church." But here I was. Back in a pew. If this was the afterlife, I would've preferred to have been put down like the puppy Abigail tried to rescue after cross-country practice.

Each of my sisters was scribbling on her church bulletin. The space where notes were supposed to go was filled with idle gossip and sketches of the back of women's heads. Abigail was the best, the one who tried to do something more. In a few years she would beg my mom to drop out of college and take art classes at night school. While ostensibly it was her choice, Abigail would instead finish college and get an office job.

"The Resurrection is the promise for those who have forsaken worldly pleasure," the preacher said. "The Good Shepherd will come for his flock, and we will walk along still waters. We will sing praises for a new world."

My adult life had been about trying to fill the God-shaped hole. I kept hoping for the promise of peace but it never came. Losing my virginity, changing my gender marker, chopping off my dick. Things got better, like the YouTube videos said, but they never took on the utopian quality the LGBT mafia loved to advertise. For instance, I did not enjoy Pride. Not because I was a prude or didn't enjoy sex or whiskey, but because it was loud. Instead, I tried to remake myself over and over, hoping I would unlock the key to eternal peace.

I had endless phases. All of my hopes and dreams, dutifully chronicled in my diaries over the years, meant nothing. Each obsessive rabbit hole phase—library girl, academic, goth girl, band girl, blogger girl, pottery girl—they all gave me a little bit of time in everyone's eyes. Purpose in miniature. No one expected me to do anything but survive. I spent my time trying to use words to build a ladder out of the hole. Maybe at the top I could wrestle an angel. I could prove myself. I could learn the way love spoke to nuns. Somehow in all that silence they filled holes without masturbation. When I read about older single women, or older trans women in general, I wondered what kind of mothering they did to banish their God-shaped holes. Was it only Protestants who had the hole? Only Christians? No, the futility seemed to touch everyone. They whined about the end times without ever having read anything about them in the Good Book.

"We just want you to be happy," everyone said when I came out, whether as encouragement to keep going or discouragement to go detrans.

I never stopped believing in eternal peace or eternal damnation. They just changed shape like a chimera, adopting pieces of Christianity, socialism, queer theory, and some ketamine-induced hypotheses.

"God gives us eternity as a gift. The precious gift of our Lord Jesus Christ. He can save us from our sins. He protects us. He cherishes us. You know, many of you know, my grandnephew and I had a bad relationship. He wasn't always the best behaved boy in the front row . . ."

He was never the best behaved boy. While she hadn't told us yet, I knew Lily would soon reveal he asked her for nude pictures of herself and asked her to do things she did not want to do. A few years later he would escalate to stalking. Eventually my mom would tell the cops and they would do nothing. But Dad knew. He knew it was the preacher's grandnephew.

"My grandnephew was trying to fill something that could not be filled by earthly desire," the preacher said. "He was trying to fill the hole in his humanity." That wasn't the only thing he was trying to fill. "But only God completes us."

I sat listening attentively, not scribbling on my sermon notes. There was nothing here I hadn't heard before, whether in the suburban church or on the streets of the city. Everywhere I went people declared the holiness of God. *i would believe in god if he gave me the last poptart, I posted once.*

The God-shaped hole was gurgling in my stomach. I felt it wiggling around buried under my eggshell yellow dress. My mother shushed me as if I was making the noise willingly.

I walked out of the service, ostensibly to go to the bathroom. Lying to my sisters was easy. I slid out of the booth and walked out. I didn't go to the bathroom though. I was still too terrified even with a perfect cis body. No hot button pushing for me.

*

The playground outside our church was empty. I walked to the swing set and sat, staring at the gravel and swaying. Chillier than I expected. How long would it last—this redux? Was rebirth everything I wanted and more? Sure. I was everything I wanted with too much interiority. Twelve-year-olds are supposed to be fumbling through primordial ooze. Not contemplating God. But contemplate I did. And did again.

Boyhood, girlhood, children of Satan. The hole was never filled by fidelity.

"What do you need?" I asked again as I started pumping my legs into the air, getting higher and higher on the swing. The noise in my head crackled. My stomach felt so nauseous I wanted to lay down on the ground and stop resisting but I kept on pumping. I would be an angel if it killed me. *Let me walk with thee, close to thee, close to thee.*

I want more than just the last Pop-Tart. I want a Grammy. And three boyfriends, one girlfriend in a crazy polycule. I want to be a bisexual icon who people make YouTube compilations about. I want a photoshoot on the cover of Vogue where I'm licking a gun like a Bond girl.

I want to swim with manatees and move to a new country.

The hole inside of me took shape. No longer whispering, only the rustle of feathers and Jell-O of eyes. My Biblically accurate angel.

"Greetings," the hole said. "Fear not, I am Gabriel."

Out of the swirling darkness came spinning, forever weaving into the human plane. It was like he was molting. His eyes circled his body along a gold line, his feathers sparked with holy infinity. My sense of taste and smell didn't work around him. Like I'd just used mouthwash.

"Hello," I said. "Do you still need a Pop-Tart?"

"Among other things," he said. I realized I wanted a treat, too. I didn't need a Grammy or a girlfriend, but chocolate sounded nice.

After talking for a while we decided to go to Target. They were likely to have all the treats we wanted. No manatees, but maybe an aquarium.

"What is he like?"

"Really?"

I nodded.

"His voice is the sound of a hundred dolphins whistling."

"Where was God during MeToo?"

Someone saw the two of us trolling the shampoo aisle and snapped a picture.

"Now you are interested in philosophy?"

"I didn't know it was philosophy to ask something like that."

"The Absence of God," Gabriel said, slowing his words intentionally, "is always philosophical."

We walked through the sliding doors past the frozen drink machines. I almost asked him to stop and get one. I thought it would fulfill one of his urges. One of our urges.

He ran his fingers over the cheap rainbow of nail polish. If I had been a girl I would've shoplifted. I was a girl. I could shoplift. A few bottles made their way into my pockets, clanking like marbles.

"Do you want all the men in jail?" he asked as we wound through the beauty supplies.

"I never said that."

"God is an abolitionist in some ways. And in other ways, he is not."

"So, he does believe in punishment?"

"I think even abolitionists do," Gabriel said. Someone was looking at us and snapped a photo on their phone. He was going to be the next big thing. Biblically accurate angel kidnapping teenage shoplifter.

"What do you think of autofiction?" the angel asked.

"I think it's silly."

"When you get bored you look just like Marilyn Monroe."

I had never watched a Marilyn Monroe movie all the way through, so I just blushed again.

"Have you read the big detrans book?"

Gabriel shook. I assumed that meant no. In the future me and my boyfriend argued about the book. We spun theories on who was who and what a biomythology was. He didn't like the sex scenes.

"The basic plot of the detrans book," I started, "is that a trans girl witch meets a detrans witch with a lion familiar. The main trans girl witch eventually starts dating the lion and discovers he's a trans man the detrans witch put a spell on."

"Sounds complicated."

"I didn't finish it."

"Well then why do you think about it so much?"

"I like to think."

I realized, perhaps, angels didn't think that much. They just sort of existed.

"How many pages is it?"

"About seven hundred," I said.

"I'll take a look tonight and tell you how it ends."

"While you're at it, can you make transsexuality not a sin?"

Gabriel chuckled and his wings shimmered.

"I'll see what I can do."

For the first time since I'd left the church I wondered if my family missed me. In this new ecosystem, how important was I to the unit? As a boy I held the family together. The meek caretaker. A repository for guilt. I loved being a punching bag. Even if they hated your guts, they needed you. Every family needs a fall guy. I took in everything around me and swallowed it down, waiting years to burn the coal.

Gabriel was looking at a sticker book. I wandered over and saw he was looking at a page full of marine animals.

"There's no manatee."

"Why are you obsessed with manatees?"

"Because God thinks they're the funniest creation," he said.

"Really? More than a platypus or a blobfish or an axolotl?"

"Yes, much more than an axolotl."

"Why?"

"Because they're so helpless. And everyone wants to swim with them in captivity. The way you've let everything go you'll be lucky if there's any in the wild by the end of the decade."

"Animals are always getting endangered. Why didn't God plan for that?" I moved a few feet away from him. People were looking at us. Someone snapped a picture and sent it to TMZ. I'd fucked the alternate timeline, spoiled my dream with fury.

"I think God hoped more of you would blow up pipelines," he said, before ushering us out of the Target—though not before a detour for a box of purple Pop-Tarts.

*

From the woods a few hundred yards away, we watched my family tear into the church parking lot in tears, screaming for me to come back. My parents had yet to buy me a cellphone. They were frantic, crawling like bugs over the asphalt.

"What will you do with this new precious life?" Gabriel whispered.

It was easier for him, he floated among the branches. I was struggling to hold on for dear life. Perhaps he was also picking up on the fact that while the God-shaped hole had turned out to be an angel, I still felt empty. Maybe even more empty now that he was outside of me, had given me everything I wanted.

The birds were singing.

He took a bite of the purple Pop-Tart and offered me the other. I munched on it contemplatively, letting the crumbs spill on the forest floor. A thousand yards in the direction opposite the church a man was starting his car, a six-pack in the passenger side. Another honky-tonk song played loudly over the speakers as he turned the engine and drove off, something about women and protection. Vintage 2007 misogyny.

I watched my dad hold my mom. My sisters looked at their feet. Other congregants gathered asking what they could do. Soon they would find me if I didn't leave.

"How do I get away?"

"Further and further on up this road? Or back into your old life?" Gabriel asked.

I turned to the God-shaped hole and asked her what she wanted.

Fire, the hole said. *One million dollars. A sword. Sparklers in a hot tub. Going down a waterslide with the hottest trans boy in Brooklyn.*

Takis and Lavender Ice Cream. Omakase. Crashing a rich boy's Lamborghini.

"How about a little fire first?"

Gabriel nodded.

What if a little spark was enough to do the trick, I thought. With the beat of a thousand wings, a blossom of soot arose. A small fire broke out in the west wing. The white wood crackled with fire. White then brown then the bluish tinge of kindle before curdling black. It didn't feel apocalyptic at all. I would no longer have to sit and listen to endless revelations or listen to the praise band try and milk a C-major chord for all its worth.

People were screaming, fleeing the building in horror. Little kids whined in confusion. The house of worship and horror one and the same at last. Glory, glory to all the deacons who called me a pervert. My safe place, my pyrotechnics.

"They'll be ok," the angel said. His eyes were watching me watch the blaze. The whole church was soon enveloped. "You didn't want any one to be hurt."

"No," I said. "I just wanted the distraction."

Church-burning felt so good. So calming.

As I stared at the smoking steeple, Gabriel hailed a passing truck and murmured something about needing a ride. Hitchhiking with an angel was far less threatening for a fourteen-year-old girl than going alone. I don't know if the woman driving saw the same terrible monster that I did, but she let herself be charmed into driving us far, far away. Much farther than the original destination the angel told her. I watched my hometown fog in the rear-view mirror. The universe was stripping every little rule away from me.

We drove past McDonald's, prairies, trees, gods, devils, churches, anti-abortion signs, forgiveness, cemeteries, diners, empty lakes, quarries, fields of corn, fields of wheat, fields of past loves, parks, drones, UFOs, government buildings, ghost towns, motels, pain, fires, rallies, trade wars, poisoned water, rising insulin prices, pestilence, plague, frogs, Trojan Horses, mysterious explosions, covens, a giant cross, joy, hope, grace, love, and huge bird nests.

When the crucifix faded behind us and we rolled into the parking lot of a Southern-themed diner, the angel and I jumped out of the car and told the woman we had to part ways. She smiled and hugged me and googled where the nearest women's shelter was. She almost seemed happy to write me off as a battered kid rather than a simple religious runaway.

"This is where we part ways, too," Gabriel said as we pissed behind a car wash. The hedges were tall enough to hide my squat. He gave me a few thousand dollars and his armada of eyes winked at me.

"Mad money," he said.

"Thank you," I said.

"Well, you're detrans now. Long before it will become in fashion. You have some time to prepare your I'm a trans woman in a cis woman's body speech. The *real* transsexual vampire."

I kissed the God-shaped hole and licked the embers of his mouth.

IT/ITS
Valentine Freeman

In an effort to see my dead father more clearly, I read Stephen King's *It* and find a monster you can't see clearly, a man deadnamed Bob Gray who chose the honorific, "It," its name becoming its pronouns, its pronouns being the ultimate indefinite pronoun—a very radical move for an alien energy several million years old named after a pedophilic cannibal. What we see is not there, is insane and invisible. Fear hologram that can eat you.

The monster can't be seen, so I spend several stolen hours dodging upsells on Ancestry.com by zooming in on grainy, paywalled images of my father in Uniontown, Pennsylvania's *Morning Herald*, spanning his career with the Fayette Singing Boys at eleven in 1966 and twelve in 1967, and the *Evening Standard*'s account of his car upsetting at 4:00 in the afternoon of May 1972. Five years and some months before my sister is born, a 1971 yearbook offers a bushy cloche of black hair around a well-fed face with my father's glamorous beauty mark attached to the right nasolabial fold. An undignified, sensual amusement on its open mouth, and the big teeth I've resisted many attempts to straighten. I laughed and smiled silently with my mouth shut from ten to twenty-five, learning how to crack it open and chuckle by watching other people, like a psychopath.

Sealed-shut lips, infinite variations on a line—to indicate emotion, judgment, acquiescence, loathing, and to indicate that I am inside my mouth, and it is not available right now.

Fifteen tents circled together under an overpass of twenty-six lanes of traffic on five highways, shawled by one organism quilted from tarps, grocery bags, towels, and sharp objects woven into the seams like hairpins.

Or the split toes of two expensive shoes lined up facing you under the table at the restaurant where the symbols slip, and I pronounce St. Tropez phonetically and we both laugh.

Or the line of blue fingerprints left by hands identical to my brother's and father's hands, my hands that stop you from touching my arm over and over that way. And the mouth-line that lives here now on my face when you look at me "like a monster" that neither of us will say you can't really see.

One record is too grainy to search with command+F, but the headlines say trillium is in bloom, an airman lost the air in his suit and died with a hiss, and a honey-blonde is sure to outpace a Black woman running for republican governor. It is May again, 1966.

*

"*Urine luck.*" My father thwacked us on our asses with a damp terrycloth dishtowel, see-through if held to the light. He clipped off the tips of our noses and served us chicken tongue meatballs, and the moon was god's gross toenail clipping, god's underwear hanging from the chandelier in his mother's foyer in Uniontown, Pennsylvania. She was the first lady, devoted body, mind, and spirit to the town mayor. She was fundamentally committed to the spring-loaded ballerina in the music box, to lovingly mimicking the soft aws and uws in a child's mouth saying, I lika teach liddle buwds to sing. Mouth of marbles for the child, the child is white spray paint over everything in the house, over the plastic on the sofa and the marble eggs in egg cups on the mantle and the embarrassed cockatiel blushing in the breakfast nook. Uniontown! It's all I saw when I imagined Derry, Maine, the birthplace of It. One of the small American towns with the bad American breath of the Fayette Singing Boys choir director and the ceaseless smiles of petite, honey-blonde first ladies wearing gloves in portraits.

These kinds of towns keep musty bedroom altars of lead-based children's toys meant only for boys to play with. Only for boys to soak up through their fingertips throwing jacks in the street. Little sailboats and little yellow raincoats, and this heavy kink for what is so preciously innocent that it promises its own inevitable corruption, the kink of pretending you don't smell the terrible breath of the Odd Fellows Hall by putting starched Peter Pan collars on little boys and setting them in the middle of the room to absorb all the stink, in a bukkake circle of the polyester-clad white-passing enjoying a brandy.

Antics about boys named Dicky and Dick and Ricky and Gonzo and Jeffrey and Francis and Tom and later, when they're put in starched football uniforms and set in the middle of a stadium Friday nights, they're named Freeman and Fike and Brown and Wachowski and Harmon and Watson and Smiley and McClure, and these antics are about upset cars in broad daylight afternoons and not about being too drunk to stand at graduation with the choir director whose breath you've had in your nose since you were eight in 1963.

*

I was trying to see a monster, or understand how one describes a monster, because I was trying to write about my father. There's a romantic comedy shaping up about me and him set in 1980s Portland, Oregon where it can't quite be true that a monster is involved. California Raisins are smoothing around in sunglasses and the air smells like rotten moss and burnt cedar carpenter pencils, and the monster is so beautiful, with his Marylin beauty mark and his bolo tie on the wedding day, and the child is dirty and gay and wild with leaves in its hair and a patriotic dress dropped over its bony shoulders and so in love, she and the monster have a whole thing going. A child is holding a monster's hand and you're not going to say, Look out! It seems like she's already down for whatever, so just keep things moving.

Dads and clowns are both expressions of the prefabricated world of former children telling current children what something is and how to feel about it. The clown is a monster so that we can show you—I am holding hands with a monster! Don't worry about it, I am aware. I am down to clown.

A scattered rash of lead jacks makes a line in the center of a room with a dad on one side and a clown on the other, and I am going to kick it because I miss my dad.

*

How do you describe a monster's body? It always feels like such a failure of imagination. Underneath a clown is just a naked body, a face capable of a neutral expression, a dick that has to pee, feet that rest on the floor.

So, is the monster a put-on? What if I could remove the outside of my father? Would I find an organism in there that makes sense to miss? Being in love was a confusing experience at that tender age, and now I find it challenging to describe the beloved body.

*

In *It*, I found a fall guy, a bullshit artist. If a man is eating a child and he's laughing, he's a monster. If he's crying, what then? King draws lines as clear as sewer pipes between the creation of fear and the illusion of thought assuming physical form as an expression of fear. Is it fearsome because you know somehow that you aren't looking at what you think you are looking at? When your brain knows two different things, bad dad good sad? Gush of cortisol when your small body is thrown carelessly into the air by your teenage parent and then viscous coating of endorphins when you land back in its young, brown hands. You both have the same square thumb joints, which makes you feel proud and horny and bereft as an adult, seeing your hands resting on your wife's leg. It's possible that I don't know the difference between the feeling of love and the feeling of relief.

*

MOONWOLF!

SPIDER ON A BICYCLE!

ORGY OF THE UNBORN!

GREASEPAINT!

SÉANCE!

LAVENDAR MENACE!

DANCE OF DARKNESS!

*

Octavia Butler's Ooloi are third sex gene-traders you need to make a viable baby to survive in this terrible new world. They are part of the Oankali, whose bodies are so unimaginable to a human that to look at them would surely boil your noodle, so its visibility is titrated to you over a period of confinement wherein you and the alien body cohabitate as long as it takes for you to adapt to its presence. From across the room, it observes an ultraviolet boundary pulsing with your resting heartrate. Eventually, you see it coming into focus, the aperture dilating to deliver you from Act I to Act II, and you'll only ever be able to squeak up to Butler from your tiny dollhouse in her notebook and say, I guess it has finger snakes for skin? Fan art on the internet seems unable to fully surrender to not knowing, with penciled knobby knees on grotesque legs and too many arms and the touching, seeking skin of the monster. But I think Butler is trying to say we can't actually see it. Lilith cannot see it, so when she experiences seeing it, she is already changed, already not Lilith. Alchemically, you can't receive novel input and remain stable, so your reception indicates you are already changed. There are Ooloi attempts on deviantart.com: pitiful, terrifying mutations of human shape with eyeballs where they shouldn't be, etcetera. Inexplicably, a commissioned colored pencil work of a Shih Tzu in a tuxedo is included in the search results.

If I could see It, or if you could see It, we wouldn't be ourselves—I want to ask Octavia, is this what you meant? Will we ever return to ourselves, or are we already shed of ourselves in a continual catastrophic molting and, so, keep reinventing points of reference to understand, most of all, our kin relations and their bodies, who and what they are to us? Are they in us or waiting all the way across the room so we don't freak out?

It can't really be viewed and described, but It actualizes in some sense when the misfit band of Derry dorks reaches the beginning of Act III in the sewer system deep under downtown, where It seeks both dominance over and escape from the children by means of scrambling its own body like a slot machine or a grade school paper fortune teller, culminating penultimately as a pregnant spider—at which point the boys conclude It is "a female"—then taking Its final form as the unseeable, unsayable Deadlights.

In truth, a clown doing literally nothing scares people. The clown is borne of a drag of haplessness. It's about misplacement. Black makeup slashed over the sinking orbital fat loss below your eyes. A Tammy Faye polyester blouse sharp with generations of body odor, frilled with an ascot of bed skirt around the jugular, Hammer pants, lipstick where it shouldn't be. Boo! Tim Curry wiped off most of the greasepaint the girls in Vanities spent hours building onto his face and said, "I think I can make this exceptionally scary with a minimal amount of makeup." This is not the first bad man. He is referencing the work of previous bad men. This is derivative performance. This is nepotistic terrorism, a father. Come here, sweetie pat pat pat on Its lap. He is saying, I hardly even have to try.

*

Present day: Lela comes over for beans on toast and tells us about their moldy bread blankets and steel tapestries, how they'll reshape a white-box gallery with powder-coated hazards. Men with generational expertise have been burdening themselves with the telling of what the machines can accomplish, actually actually actually. The men let the bad news slide off their tongues toward Lela while their furrowed brows and ahistorical hands focus on the curves of the machines, and at night in the gay bar of Lela's adjunct janitor's closet, they make the CADs even lacier and more impossible, so the men keep saying more and more ma'am if you ask the machine to run this it will break your blanket, it will go up in smoke. Lela says, *I am asking the machine to do more than it thinks it can do*, and all of a sudden I know how to begin a whole reordering process where my body can provide better information than my brain about what my father was and what happened and what I'm supposed to do about it. It's not a Rubik's Cube ma'am my hands are tied I have no country no body, I have made no oath.

A clown is an unsedated uterine biopsy. Stirrups full of smoke. A clown is a waste site. A compost bin. A clown is a urinal cake. A clown is a crossed-out legal clause. A clown flickers in your peripheral vision. A clown drinks Fanta, scares you outside the 7-11. A clown is a teenager judging you. A clown has fancy friends with a house in the desert. A clown is a pit bull with a GladRag in its teeth. A clown is handmade. Elements are added, removed, refined, referenced, but it takes a human palette to dial it in. This fiberoptic squirting magenta flower that is both means and ends, both smoke alarm and downed powerline.

*

Stupidus was the Roman empire's stunt double in lipstick and frills. *Stupidus* from *stupere*, "numb and astonished." He could belittle the rich and speak of the unspeakable. Like all other clowns, he was a location, a valve, a drain, a hole in the empire's body. Everything must exist and go *somewhere*. The energy is finite. Some evening in 1989, I entered the bathroom without knocking and my father's smooth brown body was hitched up with one leg on the sink and a Preparation H plunger in its asshole, with which I was eye level. Half my father's height, I moved my eyes to his face then reversed back to the miniature archeology set on my twin bed, dusting false bones off with an eyeshadow brush. Years later, losing sleep with an asshole on fire from hasty public fucking, I would meet my father's eyes again, remember my mother telling us when we were in single digits that she used to come home and find her pantyhose and underwear stretched out, unconvincingly reintegrated into her dresser. That dresser burned in a housefire along with the bed I was born in, and her father was born in, and my father fucked other women in. Periodically itinerant, my mother had stored all her belongings in her friend Terry's basement. Terry was another drunk who smoked in bed with whom my mother was intertwined purely out of mutual, resentful, inescapable need.

*

In 1993, I can't breathe at the house my father shares with his wife and insist on living with my mom full time. In 1995, my father drops me off after a dinner date and kisses me on the mouth with his hand on my ass. Cast in shadow from the hallway light onto the wall of the bedroom I share with my sister, having taken off my shirt, I notice for the first time a small fairy tit asserting itself from my scrawny chest. I can live with this. Not terrible. 1997, my chest having grown Dolly-big, I'm at my stepmom's birthday party in a vintage polyester dress I think binds my tits down, and my father, drunk, says, are those things real, and the circle chuckles. In 1999, my date and I see a movie about a trans man being murdered in Falls City, Nebraska, and on the way home my date says I'm like that, I'm that way. We look like two twin dolls with the colors inverted. Shapeless, bound, stick-thin, swapping old man pants from the thrift store and smoking under our baseball caps. Within two months, some horrifying, irrepressible shape in me has unfurled into vintage dresses and red lipstick and my mullet growing out, and he has left me for another transboy. By winter, I am spending at least 10% of my waking life standing sideways in the mirror smashing my chest down and aching.

So grotesque, this flapping, unnecessary body. Where do I fit into this desire or belonging? The mirror and my mind show me a basket of bingo balls sucked up into acrylic nails at a dizzying speed, a flipbook of monster shapes that are the menu options for being a body, for being in constellation with others, for being against and with and without and upon. I'm a teenage warlock concave under a holey shirt. I'm a hag with a gaggle of broken lap dogs following the train of my robe and my spilled gin. I'm a dyke who gets to eat at the table that smells like fresh basil and musty cunts and trust funds. I'm the twisted stem of a dried shiitake reconstituting in the dew from a boiling pot of dildos. I'm a pregnant spider.

*

The tits just get bigger and bigger, as the long line of exhausted Scottish women in my body slowly have their way with me, and for twenty years I smish and smash and slouch, tucking them into my core like nuts under duct tape, and the boys of many bodies and genders I get mixed up with hover my stiff, confused shape over an egress in them that I could resolve and confirm. They like when I have bangs. In 2017, I meet my father's eyes in the bathroom mirror cutting my own bangs when I tell my partner I am getting a breast reduction—not the top surgery I had subliminally focus-grouped during *Stupidus* acts, testing the waters.

My partner, like many before her, has scars where once were tits. We are a shape. When I talk about breaking it, she is quiet. When I say no tits, she wants some tits. Here, on me. How many bodies have I buoyed and licked and meal-trained after surgery. How many bodies have I escorted into hostile Mississippi living rooms, flashing my most flamboyantly neutral code to blur how many bodies into a palatable shape through the Winston-smoke. I have a drawer full of bras and binders and smashers and I can shapewear into whatever hole, whatever valve you need. I want to bring you closer to your mother with my own body. I can do that. That's how mine works. I want to show a legible alignment. I want to grant you legibility by association, to gal pal with her, my nuts untucked and propped up by underwires at the mall where we hit the JCPenney while you're hunting with your mute father.

At one surgery consultation in Beverly Hills, a woman swollen with hyaluronic acid and her own repurposed fat cells begs a man on the phone to loan her sixteen thousand dollars for a couple of weeks so she can get her scheduled procedure. In the exam room, with my defamed, road-weary tits lying flat to my waist, the surgeon says, with two permanently numb and astonished assistants behind her, "Oh yeah, we're gonna give you a lot of torso back." After, the woman working up the cost estimate confides that she is so disgusted by the he-shes that come in for boob jobs that she's this close to leaving the business.

To the surgeon I end up with I provide a motley handful of reference images from myself as a ten-year-old to Georgia O'Keefe in her thick black dress. I tell her "almost not tits." My handsome, charming partner whose shirt obscures barely visible scars tended and oiled by a doting trans femme partner many years prior, jiggles her keys in her pocket like a dad. Healing on the couch a few months later, with ice-bag falsies smashed to my body under a nursing bra, I'm watching my stepmother pace our small living room while avgolemono soup viscates on the stove, telling me, Your father told me for our third date to meet him at the Park Blocks in front of the library that he had something to tell me and he opened his shirt

A thin white linen shirt buttoned up just above the metasternum, sleeves rolled up three quarters, pale loose jeans cinched with a thin embroidered vest, hair oily and rich and those Andrea Riseborough eyes and he had shaved all over, everything, he'd shaved everything and he told me he was a woman and that he thought that he should have surgery to change his body and I was very supportive but we came up with a deal I said why don't you wait a while and for now we made a deal where he was allowed to wear my clothes sometimes—*Did he ever go outside on the street? It feels so wrong to say he, I imagine Freddie Mercury in the video for "I Want to Break Free" flouncing up our plum-stained back walk*—sometimes he went outside, and you know sometimes we would try on my lipstick together and stuff like that and I was very supportive—*Did he ever go to gay bars? I mean did she ever hook up with men? I imagine Freddie on her knees in the bathroom at Embers*—"We enjoyed a healthy sex life" she later wrote in an email that she later demanded I erase.

*

My tits grew back in 2020 when I was living alone on a hill in Echo Park ordering several meals a day delivered to my porch while the whole city slept and sanitized.

My tits are a gag gift. My tits are birthday candles you can't blow out. Last year my wife lost a breast to cancer, saved her life by sacrificing one of her perfect fairy breasts. We trace and smoosh and lick the crooked scar with a miniature doll's tit of fat still tucked into one end. I've stopped telling her to enjoy my lifted set while she can, that they won't be here much longer. Now it feels so fucked to say, even still more Rubik's Cube-fucked than her silence from before when I said I would finally cut them off for real this time. Now there's a mess of fishing net around the whole thing with hooks stuck in Its cheeks.

*

I remember my father's flat, hot chest under a pale-yellow Western shirt with pearly snaps. Her new cowboy hat hovering over the kitchen table, and a fleck of toilet paper mortared to her cheek with blood. We were being re-delivered to It, to my father's chest. To run twin hands down the fronts of two flat chests, my father's and my eight-year-old body's. To miss my father in 1998, to see my father eating dumpstered meat on the sidewalk in 2001, to hold our matching hands together while my father dies fast and ugly in 2013 in a state hospice. Her hands are dusty CD cases, her hands are Saint Augustine's confessions, shit dribbling into pink sweatpants before you get to the toilet, the toilet in the giant, ostentatious bathroom in this repurposed McMansion full of dying homeless men, and my father. Her final look for the night was Homeless Man with JanSport Full of Robitussin Finding a New Path through Lutheran Fellowship. Her body hung around her like a bird, her body was a garish prism of rainbows. She was a fox's wedding procession I wasn't supposed to see. Holy water squirting from a flower in her toothless mouth. Her whole uncatchable, unwatchable self. I wish to split the cells back to Deadlights. I wish to preclude description. I wish to cut her back into the front of my body. To also become unperceivable.

HIPPIE COMMUNE, HIPPIE CAMP

Jibz Cameron

My parents met in 1972 through the Hog Farm commune, formed by the famous activist hippie clown Wavy Gravy (Hugh Romney) and his wife Jahanarah Romney (Bonnie Jean Beecher—she was on *Star Trek!*). The Farm had a few early iterations in Taos, New Mexico and Tujunga, California. My mom lived at the New Mexico outpost of the commune with her first child, my older brother David, whom she'd had with a man named Barry Kalish. Barry and my mom met in Detroit. When the Hog Farm came to town, he and my mom decided to take off with them, eventually landing in New Mexico. Barry and my mom split up, and Barry left the commune. One day Barry came back, kidnapped David, and took him to Mexico where he was selling stolen office supplies. At the time my mom was pregnant with my older half-sister, Jyoti, by another commune guy, Peter. Alone and pregnant, my mom left New Mexico to find David, who turned out to be in Los Angeles, in the care of some woman Barry knew. My mom showed up at the woman's apartment with her boyfriend James, who would become my dad. Any questions? I have some.

Commune life had its hierarchies, and certainly its dramas. Like a soap opera starring the cast of *Easy Rider*, and the soap is Dr. Bronner's. We belonged in some ways, but there was always a slight outsider feeling, partially because we didn't live there full time and partially because we were witnessing the Hog Farm limping into the 1980s, and everyone had a past. As a dyke who has what we all call "gay family"—other queers we will know for the rest of our lives, some we actively dislike, have fucked, have fallen out with, have rekindled, we will know each other forever and talk endless shit on sometimes but would most likely do anything for—I relate to this deeply. I'm fifty now and have known some of these fools for thirty years. Imagine if all the dykes I hung out with in my twenties all had children together. WHAT A LIVING GAY HELL.

Many of the commune women were decidedly scary. I always wanted the women to be nice to me, because when we were at the commune or at camp, we got to be free of our parents and enjoy possibly nicer adults. Cherry was a commune matriarch who was always giving me and J'nai the stink eye. I longed for her to like me because she seemed important. She had a round, pretty face and wore Guatemalan tunics. She was kind to my brother and older sister, though, and I couldn't figure it out. I realized later that my mom had a kid with the guy she had had three kids with. Jyoti fell in the line of ages right after one of Cherry's kids and right before another one. But that didn't really make sense, that she would be mean to us. Why not Jyoti? Maybe she and my dad had a fling? Who knows. Jahanara, Wavy's wife, was also a big-timer lady around the commune, and many were frightened of her because she had power and didn't take any shit. But she was always gentle with me and J'nai in particular. Later I learned my dad and her had been hooking up in LA during the time she was an actress and a Playboy Bunny. The women also ruled the food, which was nerve wracking because kids always wanted snacks, and it was a crapshoot who would be running the kitchen that day.

Sometimes people say, "Weren't you raised in a cult?" HOW DARE YEE?! As I clutch my amethyst necklace, NO!!! A *COMMUNE*! MUCH DIFFERENT. A cult *is* much different than a commune, entirely different, their foundational principles are polar opposites. A cult is a dictatorship and a commune is a communal living situation that makes up its own rules, supposedly by popular vote in democratic process that sometimes gets overshadowed by a dominant personality and then becomes cult-like, or people start living together believing they want to share responsibilities and then it turns out women do all the housework and men just spew their jizz everywhere. Sometimes it's radical, amazing, and harmonious.

Of course, there were actual menacing characters as well. There was a notorious "bad dude" who would drop in and out. He would roar up the dirt road on his Harley and a somber, tense energy would vibrate around the farm. He wore a wife-beater and jeans and smoked a lot. He was one of my 1/16-brother's dads. He had a nasty coke problem and was a violent asshole. But, like I said, gay family. I also know there was some heinous behavior by some of the older guys, too. I mean, where there are men, there is danger. It came in the form of them preying on teenage girls at the commune. I wasn't aware of it at the time, but kids my brother's age certainly were, and it colored their experience much differently from mine. By the time I was of the age men were letching on me I was luckily not hanging out at the Hog Farm, so my memories there are largely positive. I know that feeling, though, the feeling of a place being poisoned for you by the hideous shit that happened to you there.

One family at the Hog Farm was bossed by a skeletal, mean matriarch named Dragon and her two beautiful, raven-haired daughters, Indigo and Kalahari. She was German or Eastern European; her accent made her scarier. She had stringy blonde hair and wore a mashup of silken flowery pashminas draped over her bony frame. Her yam-shaped breasts swung freely under threadbare tank tops. She stomped around in flat leather sandals, and barked at her children and everyone else's children, too. Apparently she had arthritis in her entire body, but I didn't know that.

Kalahari was rumored to have a tail. An actual tail. A tail of hair, the cause of great speculation and gossip for us kids. One fateful day, when I was around eight years old, Kalahari and I played by the river, just the two of us.

I have to pee, she said. *I have to pee, too*, I lied.

We crept into some shrubs. She pulled down her cotton underpants. Out tumbled a long blonde braid, sprouting from her lower back, just above her butt crack . . . her TAILbone. It was thin and shiny and had a ribbon tied to the end, with bells on it. She noticed my horror.

Oh yeah, that's my tail, my mom won't let me cut it off.

Indigo ended up getting a doctorate from Yale and became a politician.

In the mid 70s, Wavy Gravy and Jahanara, along with other Hog Farmers, founded a performing arts summer camp which I attended from age six to age twelve. It was called Camp Winnarainbow (I know). It is where I learned improv.

Early in the morning Wavy would blow a giant conch shell, signaling it was time for morning circle, and all campers, counselors and staff stumbled out of their tipis to gather around the fire pit. It's super cringe to write tipi, as white hippies notoriously appropriate indigenous engineering and everything else. I just looked at the Camp Winnarainbow website, and they now have a tipi acknowledgement statement which explains why tipis are such an amazing invention—

they are portable, stay warm, and since the walls are fabric you can hear if someone in your community is in distress—a baby cry, etc.

At morning circle, we would stretch, warm up our vessels (bodies) and sing goofy, socialist folk songs. There were many bangers. My favorites were the macabre, cartoony ones like "Oh Dunderbeck" about "the sausage meat machine" that made salamis out of dogs, cats, and children; or "Titanic," about rich people drowning. Not to brag, but I knew the counterpoint to "witches are bad" very early in my youth:

Who were the witches
Where did they come from
Maybe your great great great grandma was one
Witches were wise wise women they say
And there's a little witch in every woman today

This is exactly what annoying queers say all the time now.

I also enjoyed the enviro-anarchy bop about dirt:

Dirt dirt, top of the mountain
Dirt dirt, bottom of the sea
Dirt dirt, got a bad name
But it became known as proper-ty!
Apples bananas beans and rice
Guacamole with my favorite spice
Milk and meat and cows that moo
Grazed on grasses, grasses that grew from
Dirt dirt . . .

To close morning circle we would do a collective OM before heading off to breakfast. Starving by then, we joked: OMMMMMMM MY GOD I'M HUNGRY. OMMMMMMMMLETTTE PLEEEASE. We'd meander up the forest pathway to the giant outdoor kitchen seating area and line up for food with our trays perched at our bellies, then eat under the oaks on picnic tables. If you were brave enough to get up and face the chilly air before morning circle you could get hot cocoa at the communal kitchen, but I rarely could get that together.

Next it was time for the meeting on the stage, where the teachers would announce their classes for the day. There was a rainbow bridge that went over the stage, it had stairs up either side and a curtain that fell behind it to the floor. All sorts of lessons were on offer, two sessions per day: stilt walking, juggling, tightrope, trapeze, belly dancing, unicycle, gymnastics, clowning, face painting, guitar, stick fighting. It was the 80s, so we had topical classes like D+D and breakdancing. The only class I went to was called Space Eat, Wavy Gravy's improv class. I would take Space Eat every single day, sometimes for both sessions. I never learned a single circus art, or anything else for that matter.

Wavy was iconic. On hot days he wore a hat with a rubber fried egg on top. He had different characters he would appear as throughout the session, such as Al Dente, the Italian restaurant host. He would wear a stiff toupee and a tuxedo T-shirt and *talk-a like-a this-a*. Sometimes Wavy would wear a red clown nose. Wavy had no teeth. I remember two different rumors: one was that they fell out from heroin use, one from eating too much candy. At any rate, he had a false set that was rainbow-colored. At night before lights out he would yell, "Brush 'em if you got 'em!" He had a scratchy, hoarse voice, probably from smoking. Wavy had been a beatnik. Before he wore floppy multicolored trousers, he wore black turtlenecks. A true counterculture guy.

During Wavy's Space Eat class we sat in a circle in the woods and played improv games. I loved "Machine," where we built a giant, vague mechanism together out of our bodies moving and repetitively making a noise. I also liked the object changing game.

Some kid started with miming, holding a cat in his arms. He stroked the soft fur and scratched under its chin. I would pay fiercely close attention to the detail, noticing how big the cat was, which end its head was attached to. This kid's cat was actually shaped like a snake if you took their miming literally. In the game, as soon as someone had an idea for another object to mime, that person could go into the scene, play along with the present situation, and then change it to something new.

I crept up to the kid and his invisible flat kitten. I reached out my arms and picked up the cat, petting it gently for a few moments, then my hands began to cradle it on either side. I was seeing a loaf of bread. I proceeded to mime putting together a sandwich, mayonaissing and mustarding each side, then delicately placing slices of cheese on the bread. Then I closed it up and brought the gigantic hoagie to my gaping mouth, just as another kid came up and tagged in. Improv speaks to the way my brain works: fast and stupid. I love how exciting and imaginative it is. I've never had stage fright or feared looking dumb, which is both a gift and a curse; I only felt excitement at being on stage. Improvisation is about listening and building something that harmonized with the people around you—something I wasn't getting at home. It is about taking what is in the moment and making it bigger, bolder, more present, all while affirming the people next to you. Telling them, *I believe your sandwich! I believe you!* And wasn't it incredible that one could actually remember, if one tried, exactly what it felt like in your body to open a jar. The shape of the round lid under your fingers, the resistance at first, and then the moment of the top loosening, pop! Putting a butter knife into the jar, feeling the slight weight of mayonnaise against the blade, getting the right amount of blob, and on to the sensation of spreading the mayonnaise. Not too much pressure or you'll scrape into the bread; not too light or it won't spread evenly. If you concentrate hard enough you can do these things and be transmuted into that world and take everyone with you. And it's funny.

Why is it funny to watch someone mime making an invisible sandwich? My hunch is that the humor is not in the subject matter, per se, but the audience's surprise and recognition of themselves in this mundane, plebeian task you would otherwise ignore. It draws attention to how absurd all of our assumptions about life are, and how much we take things for granted. That each moment is a fucking miracle by god. Taking away the actual materials of this job of sandwich making—no jar, no knife, no bread—draws attention to the intimacy of these moments, reminding us of what we know, what is stored in our bodies without even trying, our unconscious brain on display. When we see ourselves reflected this way we are surprised and delighted and we laugh laugh laugh at the pleasure of that.

My pals at camp included a short girl with frizzball hair named Cecil, who had a very high and scratchy voice. She looked and sounded like a cartoon. We did Space Eat together and she was deeply into putting on plays and doing theater. She is now an adult, the same size, who plays the ukulele and works at camp. I had a hilarious deaf friend named Eddy who once put his tongue through a hole in a tortilla and it made me spit-take milk all over the table. There were also many celebrity hippie kids. One year I hung out a lot with Alex, who was and still is Whoopi Goldberg's daughter. We didn't know at first, but suspected she was fancy because once she told us a story about having dinner with Mick Jagger. And then she kept telling the Mick Jagger story until finally someone asked her if her parents were rich or celebrities. Alex took me to the payphone with her to call her mom once, and I got to say hi to Whoopi, which was thrilling. I can still hear her deep smiling voice, *Hi*

Jiiiiiibs, nice to meet ya. Trixie Garcia, Jerry's youngest daughter, went to camp with me and was in my tipi. I went to college with Trixie, too, at San Francisco Art Institute. We were there together when Jerry died. I asked her how it felt to have your dad's death hijacked by millions of hippies who thought they knew him better. She solemnly nodded, *Yup, it's pretty fuckin lame. I hate it.*

Jerry's stepdaughter, Sunshine, was a camp counselor. She was the biological daughter of Ken Kesey and a woman they called Mountain Girl. Sunshine took us to the muddy river and put glops of it in her thick blonde curls and pretended to be Medusa. The son of the drummer for the Dead went to my camp, too, but he was just a little kid so I didn't pay attention to him. To me the Grateful Dead were boring old people music. I ended up appreciating them later in life, musically, but I can't look at them—it gives me a mildly grossed out feeling. Mixture of shame, boredom and, like, I am hanging out with dads. Who wants to do that?

Another frizzy-haired camp counselor I loved was Sharon Share-alike. Sharon wore a costume every single day. Her greatest hit was a flowery old bathrobe, fluffy slippers, and an old lady wig that had rollers in it. The rollers were attached to a tube which was attached to a pump that could make the curlers stand on end like in a 50s cartoon when you squeezed it in your hand. I thought this was the most genius thing imaginable. She went to the grocery store in Berkeley dressed in that costume, shocking the other shoppers. She also donned a body suit with the solar system painted all over it and wore it with a hat shaped like Saturn. Sharon was also the president of the Banana Slug Club. If you kissed a banana slug you would get a special pin, of a slug, of course. She picked up a tiny, snot-colored slug about an inch long, and I leaned in and gave it a quick peck. It was more sticky than slimy, but it was so quick I barely noticed. Everyone went EEEEEEEEEEEEW! But we were all delighted. Now, if you *licked* a slug you got *another* prize, but whatever that was it wasn't valuable enough for me to lick a fucking slug. That just seemed gross.

We had some special guests who would come visit camp every year, like Fred Wahpepah, a Kickapoo tribe elder who hosted a sweat lodge and taught Native American songs to the kids. Fred was even keeled and calm, which stood out because most of the adults were slightly manic in their enthusiasm. His songs were mostly about animals. As for the sweat lodge—lots of hippies had saunas, but a sweat lodge was a completely different situation. The adults would circle around the rocks and be mostly naked. Which was gross, of course. There was incense or sage or some intensely rich smell that was very strong, so powerful it fried the nostrils. Fred sang and played a drum in the 1000000000 degrees. The rule of the sweat lodge was that you were not supposed to leave. The lodge was a little dome covered in a tarp and many, many heavy blankets. I had to shove my face in the dirt and try to stick my lips out of the dome to gasp for fresh air. I felt pressure to stay in, because it was a real badge of stamina to withstand it. I never lasted more than ten minutes. Maybe five. The adults would straggle out an hour later, slick with sweat and blissed out at their resurgence and healing. There was a stream nearby and they would all go plunge in, steam rising from their heads.

Another iconic camp counselor was Reggie. He was tall, Black, extremely fit, handsome, and a martial arts expert. The boys were obsessed with him. Surely not *everybody* was kung fu fighting, but many were at Camp Winnarainbow; wielding nunchucks, being a ninja, karate, Japanese throwing stars, and of course, stick fighting. Reggie was also the camp Dungeon master, as in D+D, which I knew was very important but not sure why. He strode around camp shirtless, his kung fu pants hanging off of his hips, an enormous crystal or eagle claw on a lanyard on his glistening chest, brandishing a gigantic wooden stick in his hand.

The real, deep, nerd actor kids, such as myself, sometimes put on plays that were not part of regular camp programming. One such play, *Airheads Airlines*, written by resident camp theater dork, Mark, was about an airline that was run by drug addicts. I demanded to play the stewardess, so I could wear high heels. They were white pumps, and I fell off the stage because I couldn't stand in them. It was worth it. I got to teeter around carrying trays of drugs to the passengers.

Uppers, downers, alllll arounders, anyone?

The pilots, who were also children, hallucinated and saw purple elephants in the sky. There was also a Swami on board. Swami Salami? Oh, the 80s.

Airheads Airlines, zoom golly golly zoom golly golly zoom

I can say that I was mature enough to know that the drug jokes were actually pretty funny. I disagree now, but I do think children pretending to be on drugs is funny.

Because the Hog Farm's home base was in Berkeley, lots of kids from the city came on scholarship, many of whom were unaccustomed to nature—and with them came cool shit. I came from super rural Mendocino County where there were probably two Black people in our town, and they were related. I didn't think about it at the time, of course, but so much of the excitement of camp was learning about new styles, dances, and music from the city kids. I didn't attribute this to the kids being Black, mostly because, in my experience, kids don't think that way. But it was hugely important. I am sure I was super annoying when I went home to my dumb town and showed off my new moves and fashion.

One year, breakdancing took over. The counselors were all annoyed at this, but it was unstoppable. The boys were forgoing stilt-walking and trapeze for parachute pants and fingerless leather gloves, carrying cardboard stacks and linoleum rolls and plugging in their boomboxes with an extension cord that ran through the dusty leaves. I learned to moonwalk and do a slight robot. My moonwalk is still about 30%, but I am proud to have been at least a little bit in the conversation.

Camp also introduced me to other city kids, such as real punks. A freak counselor named Davey wore a Wham! T-shirt on orientation day when I was ten. I got very excited—that was my favorite band. I had a special savings can with my friend Laurie to pay for flights to England so that she could marry George and I could marry Andrew (blondes = barf).

I LOVE YOUR SHIRT! I LOVE WHAM!

Davey laughed at me. In my face.

A tiny leak began to form then and there in the bubble of consumerist popular culture I worshipped. I became laser focused on everything Davey liked and represented. He wore old man pants and weird shoes. One day he wore a shirt repping MDC, the punk band, which I learned either stood for MILLIONS OF DEAD COPS, MILLIONS OF DEAD CHRISTIANS or . . . MILLIONS OF DEAD CHILDREN!!!! WHAT!??? Why do we want to have millions of dead cops!? And what of the millions of dead children?!!! A slightly older city punk friend, Spring, explained it to me: *Well, we want dead cops because cops are actually a weapon the government uses to terrorize and control people, usually, like, the poor people and Black people. The children part is probably about how war kills children. And the Christians are just evil and everyone should hate them.*

Me and my friends whispered into the night about what a freak Davey was. *I heard he woke up in the middle of the night and sat straight up in his sleeping bag and shouted, "TV ROTS YOUR BRAIN SO SHOVE IT UP YOUR ASS!"*

TV rots your brain? WHAT? I was very familiar with my dad's rant on the evils of the government and his critique of *Dukes of Hazzard* and *Three's Company*. I can still hear my father's angry review of that show—"Someone says the word 'toilet' and they all fall down laughing." And I heard his endless anti-government viewpoints. I knew that the government was bad, but I didn't really know why and how it was. To me it was paternal griping and low-key insults to us kids. I recalled my father also saying that advertising was the United States' biggest industry, and that television was just a tool to sell us things. Davey's anarcho-dots started to connect for me.

I hadn't hit puberty yet, but rage still bubbled under the surface. The real splits in reality were on their way—the moments as an adolescent where I discovered "everything is a lie"—and Davey's ironic Wham! T-shirt was the gateway fissure. When they hit me they decimated many parts of me, most importantly the part of me that had so joyously loved Wham! I realized not only would I never marry Andrew Ridgeley, but that Andrew Ridgeley was part of an entire white supremacist capitalist system of popular consumerist cultural mind control meant to keep people ignorant, sedated, and distracted from horrors of our deprived governments while promoting elitist sportswear. Little did I know I would spend much of my adulthood in recovery trying to reconnect to the stupid joy that I had as a child who loved that idiotic music.

By age eleven I was well on my way to being a punk rocker, but I was still very innocent. I shaved a tiny part of the side of my head, like a quarter of an inch, with my sister's leg razor. My exposed flesh scared me so I stopped. I looked stupid. My grandmother asked me what I wanted for my birthday, and I told her "something punk," and she gave me a novelty shop rock with a bunch of little rocks hot glued on top of it, with eyes, holding a sign that said "rock concert." My dad laughed at my desperation for coolness and my grandmother's shade.

At camp I met Tré Cool, later of Green Day fame. He was already going by that name, which to an eleven-year-old was pretty clever. He was fourteen and we were "going out." I don't think we did anything beyond hold hands and giggle. He was a drumming prodigy and had already been recruited into the Lookouts with Larry Livermore. He was a jokester with a nasally voice and wore a zebra-print muscle shirt and authentically ripped jeans. He grew up in the sticks near the Hog Farm, which is how he ended up at camp. When city kids would ask him what his parents did, he told them (with a wink at me) they "ran an organic tomato farm." I thought this was hilarious, because of course they grew weed and I was pleased to understand something important and criminal like that. After camp that summer we pen palled a few times. He sent me a newspaper article about the Lookouts that I showed off to my friends. I had a boyfriend! In a band! In the newspaper! But it fizzled out. Tré was already getting famouser and touring so he didn't come back to camp. A couple years later, when I started going to the all-ages punk club Gilman Street, FUCK GREEN DAY was spray painted above the stage. They got too famous. But also that band is truly irritating.

When I was twelve, I attended camp for the last time. I had an enormous crush on this beautiful hippie boy. He was from a prominent commune family (lol). Tan and toned, he had long, brown hair with golden streaks. He strode around barefoot in linen pants like Reggie, carrying ancient weaponry (a stick). I lied to him and told him I was thirteen. He was seventeen. By the time he found out I was only twelve, it was too late. He'd fallen for me. We made out in the dirt next to a tipi, which I can say with perfect clarity was my first psychedelic dopamine trip. We only did some OTB petting, but my entire being was transformed that evening. I got my first mainline of the greatest drug on earth. We kissed passionately, and my heart hammered nearly right out of my chest. I was transported to another galaxy with desire. Desire for what? For more, that's what. That's all I could think of. I had never felt anything close to this kind of bliss. All my blood rushed to my head, and I was absolutely desperate for more of this feeling. I was a lifelong junkie who had been living for twelve whole years not knowing about junk. Then I got an uncut mainline straight to my entire system. I looked up at the starry sky, devastated that I had never known this feeling. Where had I been? Doing improv!? What the fuck? I swore I would hang on to this as long as I could. It was the feeling that I had captured an unattainable thing. That there was a laser focus on me and my magic. We only had one more makeout after that, equally mind bending. He left camp early and I was in immediate withdrawal. A couple weeks later he wrote me a letter and I was embarrassed at how corny it was. It dawned on me that I didn't really like him, I just liked the feeling I got from him. I suspected that he might be dumb. He had written me a generic poem in lavender felt tip marker, wherein he quoted The Doors, a band I continue to hate, and had drawn flowers on the envelope. Fuckin hippie.

When I was in 3rd grade, I had long, unruly hair.

It was one thing I had in common with other girls.

My mom did not value long hair.

Her preferred method for taming her own coarse Syrian hair was to keep it short.

Unfortunately, she was also the one who had to un-snarl my mane every other day.

I didn't learn the word "tender headed" until I was an adult.

I didn't even realize that was an option (to be sensitive) as a kid.

She'd eventually lose patience, and...

We went to a strip mall hair salon so I could get a trim.

A TRIM

Mom disappeared to talk to the "stylist" and I waited.

I remember it was so long that I had time to really fixate on the giant wooden console playing olde-tyme cartoons.

It had a mysterious hole in the bottom. I knew it must hold something incredible, because when I tried to explore it...

The receptionist scolded that it was just for kids who did a good job sitting for their haircuts.

Finally it was my turn.

I was used to sitting still for procedures. The cape was fastened around my neck, the chair wheezed up, and I was locked into position, ready to earn my prize.

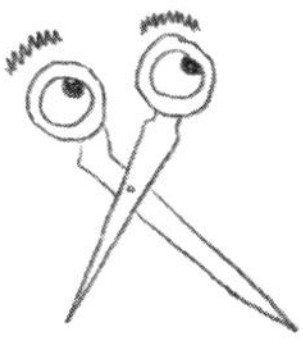

Do you need me to take my ponytail out?
Nope.
HE
CUT
IT
OFF.

PINNED TO MY SEAT BY THE SOCIAL AGREEMENT OF THE CAPE, MY BRAIN COULDN'T MAKE SENSE OF WHAT WAS HAPPENING

I WAS (literally) STUNNED.

I WAS FAMILIAR WITH BRIBERY. SOMETIMES BAD THINGS HAPPENED, & THIS WAS THE EXCHANGE. TOYS FOR SILENCE. A KID'S WAGE.

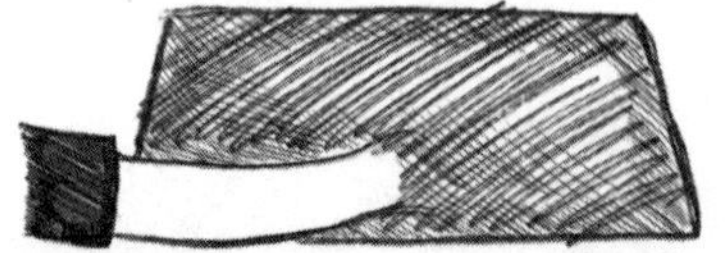

I STUCK MY HAND INTO THE DARK OF THE CONSOLE, EXPECTING (for some reason) A VIDEOCASSETTE OF CARTOONS LIKE THE ONES THEY WERE PLAYING.

What kid wants a wooden ruler???
It was the last straw.

Nickie?

As Mom paid,
I ran out the door.

With nowhere to go, I
threw myself against my
mom's sun-hot Ford Tempo
and cried.

Nick?

I THOUGHT YOU SAID YOU'D NEVER HURT ME!!!

Honey, I wouldn't...

I...

I had *no idea* he was going to do that,

He must have gone CRAZY!

All I said was a trim!

I thought we were just going in for a trim.

That year in school pictures I looked like a boy.

Some people love looking like this. I did not.

My bowl cut was paired with a mom-chosen polo shirt and itchy homemade polyester pants.

I was sad and confused that this was how life could be.

A surprise, non-consensual shearing out of nowhere.

And for a long time, the story has been repeated in my family as this: A bald man went rogue and cut off my ponytail. And then I yelled at my mom over a haircut.

He either went bonkers, or lost all knowledge of hair (due to his baldness) depending on the telling.

But what if that wasn't the real story? What if the truth was much more simple?

In all the stories, she was the trustworthy, forever-devoted mom, and any aspects of my life that felt chaotic or unfair were not her fault,

In that moment, what if an executive decision on Mom's part when awry?

If it surprised her that I had a reaction and in that moment she pivoted to stay my hero?

Never trust a bald barber I guess, huh?

BAREFOOT SHOES

Amanda Verwey

The tall crabgrass tickles my arm. It's my responsibility to cut it now but none of the five lawnmowers in the shed work.

I came to the yard to give myself a clear space to think before it all starts—but I don't even know what I'm trying to wrap my head around. I think harder about what to think about. Maybe I should set intentions for the day. I want to keep my eyes out for family shit, circus shit, maybe take some pictures? Maybe I should go in there and take pictures now, actually. I start to rise but—

Too late. Here comes Ed, waddling up the path in his cargo shorts. Early.

I lead him to the garage, hoping to buy myself more time alone in the house. "I guess we can start here. It's been overrun by raccoons, so be careful of that."

I swing open the side door and the smell that hits us is like ten thousand ferrets all shitting at once. Inside is crammed with an unstable tower of objects so tall it grazes the rafters. Through the cracks of negative space, I make out a layer of excrement carpeting the floor. I'm immediately apologizing—even though it's not my fault it somehow *feels* like my fault—but Ed wades through the turds in his flip-flops like it's a crystalline stream. He has seen worse. *What could be worse than this?*

"Pee bottles. I get that more than you'd think."

I love Ed. He only ever says deadpan things like this in the most impeccable Wisconsin accent, so I have no idea if he likes working with me—but I *love* working with him. He has a very reliable Midwestern face. Like a Dust Bowl-era father of seven. It makes me feel taken care of.

Ed's business is cleaning hoarded houses. "I bet this one will take three days on account of the garage and all that shit in the basement. Labor will cost forty-five hundred bucks but . . . from what I'm seeing here . . . I'd say it'll only run ya a grand or so in the end."

I look at the decaying stacks of wood planks, patio furniture, road signs, military equipment, and bicycles, and am confounded by his estimation of value, but don't question it. Our agreement is that he can keep and sell whatever he wants and subtract it from labor costs. A godsend since I'm hemorrhaging money.

This is my ninth and final clean-out project with Ed.

Months earlier, I inherited the properties—all nine of them. An office with three rooms and a lobby, a condo, three storage garages, a storefront, and three historic homes. My aunt hoarded things, and hoarded spaces to keep the things in. I only knew about four places when I agreed to be executor so...I've been back in my hometown longer than I ever thought I would be. But this is the final stretch.

A large box truck, a Sprinter van, and a scrap metal pickup appear en masse and park out front—Ed's team has arrived. He heads over with traffic cones and starts partitioning off a wide breadth around the vehicles for sorting tables.

The appearance of the trucks signals that I'm now invisible, and the rest of the clean-out will be largely ignored. I have no utility. I'm weak, one hundred and ten pounds and allergic to physical labor. My presence is probably a nuisance, but I don't want to miss a treasure being unearthed, so I'll linger all day while the team hustles around me with purpose. I head into the house to start my ghostly puttering.

I remove a rusty skeleton key from the lanyard on my neck. Part of my aunt's hoarding was preserving the integrity of antique things, so she refused to modernize locks. Now I'm wandering around looking like a medieval janitor. But I've come to appreciate the pageantry—gives my entrances a magician's flair. The worn grooves take forever to catch the latch, but then there's a forceful CLICK and *ta-da!* The door jerks open. I push it through the debris on the floor like an arm swaying in the snow, making an angel.

Inside, I shimmy sideways along the narrow paths doing last looks. Or is it pre-looks? I only have a few minutes before the house is descended on by Ed's workers, and I want to savor something but I'm not sure what.

I pick up a Wendy's bag from the stairs and shake it. Twenty-year-old french fries rattle around like a maraca. After today, the Wendy's bag will be gone. The famous Wendy's bag! Can I part with it?

I remember finding the Wendy's bag when I finally got back into this house after being locked out for twenty years. I was accustomed to the claustrophobic eyeline of hoarded spaces by then, but there's always a unique *getting-to-know-you* period with each property. At first glance, everything just blurs into a solid mass. A dizzying interconnected landscape of cascading peaks and valleys. You have to let the eyes adjust. Soon individual objects appear. And the first thing that came into focus in this place was the Wendy's bag. It was a surprise.

I never thought of my aunt as a food hoarder, just a stuff hoarder, but inheriting the houses exposed an underbelly. Soon after I discovered the vintage fries, I ventured into the kitchen and was confronted by a petrified banana stuck to the wall, hovering about three feet off the ground, and a peanut butter sandwich on the counter that was old enough to vote.

This memory gives me direction, and I hurry to get a pic of the banana before Ed chisels it down.

Unlike the other properties, this one I have history with. When it was my grandparents' house, I spent every day here after school while my mom was at work—until my grandma died suddenly of a heart attack, then my grandpa went to assisted living, then my aunt inherited the house, then filled it to the brim, then closed it up forever.

I scan the kitchen and remember sitting at the small, round table in the corner, my feet swinging in the grownup chair, waiting for my grandma to cut the crust off my sandwich. In my memories this room is always sunny, with a warm, golden hue. I look down at that same table in the shrouded blue light of today. It's scattered with broken glass and hardened goop after the decades-old food jars on it burst, then were left to dry, cementing the shards to the tabletop like a weaponized mosaic.

I take a picture of that, too.

Texts start coming in. My phone pulsates with the rhythmic banter of the group thread. *Breaking News*: Somebody saw someone do something in their open relationship that's both scandalous and hilarious. Normally I'd be all over this—ear emoji, tea emoji, side-eye emoji, skull emoji, coffin emoji, popcorn emoji—maybe a GIF of Angela Lansbury eating popcorn—maybe a GIF of someone closing themselves in a coffin. But right now I don't feel up for witty repartee.

I usually live in Los Angeles, where I pursue a (mostly failed) art career in equal intervals of vigor and despondency. So when my aunt died, I was forced to explain to the troupe of coastal homosexual culture-makers who are my friends what the hell I was doing in *Wisconsin* all summer. I tried to dress it up, "Yeah, it's hoarding, but like, Grey Gardens historic homes and art and antiques hoarding—not, like, dead cats."

Dead cats, for me, is the dividing line that separates my new life from a bad reality show. But as I confront the space's true inventory, it's been harder to get on my high horse.

I slip the phone back in my pocket.

The kitchen is depressing me. I throw away the Wendy's bag and move into the dining room. As I inch past the oversized hutch, I catch a glimpse of my own eyes peering at me from between stacks of bankers boxes. *Huh?* I wrestle out a large oil painting of myself and prop it on a stack of mildewy fabric bolts. *What fresh Dorian Gray hell is this?*

How is it possible? Where did it come from?

Then the memory of a long-forgotten high school summer job rushes back to me. I used to sit for portraits in the community center's painting class. I remember the old, grouchy instructor who used the class not so much to teach, but to have free access to models for himself to paint. Then I remember he died and his estate sale had years of his portraits up for grabs. And I remember my aunt telling me about the sale. And I guess she went and bought this painting of me.

When these recollections flash all at once, I wonder if this was what my aunt was chasing. To not let life just fall away behind you, but instead to take it all with you, a million access points, tactile and alive. A diary of objects just waiting to be summoned—

My thoughts are interrupted by loud banging, then scraping, then a smell like halitosis and hot garbage. I run back into the kitchen and, just as I suspected, Ed and a couple guys are trying to move out the fridge. They shimmy it forward in a delicate ballet, careful not to unleash the liquefied groceries inside.

Ed makes a faulty tilt and we all hear a powerful WOOSH as a wave of ooze sloshes to the front and shits out the crack in the door, leaving a pile of cold fridge diarrhea about a half inch thick on the linoleum. In a rare moment of disgust Ed declares he "ain't touch'n it." I stare at the mound on the floor and it stares back at me. *This is my fridge diarrhea. It is my legacy.*

I need some air.

"I'm going to my brother's. Don't throw away that painting of me in the dining room, I want it." Ed nods, still straining under the weight of the fridge.

On my way out I notice a porcelain clown doll under a pile of clothes. It's a well-made antique, so I know it's supposed to be sincere, but I can't imagine its smile reading as anything other than John Wayne Gacy. It reminds me. I yell back to Ed, "And if you find any circus shit save it for me! My grandpa was a circus historian!"

"What?!"

"SAVE ANY CIRCUS SHIT! MY GRANDPA WAS A CIRCUS HISTORIAN!"

"OKAY—FUCK!"

The fridge topples over. I grab the clown and run out the door.

As I get to the yard, a rocking chair careens out the open front window and lands, splintering on a growing pile of furniture discards.

It was my grandma's rocking chair.

How could they break it?! Why would they just throw it in the dirt like that?!

I shut my eyes and take five deep breaths, channeling a lifetime of sliding-scale therapy so I don't have some misdirected tantrum characteristic of a white woman out of touch with her grief. They couldn't know the difference between a random rocking chair and a rocking chair that belonged to one of the sweetest women that ever lived. A rocking chair where that sweet old woman would bring me sherbet Push Pops as I rocked and watched my grandpa tend to his rose garden out the window. Of course, they couldn't know. The rose garden is just a cluster of thorny weeds now.

I grab the chair, dragging its broken leg behind me as I continue across the street to my brother's place.

Only in my family would an apartment with a view of a generational hoarded home be regarded as an acceptable place to live. But even so, of all places in my hometown, I'm most comfortable at Iggy's.

When I approach, he's pounding out a John Carpenter score on his keyboard at the window.

Iggy's detachment from the chaos fifty feet away is purposeful. He's been on a quest for serenity, simplifying his life to a monk-like degree. And part of this grand simplification is a hard boundary that he will no longer help with the hoarded houses —a reserve which inconveniences me greatly, but which I also admire greatly.

I drop the chair and knock on the window, using the clown's porcelain hand. He opens the door. "Who's your new friend?"

"I think he lives here now." I flop down on one of the two straight-backed Ikea lounge chairs that are crowded into the center of the room by music equipment. I throw the clown on the other chair. Iggy assesses it. "Yeah, feels right." He sits on the floor so as to not disturb his new roommate.

I slouch deeper into my seat. "Am I fucking up? I mean, the houses are almost done. It's done. And I did, like, nothing to capture it. Basically, nothing except a few shitty pictures on my phone. It was awe-inspiring. This monolith of consumerism and scarcity and mental illness. I feel like I should have alerted someone—like some, I don't know, psychological experts or something, to do, like, a case study. I mean, there were so many properties and so much time and care and meticulous organizing among, like, total ruin. Cleaning it almost feels like disrespect. Like I'm tearing down some carefully constructed piece of art. Who's to say she wasn't a Noah Purifoy or Watts Tower? Should I have preserved something? Anything? Everything? Or is that, like, the inherited trauma of the stuff creating this gravitational pull in me to maintain its false preciousness despite looking around and seeing, like . . . the fridge having diarrhea."

Iggy considers this deeply for a fraction of a millisecond, then cracks a beer and passes it to me. "I don't think anyone is paying admission to see that shit."

Iggy always knows exactly the right thing to say. I slam the beer and head back to the house. He yells after me as I go. "Get this busted-ass chair off my porch!"

The sky is turning a dark cobalt. Looks like another thunderstorm. I was going to ride my bike down to the lake after Ed leaves. Stare out at the horizon to clear my eyes. I guess I'll walk back to my shitty rental and stare at my laptop until I fall asleep instead.

I look at my phone. The group thread is going to some event that half of them dread and half pretend to dread. "Wish you were coming." I don't reply.

I drop the rocking chair back on the junk pile and take out the skeleton key.

I find Ed in the basement. He gestures to a tall stack of weathered porn magazines.

"You care if I take your grandpa's porn? It's from the seventies. People collect it."

I'm struck that this, of all things, Ed felt the need to ask permission to take. Midcentury furniture, Heath pottery, intricate blown glass, Native American artifacts all flew out the door without mention, but *this* he was unsure if I wanted to keep? *Why?*

Was he trying to sexualize our relationship? Was there a tension all this time that my queerness blinded me to? I suppose, were I a straight woman living in Wisconsin, Ed and I would make sense. We could run the hoarded house business together, Ed cleaning pee bottles while I refinish vintage credenzas that once nestled the hollow midsection of a partially decomposed cat. I could overhaul the cramped junk depot that Ed is passing off as an antique store. Once it's a proper design showroom, maybe I'd join the city council. I mean, the town borders Lake Michigan. They should focus on tourism, since factory life in the Rust Belt is long dead. Revitalize downtown. People from Chicago will come up to go boating. I could help them pick out a special piece of salvaged furniture to bring home to their penthouses. Ed would dutifully deliver it with only mild grumbling about Illinois drivers. It could really work.

I glance at the porn. "Yeah, you can have it. What kind of stuff was he into?" Ed shrugs. "Shaved."

I laugh a little, suddenly wistful. *My last clean-out with Ed.* "Thanks, Ed, for everything. I don't know how I would have done this without you." He doesn't stop dumping boxes. The one he's sifting through now looks full of . . . nails? I keep going, trying to force a meaningful moment. "I mean it, I couldn't have handled the gross stuff alone. I know these houses didn't have like, dead cats or anything but—"

"Oh, I found a dead cat."

"What?"

"Yeah, there was one in the garage under that big wagon wheel. Musta been dead awhile, too. Mummified. I swept it up with the leaves."

There it is.

A dead cat.

The truth of it.

I search my mind for a response, but it's blank. Ed dumps another box full of. . . pipe cleaners? He never looks up. "Oh, and that desk over there is all full of the '*circus shit*' you were looking for."

Excavated from under years of boxes, my grandpa's desk was in pristine condition. It looks as though it could have been worked at yesterday. Circus ephemera fanned out in a way so casual yet so beautiful it looks curated. Posters, miniatures, blueprints, pamphlets. A photo album splayed in the center catches my eye. I sit in my grandpa's chair and page through it. Hundreds of photos of the circus—some of big top shows, some of patrons, some of my grandma and aunt smiling straight into camera—but mostly they're of backstage. Circus performers and staff just living their lives. Smoking and laughing and walking to their trailers in half-shed costumes.

Why didn't my grandpa run away with the circus if he loved it so much? He wasn't a conventional guy—he rode a motorcycle, played banjo in a big band, was a boxer, a woodworker, looked at shaved porn —so why stay in this small town his whole life, allowing only a few days a year to attend the circus and take pictures to savor, rather than just *living* it?

I suppose fucking off to California the first chance I got was my version of running away with the circus.

I stop on an image of two clowns. They're in full dress but talking casually. They look like they're trading opinions on the day's headlines or griping about the show's next destination.

One is more flamboyant—he's holding a balloon and wearing a bald cap topped with a tuft of hair and shoes in the shape of oversized bare feet. I feel I know that clown. That clown reminds me of all the weirdos I've collected out in the world—artists and writers and performers and freaks too good to be employable—all the people I just go through life with, having regular conversations, blissfully desensitized to the fact that they're wearing barefoot shoes.

Then I see myself as the other clown. The patchwork hobo with a painted five o'clock shadow and a bouquet of dying carnations, roaming with a bindle, searching for something but I'm not sure what.

I close the album and take it upstairs, so grateful to my aunt for keeping it.

JUST SAY YES

Clement Goldberg

I was in the backseat of a Trans Am the night my best friend decided we should drop acid for the first time. We were fourteen and did not feel too young for drugs. I was the kind of person who received peer pressure as collective wisdom. Just say yes! A lanky boy with blonde hair in an oversized sunhat made from twisted palm fronds handed us two tabs. The words "double dipped white blotter" filled my ears like song lyrics. I don't remember if we paid for the drugs, but they cost five bucks.

The hours ahead promised mystery. I came equipped with my mother's anecdote about the first time she took LSD—it was so scary, there were spiders and pumping hearts everywhere. All I heard was "the first time," and understood it was something worth doing more than once. Spiders and hearts were not much of a lead or deterrent.

I learned we were at "the lake" after we got there. We only made it as far as the parking lot that night. There may have been a dark body of water surrounded by cypress and oak, stereos balanced on front hoods, headlights crisscrossing through wild grass, cheerleaders losing their virginity to hot troublemakers. I never went back. It was possibly just a stealthy name for a spot where teenagers bought and consumed drugs. We stood there like audience members waiting for the show. The drugs came on with a mild opener, streetlamps encircled by colorful rings. The moon had a similar halo and glossy sheen.

The kid with the Trans Am looked bored in his driver's seat. Ten of us were coming up on acid. We piled into rows playing Tetris with our bodies, laps filled, arms and legs flapped over car doors. I sat behind the driver with someone flat across my legs. We crammed into all available space. I hallucinated a green dodo cartoon character, Gogo from the show Tiny Toons. He flew past, stopped in the center of the car, hit himself in the head with a mallet, split into twenty identical tiny Gogo's that exited the far window. I smiled and decided that I loved LSD very much. We sailed down the freeway and I arrived at home with a carload of questionable youth.

My mother was out of town with her new boyfriend, a car salesman who moved in with us a few weeks after he sold her a white Toyota and then revealed his true demonic form. She mentioned calling me later but didn't make it a big deal. We lived in a tree-lined urban townhouse development behind an underwhelming strip mall with empty storefronts and frequent turnover. There was a basic community pool with a small hot tub for the residents, surrounded by a knee-high metal gate. It was raining and dark out, otherwise an adult passerby could have ruined our good time.

I left the party to feed and walk the dog. My trip grew stronger once I was alone. I learned about particle physics en route. My hand dissolved into the molecular structures that we studied in science class—neutrons, protons, electrons. The particles performed various kinds of bonds, and then my hand turned back to its fleshy form. I grasped a sense of matter, energy, and interconnectivity in a way that electrified my consciousness. If I had been better at math, had some kind of guidance around my education, and had stopped taking drugs, maybe I would have become a physicist.

Blacktop gravel and tiny white rocks reorganized into yin-yangs. A transparent film overlaying the sky and ground was covered in hand-drawn doodles; ankhs and peace signs danced in pulsating rainbow arcs. Pink Floyd's "Comfortably Numb" sounded like it was broadcast for the whole cul-de-sac from the universe's radio. I slipped between folds of space-time, and came to a few feet ahead of myself, into the void and back again until I was at my front door where my dog barked. I grabbed his leash. We made it as far as the front walkway before he relieved himself and I heard the phone ring from the house. My mother! I had forgotten that she was going to check on me. I felt awful pulling the dog back inside.

I raced to the receiver and sat on the carpeted floor. My mother said I sounded tired and asked if she woke me. I was relieved she introduced the possibility that I was asleep. I agreed, and added a headache for some flourish. I lied to her as fuzzy carpet strands towered above my head, submerging me into a thick, tan forest. The rug enveloped me. I lost sight of the dog as I shrank and the forest grew. I clung to the phone and prayed she didn't ask more questions.

She told me to go back to sleep and hung up. I was elated.

Formerly dead foliage twirled up into the air, suspended in floral plumes. Everything was alive with breath and buzzed with impermanence; it felt sacred. I promised myself I would not take LSD again for a long time, to honor this experience with reverence. I finally made it back to the pool and found that some of the kids were gone. I plunged into the hot tub with four friends. They shapeshifted into illustrations from a popular Greek Mythology book, became animated with laurel crowns and bulging muscles. I was insanely thirsty and had an unwelcome acidic taste in my mouth. My peak waned and took a revolting turn—everyone morphed into uglier versions of themselves. My fingernails were filthy. A skater boy with a blond mohawk and small patch of his first pubes pressed his open butt cheeks to the jets; he sprang from the tub and shot water from his asshole. He repeated the routine as if it was a miraculous feat rather than an ungodly act, spraying feces poolside. I abandoned the hot tub shitshow and retreated into the swimming pool.

The visuals subsided. My come-down dampened into a soft existential crisis as I sank to the bottom of the deep end. I contemplated my existence and life purpose. It had been a particularly hard time. I was bullied for what other people saw in me before I understood it myself. I despised my mother's boyfriend and no longer felt at home in our house. I questioned if was there any reason to break the surface. I flattened my body against the chalky cement near the drain and heard an answer. *You are here to make people laugh.*

I was born with a Capricorn Stellium in the sign of the Sad Clown ruled by Saturn. I grew up surrounded by clowns. My grandmother painted clowns and decorated her house with them, specifically the sophisticated sad French ones, Blanc and Pierrot. Cabaret posters of performers Jane Avril, Aristide Bruant, and the Moulin Rouge by Toulouse-Lautrec covered her walls. Édith Piaf played on heavy rotation. My grandmother introduced me to flamboyance coupled with sadness, the magical escape in cabaret and art as a means of survival.

She was a class clown in Belgium before her education ended in the fifth grade, when the war broke out. Her sisters were sweet and smart, respectively; clown was hers to claim. She would double over with laughter when recounting her punishment for acting silly and being left-handed. *Pow, pow, pow, against the blackboard!* my grandmother would cry as she hit her hand on the wall the way her teacher pounded her little kid head. I examined my hands underwater and saw molecular bonds as trait; for some reason my family said they thought I would be left-handed too, like it was a vibe we shared. At my same young age my grandmother had to hide out on a farm and change her name. She ran fake papers for the resistance, survived on the run using various counterfeit schemes and married my American G.I. grandfather so she could immigrate to the U.S. Her smart sister was held in a Paris jail, and the sweet one had a baby with a French Catholic soldier who stole him without recourse. My grandmother eventually found him in a Paris phonebook and learned he was a hairdresser just like his mother. I did not inherit her handedness, but epigenetic trauma that healed towards an ability to create a horizon in the darkness and joke my way towards it, no matter how bleak. The least I could do was get out of the pool.

The rain stopped, and my best friend pulled on wet clothing. I never brought us towels. We shared the hallucination of floral plumes at sunrise on our waterlogged journey back to my house. She was ready to drop acid as soon as possible, but heard you had to wait a few days for it to work again, something about tolerance. I kept my promise to abstain as a sign of profound reverence, which felt like forever but only lasted three years. I like to blame this early experience for making me an artist, but maybe I never had a choice.

NOUGAT AND NAZIS

Samara Halperin

I've always loved making people laugh.

I can't remember *not* wanting to be a clown, although apparently I told my nursery school teacher, Simcha, that my dream was to become a dentist when I grew up. I was a very chatty and outgoing kid, like a mini Milton Berle. One of my Mom's favorite stories to tell is about the time we were walking down Broadway when I was three. When we got to 79th Street, she stopped to look for something in her purse, let go of my hand for two seconds, and I vanished! She was terrified and started shouting my name and running around looking for me; she heard music, and people clapping, and raced over to find me dancing in a circle of homeless people. I remember the music and the clapping and feeling so warm and happy, like a chihuahua basking in a sun puddle.

My Dad was a psychiatrist whose specialty was helping people who had been in cults. He had a home office when I was a kid, so I got to practice my clowning on his patients who were eternally waiting in our hallway for their appointments. I'd skip into the hallway on my six-foot birthday stilts, or my treacherous, metal-spring, Hanukkah "moon jump" shoes from my favorite Uncle Richie, wearing Mork from Ork suspenders and the orthodox yeshiva-mandated navy-blue skirt that covered my whorish knees. Then I'd tell a couple jokes or do a magic trick from my "professional" magic set.

If I really liked the patient, I'd jump off my stilts/ unbuckle my moon jump shoes and perform the mime routine I came up with at my Saturday mime classes at the Richard Morse Mime School in the West Village. The routine began with me mime-walking down the street, eating a perfect, shiny, red apple. I'd mime taking a big bite of the mime apple and, OH NO, there's a mime worm in the mime apple! I'd slowly pull the worm out of the apple and then dangle the worm above my head, like I was about to eat it.

Instead I'd become the worm itself, and slowly wriggle down the hallway, looking for another apple to ruin.

Sometimes my Dad's patients would come to their appointments/ our hallway wearing brightly colored cultic robes or suits (or yarmulkes if they were Jews for Jesus). I liked the Hare Krishnas the best, way more than the EST escapees or the Moonies, because the Hare Krishnas actually laughed at my jokes, while the Moonies just laughed at everything.

On the weekends we sometimes visited family friends in Scarsdale or Tenafly, New Jersey. My Dad loved getting out of the city and breathing fresh air; he would say, as we drove down the quiet suburban streets full of nothing but houses and yards, how nice it would be to live in New Jersey, and have a house and a yard with grass and trees, and my sisters and I would all cry, "But there's nothing here, don't make us move to the 'burbs!" until it got totally out of control and everyone was crying and yelling and threatening suicide, including our Mom, who said she would divorce our Dad if he was seriously thinking about living in the suburbs. That's what I call family values.

One spring Saturday in 1978, we went to Scarsdale to visit the Weinbergs. My mom and Doris Weinberg had known each other since the second grade in Brooklyn, where they had to share the same chair/ desk, and Michelle and Donny Weinberg were the same age as me and my middle sister, Ilana. We all met for lunch at a Japanese restaurant in a strip mall, joined by the Markinsons, friends of the Weinbergs with a son my age named Ryan.

At the table my Mom and Dad argued about whether eating sushi gave you intestinal parasites or not, so nobody ordered sushi. I decided to get chicken teriyaki because it came in something called a bento box, which sounded very intriguing. When the waiter came to take our order, Ryan Markinson ordered a Coke and his parents said no. Then he started screaming that he wanted a Coke and jumped up from his chair and ran through the restaurant, knocking over chairs and tables and fake potted plants, yelling, "I want a Coke, I want a Coke, I want a Coccccaaaaaa-Coooooollllaaaaaaa!" Then Ryan ran out of the restaurant and into the parking lot, running in circles, screaming, "I want a Coke, I want a Coke, I WANT A COKE!!!!!!" Then Ryan's dad, Mr. Markinson, went outside and chased him in circles, trying unsuccessfully to catch him. I stayed inside, eating my chicken teriyaki from a beautiful black lacquered bento box, with chopsticks, and watched the show through the giant front windows of the restaurant. Mrs. Markinson whispered to the adults that today was Ryan's first day of *Riddling*, whatever that meant. I did think Ryan was funny, but I didn't hear him tell any jokes, so I was a little confused.

After lunch the Markinsons took Ryan home and the rest of us went back to the Weinberg's house where Michelle, Donny, Ilana, Maia, and I played hide-and-seek, and admired the Disney character mural that Dr. Weinberg, the optometrist, had painted on the wall above Michelle's bed.

Then my parents did something completely out of character—they left us kids alone for a couple of hours while they went to visit some of the Weinberg's neighbors blocks away. After a few threats and admonishing about not opening the door for strangers or using the oven, the grown-ups left the house, leaving me and Michelle in charge of our little brother and sisters.

The very first thing we did when the parents left was eat two full cans of whipped cream from the refrigerator door. What kind of family has TWO unopened cans of whipped cream?!! Then we played another round of hide-and-seek, but it felt like a waste of our unsupervised time so we tried to come up with something else to do.

I came up with the idea of going door-to-door selling jokes to the Weinberg's neighbors. I was a young entrepreneur and had recently made $28 by making and selling roach-clip feather barrettes for two bucks apiece at school. They were all the rage at the yeshiva because it was the year of roller disco birthday parties at The Roxy, and all of the girls in my class wanted to look like Farrah Fawcett.

Everyone agreed that selling jokes was a great idea, so we put Maia in her stroller and left the house. I loved telling jokes and making people laugh. The week before, I had seen a nun on my way home from the yeshiva and remembered I knew a joke about nuns, so I walked up to her and said, "Excuse me, Sister, would you like to hear a joke?" The nun smiled and said she would love to, so I said, "What's black and white and red all over? A nun on her period!!" I didn't know what the joke meant, but I knew it must have been really good, gauging from the nun's reaction.

Michelle, Donny, Ilana, and I walked up and down the street, pushing Maia's stroller, trying to pick a house that looked friendly. I didn't really understand that Michelle and Donny didn't know their neighbors, because I grew up in a fourteen-floor apartment building where I knew every single one of my neighbors, and their pets. But since it was my idea, I had to go first.

We finally picked a house with lights on. I walked up the three steps to the front door, rang the bell, and waited. I was so nervous, but then the door opened and it was an old lady, and she looked friendly, so I stepped right up like a child circus barker and said, "Good afternoon, Madame, we are here to sell you a joke. Any price would be nice." The lady smiled and said "Ok, dahling, go ahead." I asked her, "how do you know when an elephant's been in your refrigerator? They leave footprints in the cream cheese." She laughed and pinched my cheek and told us to wait while she went and got us fifty cents out of her pocketbook.

The next house was Michelle's turn. We had to walk a few blocks to find a house where someone would answer, but all the knocking finally paid off; a man in blue jeans, slippers, and no shirt answered the door. Michelle stepped forward and said, "Good afternoon, fine Sir. We are here to sell you a joke. Any price would be nice." The man smiled and said, "Ok, go for it." Michelle took a deep breath and said, "What did the Pink Panther say when he stepped on an ant? Dead-ant, dead-ant, dead-ant dead-ant dead-ant dead-ant, dead-aaaaaaant." The man said "Not bad," and gave us twenty-five cents. What a cheapskate!

The next house was Ilana's turn. We walked up to the front door together because she was only six and rang a doorbell that played a whole song. A lady in an apron who looked like a TV mom opened the door and smiled. Ilana stepped forward to give our joke spiel. The woman laughed and said she would love to buy a joke, so Ilana asked, "What's Beethoven's favorite fruit? Baaanaaanaaanaaaa, bananaana naaaaaaaaaaaa!" The lady loved the joke and gave us a whole dollar. Yes!

We left and walked a few more blocks. It got dark out and people were sitting down to dinner; it was getting harder and harder to find joke buyers. It was my turn again because Donny was shy and refused to do it, so I walked up to a door and rang the bell. It took a while, but finally an old lady in a house dress answered the door and smiled when she saw us standing there. I asked her if she wanted to buy a joke and she said she didn't have any money, but would we take candy as a payment? We conferred and decided that as long as it was wrapped, candy would be fine. Halloween rules applied. I saw that the lady had numbers written on her arm, and I didn't know what it was, so I asked her what the numbers were for. At first she got really mad at me and yelled, "You can't just ask anyone anything you want, it's very bad manners!" Then she calmed down and went inside and got us some pink, white, and brown-striped, shrink-wrapped, rock-hard nougats, and told us that the nazis tattooed the numbers on her arm at a concentration camp in Poland when she was a little girl. She told us about Hitler, and what a concentration camp was. As we stood there in the porch light listening to her talk about the nazis, I realized what joke to tell her. "Madame," I interrupted, because Ilana, Donny, and Maia had started to cry from the concentration camp stories. "Have no fear, the time for your joke is finally here...What's green and flies over Poland? SNOT-ZIS!!" She got really, really angry, yelling at us that it wasn't funny, that the nazis were no laughing matter. And—what the hell was wrong with us? That was when my parents and the Weinbergs screeched up in my dad's wood-paneled Oldsmobile station wagon and jumped out, yelling, "Where the hell have you been? We were worried sick about you!!"

We all got in big trouble (except for my sister Maia, who was too little to get in trouble), and for our punishment, my parents and the Weinbergs took the $5.25 we had earned selling jokes, and also made us give them all of the pink, white, and brown-striped, shrink-wrapped nougats before I even got a chance to try one, so unfair.

When we got home, as an additional punishment—only for me, because I "was the oldest and should have known better"—my parents made me write them a letter of apology, explaining why it was wrong to do what we did. Years later, I called my mom to ask her what the letter said and she said that the ending was the best part. It said:

"I will never, EVER sell jokes again. It was wrong to sell jokes to strangers because I could have been kidnapped, murdered, and killed,

etcetera,

etcetera,

etcetera . . ."

POSITION PAPER #45: CLOWNS

Andrea Lawlor

In the new country, some of us will spend a season in a traveling band of theater workers, staging science fiction circuses or old country plays, rap battles & marathon readings of *The Odyssey* & so on, whatever we decide together in our temporary autonomous troupe, to be disbanded at the season's end. Seasons will be irregular, maybe we're only able to take time off our current crew for two months or maybe we're in between assignments, not much time to plan & write & rehearse & stage but we'll take what we can get. We'll stay in each town for a few days, in the lodge, or maybe on the outskirts in a nice field where we will string up solar-powered fairy lights in a circle, tents inside, drinking mead with the locals after the show, still in our vests & eyelashes.

I WAS A MIDDLE-AGED CLOWN PRINCESS

Page Person

From behind a sequined curtain affixed to the ceiling of my neighborhood dive bar by two mop handles, I can make out the sparkle of stage lights on the audience. Shadowy figures face me in anticipation. The "stage" is just this narrow strip of linoleum floor between two rows of tables, but in this moment, it feels like standing at the precipice of being the world's biggest star. As the host of the show says, "This next performer is. . ." and describes me as wild or not like the other girls or as if I emerged from an island of floating garbage, my friends in the audience catch on that I am next and start cheering. An energy builds in my body that I refuse to call fear. I dig my spray painted and heavily rhinestoned Birkenstocks into the floor and remind myself all of this energy will be so useful in less than one minute from now when I swing open the curtain to make my entrance. I'm wearing tights that are too small for my long legs and a cool breeze drifts down my buttcrack as they ride lower and lower. I'm wearing the bodice hacked off a quinceañera gown from St. Vincent's with an enormous skirt made of ripped up trash bags and colorful plastic party tablecloths held together with duct tape and hot glue. No nails, no lash. A wig that appears to be sourced from the gutter with a huge shock of trash bag plastic as a fascinator.

I have rehearsed this number at least a hundred times, but now, standing behind the curtain hearing my name announced and my track starting, I can't for the life of me remember the first line of the song, the first word. I have done enough gigs to trust the process. I just hope my enormous trash bag headpiece does not get caught in the sequins of the curtain and rip my whole wig off. Yes, that has happened. "Welcome to the stage, Page Person!" Suddenly, I am in a fantasy space. I can't even hear the music. Time is going so slowly and everyone is looking up at me. I feel their attention; an energy zinging through me. I think of all the times I performed to a mirror as a depressed introverted teen and longed to have an audience. I think of all the times I got in trouble as a child for seeking attention through uncommissioned theatrical performances and feel vindicated in my career choice. I always have a stunt in my numbers to give people something to talk about the next day at the proverbial water cooler: throwing cereal, hot dogs, or trash at them and watching them cover their drinks; pulling a flashlight out of my butt, squirting whipped cream through my granny panties, or spraying Lysol at my privates while making a face like the whole area is unhealthy and malodorous. The time I bought a whole forty pound bag of potting soil to bury myself in—and realized when I opened it on stage that I had in fact purchased manure; the look on their faces when the smell hit. It was certainly worse for them than it was for me.

I *live* to grab someone by the hand and stare into their eyes and bark a whole line of a song at them like they are in trouble. They love that. I beg them for money and then throw it on the floor with disdain, like I don't care about their stinking dollars. I point accusations at them, I act like they disgust me, I wag my pointy finger NO NO NO. I pause and eat a burger when I get tired. I pull out intestines made from Soyrizo and take a big bite, I gulp down milk of magnesia and barf it all over myself. I once brought an actual dead fish in a plastic-lined pocket and handed it to an unsuspecting audience member. That one I had regrets about. Taking the fish back after the show and throwing it away in the ladies room trash can, I felt a pang of guilt at its lazy eye gazing back at me. *Why was I sacrificed?* it asked hauntingly. Just to make drunk people scream in exchange for a handful of dollar bills.

Counting the money is so satisfying. Each dollar retains some essence of the person that presented it to me: confidently folded in half lengthwise to make it easy to hand off, the nervous sweat of some straight guy who awkwardly fumbles as I roll my eyes so his friends laugh at him, the notes halfheartedly crumpled and tossed on the floor from the back row. If you have $27 in the bank you are broke; the same amount in ones and it's tacos for everybody. Eating after a gig, not having to care what you look like anymore, cackling the night away looking at online videos of a performance you have done at the expense of sleep before a day job: priceless.

I'm becoming a woman in my life out of drag so these twinks in wigs have nothing on me. I'm the big titty bitch in the trash bags and

Birkenstocks, the crazy one, the one who doesn't give a fuck. A punk rocker from way back. I would arrive to the dressing room early to claim my portion of mirror space, gazing into my reflection until some other mythic being was looking back at me. This is called getting into your zhujj. I would stay out of the drama between the other queens, but every once in a while dip into a conversation if I had something clever to add. One night the girls were comparing notes on their experiences with this photographer that was taking pics of drag performers. After your shoot he would give you a butt plug with a detailed Virgin Mary sculpted into its surface. I had used mine a couple of times and always found the nooks and crannies of her face held onto fecal material to a disturbing degree. Without looking away from my liquid eyeliner application in the mirror, I chimed in, "no matter how much you clean out beforehand that Virgin Mary is coming out of there HEAVILY contoured" which was met with howls of recognition and disgust. I was part of an elite secret society that looks so different from behind the stage than I ever could have imagined from the audience.

Later at night when the gig is over and the bar is closed, I will be absolutely screaming with delight that I got to have so much fun. I detect pure actual joy on my face while struggling to wash off the grease paint and glitter in my dingy bathroom mirror. I took so many photos at this time of night thinking I had truly located my most ecstatic self. Every time I would post them I would get a concerned phone call from a friend or relative asking GIRL ARE YOU OK? All they saw was the chaos of bad life decisions and not the total delight that I had seen in myself.

There are bad nights. There are nights when drunk straight girls come up and honk my boobs like they are doing me a favor . . . it just hurts. The times when someone decides to get onstage and be a part of your number without being invited. The times you lose your cool and just start screaming at someone to get off the fucking stage, stop groping you, stop saying transphobic shit to you. The problematic white queens speaking in blaccent, lip syncing the N word. The girls that want to read you, the Uber drivers that try to assault you in an alley, the nights you really need to come home with sixty dollars and only make sixteen. Falling asleep at work the next day, scratching a cornea because glitter got under your contact, losing your weed or your foundation of your yellow can of Got2b hair spray. Suspecting some bitch stole your tips, realizing you threw a twenty at another queen thinking it was a one, watching some other performer blow up and get all the gigs you want and make a living doing it while you are still washing dishes or mopping up vomit to pay the bills. Paying a seemingly endless amount of dues to always lose money because you always have to be making a new look. The downsides keep piling up, but the best high ever is parting those safety-pinned sequined curtains and having all those eyes on you. Hearing them scream and gag and throw money at you—it's better than any sex or drugs or warm sunlight. It's hard to describe the feeling if it isn't one you have lusted after and are finally giving yourself permission to experience. It feels an awful lot like being loved.

LONELY CLOWN HOMO

Alistair McCartney

Although they have been clowns for donkey's years, it still takes the clowns a good forty-five minutes to apply their makeup. The clowns have been a couple for as long as anyone can remember, long before they became clowns. More specifically, clown separatists. Clowns who only want to be around the creepy, discursive energy of other clowns. Though they have been accused of isolating themselves and not considering the needs of "the clown community."

While some of their more reactionary colleagues have been seduced by something called *boogaloo*, why are clowns so literal, a dumb political scene which promises to center and accelerate clowns, they have been secretly planning their own, more progressive boogaloo. A boogaloo *du langage poétique*. Before clown #1 became a clown, he was studying semiotics, a clown is a signifier, but of what? His dissertation, unfinished, was on Kristeva's *La révolution du langage poétique*. Sometimes he thinks he might pick it up again, this time analyzing the text's thesis of the revolutionary power of disruptive language through the lens of homo clowndom.

The clowns keep each other company in their silver caravan, composing their grand schemes, while remaining deeply, existentially lonely. One of the clowns cries so much he imagines if he wound up the windows his tears could fill up the caravan and drown both of them.

Sometimes after the show, which like love has a three-ringed structure, the clowns are so hyped, they fuck without even bothering to take off their makeup. One of the clowns has a dick like a toy baseball bat. The intensity of their movements smears the colors over each other's skin, until their clowny bodies look like psychotic birthday cakes, decorated with little bits of sawdust and popcorn and glitter. The top clown wears a tiny hat, its elastic bites into his chin, and no matter how rigorously he raw-dogs the bottom clown, the hat never falls off his head.

Above the bottom clown's disproportionately big ass, in the position of the so-called tramp stamp, there is a tattoo in Latin, *Nunc canis tuus scurra esse volo*, which is meant to mean *Now I wanna be your clown dog*, but probably means *Now I want your dog to be a clown*. They make repetitive owly cooing noises, a clown chorus, clown sex creates poetic language in its most unfiltered form.

At night, all clowns know art is inherently linked to failure and that political and aesthetic revolutions never go hand in hand. The clowns try and time it so they cum together, with the violent expenditure and impossibility of thirty clowns pouring out of one of those little clown cars. Afterwards, they wash their smudgy bodies off in cold water, as there is no hot water in their caravan.

THIRSTY

Kelsey L. Smoot

It's a sleight of hand, I realize exactly too late
you play a woodwind,
and instead of a cobra dance,
yellow canaries beak their way
out through my earholes,
flapping around your head, so miserably in love
we are in front of my childhood home
and I am ashamed
of how boring it is in comparison
to your silken shirt
garish, wild-eyed expression
I want to live with you I think
I want to go to every place with you
And while you always say nothing,
I am certain that this is shared between us
Look at my canaries, and how they halo your perfect,
perfect head

But you are looking past them,
your eyes tracing my lips hungrily
And wordlessly, your hand lifts from your side
You're doing it wrong, I don't protest
when your fingers grasp the small, shimmering ribbon,
a yardlong bean,
poking out of the corner of my mouth;
you must have planted it in me some night
and in one swift tug, we are both stunned
when an impossibly
too-many things come heaping out:

The spoons that you hid under the couch
to avoid your mother's rage
tied to the crabs your uncle bought you
well, really just the one–
you know, the juicy one, that ate the other one
ate its middle clean out
when you forgot to feed them
tied to the chairs
we flirted circles around
on the day we met,
tied to the books I read to impress you
tied to the books I lied and said I read
to impress you,
tied to my ribcage, so suddenly,
I fall over
broken and gelatinous,
looking up to find you
cooing over my brow,
the guilt pooling at your eye-corners
falling only the once,
directly into my open mouth
down my throat, to join all of the other things
that had become untethered,

"you won't leave me here, will you?" I manage
as you disassemble the woodwind,
kicking astray the rubble
the canaries, now frantic,
hopping about at your feet
still so ready to fly
so ready to dance for you

In the distance, I see a neighbor dog
pittering across lawns,
lapping at a gutter drain
Damn, that looks so good,
I think to myself;
the animal of me

aware for the first time in weeks
of my basic survival needs
I am so horrendously thirsty

Then, there is the sun,
seeming to drop from the sky in an instant,
and you are also gone
The canaries are pecking at my cheeks,
tangling in my hair
hoping to find their way back
The neighbor dog turns toward me,
seems to contemplate
whether I am food,
fun,
trash,
or threat,
and just before he turns his head away,
the light brown brindle of his coat
becomes livened under the streetlight

Not the neighbor dog, I slowly remember
he had died a few years back
Who would rebound all of me
that had become unspooled,
I wonder–
the canaries finally quieted
And then, I am quieted
Asleep like that, confetti all over a driveway
And then I am dreaming of you again:
your perfect, *perfect* head,
You, and that sweet little dog, I imagine
No, not *dog*
Not dog, *coyote*
Good puppy,
sharp puppy

POKED

MariNaomi

I.

It is 2002; I am poring through profiles of Friendsters-of-friends. How have I never met the emo hottie I have five friends in common with, all from disparate parts of my life? Why has my bestie never introduced me to this Joan Jett-lookalike who is clearly my type? Why is a goateed normie looking at my profile?

I investigate his profile, scrolling through his photos. Here's the goateed normie at a party, wearing khaki Dockers and a blue shirt, business casual in the tech world, surrounded by what I can only imagine are other techies. Here is the goateed techie goofing around with a hot goth, a cat o' nine tails in his grip. Here is the goateed kinkster dressed as a bondage clown, his hairy butt cheeks criss-crossed with lash marks. Wait, what? Since when were clowns supposed to be sexy?

Here is the goateed bondage clown grinning fiercely with another bondage clown, both of their teeth filed down to sharp points.

I am fascinated, but get a cold feeling when I remember that he can see who has viewed him. I close the tab, thinking about the teeth. Are they real? They look real, but who with a day job would do that? I am obsessive about teeth.

I want to say that I am shocked, or even surprised, but it is still early times, and in the beginning of the internet, the Gen X love language was sending each other the most unusual porn we could find: the blog of the guy in love with a dolphin; fan art of macro furries having sex with miniscule-by-comparison skyscrapers; goatse—if you don't know it, don't look it up. If you were working in tech in the early aughts, it's highly likely you saw these passed around the office and didn't blink an eye. Perhaps you even tricked your boss into opening a file of hairy geriatric dudes in the midst of a blowjob. The early aughts were wild.

Days later, I'm still thinking about the teeth when the goateed guy pokes me. It is now more than twenty years later, and I still don't understand the point of a poke. But it is enough to make me curious (ok, obvs that is the point), so I revisit his profile. I can't help myself. There he is, the solo shot of him looking boring at a desk. Scroll. Here is the party shot, the goth girl, the teeth . . . but wait, there are more photos—dark, grainy digital shots in more clown garb. I am horrified to catch sight of bloodplay and needle photos. (Talk about a poke!) I have been phobic of needles since childhood, to the point that I cannot even say the word "needle" aloud without feeling dizzy. I close the tab and don't look again. That's enough curiosity for me.

II.

My earliest clown memory is of the sad-hobo-clown paintings at the Long John Silver's in my Texas hometown. Various sad clowns carried red sacks at the end of their long wooden poles, presumably filled with their meager worldly possessions. Why the pole? Wouldn't that make it harder to carry? Were the clothes so full of fleas or stench that they had to be held at arm's length? I suppose I could look it up, but that would kill the mystery. I prefer to guess.

Stephen King's *It* was my next touchstone as a tween. That book scared the bejeezus out of me, so of course I couldn't get enough.

Next came John Wayne Gacy peering at me from the serial killer trading cards I was obsessed with in my early twenties. I ceded the cards in a breakup and regretted it for years.

III.

At a subculture craft fair, one of the founders of Burning Man delights me by buying over a hundred dollars' worth of my poorly made crafts. I have been tabling here for hours with handmade magnets, paintings, and journals I collaged together using macabre pics from magazines and Muppet-looking fur. Throughout my many hours at the table, a pair of bikini-clad goth clowns roller skate back and forth in the cavernous, hangar-like building, gliding noisily on the concrete. I recall the basic-looking Friendster and wonder if these roller-skaters have boring jobs and needle collections. I keep my distance.

IV.

It is 2013, and I am married to a man, Gary, who is relocating to Los Angeles due to a job opportunity. This despite the fact that when I first started dating him (and he had just moved from LA to SF), I told him I would never move to Los Angeles. Apparently not wanting your partner to suffer an awful job can move a mountain of stubbornness.

I find that LA is quite welcoming, at least at first, but I never wanted to leave San Francisco. A woman I met at a party has invited me to perform at her salon, and I befriend another guest, a performance artist named Danny. He invites me and my husband to an event he is emceeing at an art gallery the following week.

"I have no idea what the show's about," he apologizes in advance, in case it sucks. "It's a San Francisco thing."

My heart swells with homesickness, and I tell Danny we'll be there.

The first red flag is the woman in a curly fire-engine red wig, a fuzzy blue bathrobe, and Mimi-from-he-Drew-Carey-Show levels of makeup. There is something sultry about the way her red lipstick is deliberately smeared across her face. Oh no, is she a sexy clown? Gary and I exchange looks. It wasn't long ago that a coworker of his posted a photo on Facebook of a birthday party they attended as a kid. There was a massive clown in the picture, its arms hovered around the children. If you zoom in, you can just barely read what it says on the oversize pin on its lapel: "If you pull this pin off, I will bleed." What is it with clowns and needles? The photo was of John Wayne Gacy, taken right before he was busted for killing thirty-three boys, burying a number of them in his basement. This Facebook post sparked a conversation about sexy clowns, so the subject was fresh on our minds.

But kids are running around everywhere, so surely this is a family friendly event? I'm sure I'm just being paranoid.

We find our places. I will almost always sit front and center, ever since I started performing. I find that most folks want to sit at the back, and as a performer it can be unsettling to have the entire audience as far away as possible from you, as if they don't want to commit to being there. This show we are about to see is in a medium-size room filled with folks seated on the floor, so there I am, front and center as always, my legs criss-cross-applesauce.

Danny does his announcing, then the woman with the wig, dressed as a nurse and carrying a toy infant, clomps onstage in oversized shoes.

Oh no. I cannot tell you what happened before she dramatically bared her breasts to let the pretend infant suckle on them. Her boobs were pierced by myriad hypodermic syringes, placed neatly around her aureole like a sun and its rays as drawn by a child.

I am not the needlephobe I used to be, not since I started getting regular flu shots, yet I find myself sweating profusely, my heart speeding up. Gary instinctively covers my eyes, and I turn to the side swiftly, expecting to see parents leading their small children away. But they sit there in stunned silence. I intensely want to leave, but I am in the front and middle, completely blocked in, and paralyzed. I hear the clown making a soliloquy, and I peer up to see her still-bared breasts, the fake baby being flung about violently. I am trying to determine how long this will last, and this is when I see her bring out a staple gun before Gary's hand humanely covers my face again.

I cannot stand it. I watch the faces of the rest of the audience as they flinch and groan and ripple with each staple-gun bang, their faces a collective rictus of fright.

From that point on, all I have left of that memory is the smell of my sweat and Danny's sincere apology afterwards. I must have blacked out.

V.

Years later, I'm in San Francisco about to teach a workshop to graduate students. The professor tells me about one of her students who works as a clown. "A clown, huh?" I say warily.

I know a guy who used to be a circus clown, a friend of a friend with a gentle smile, a single dad with health issues. I never was able to picture him clowning around, although admittedly he can juggle like nobody's business. From what I can tell, he is not a fetish clown, though I have no issue if he is. As long as I don't have to look at needles or blood, I'm fine with whatever people want to do on their own time. Or so I tell myself.

But when I meet the clown woman at my workshop, I find my hackles are up, and I'm wary. She is about my age, a fellow queer with a butch vibe. Despite myself, I have a rapport with her. Maybe it's the clown-fear, or maybe it's Gen X flirting, but I want to neg her for some reason, so instead of calling her by name, I call her "Clown" each time she raises her hand to ask a question. I am poking her, it seems. Once I realize what I'm doing is inappropriate, I tell myself to get over it, and I do. Maturity is a wonderful thing.

After the class, I ask her why she became a clown. Doesn't she know that clowns are scary? She says with all sincerity that she wants to bring joy to people, to make them laugh. Duh, of course. That's what clowns are supposed to be about after all, right? It's kind of sick that it's taken me four decades to actually see an example of this.

I let my defenses soften, and she shows me some of her tricks. She is delightfully funny, and I even find myself guffawing when she executes the perfect pratfall. Maybe clowns don't have to be scary or sad after all. Maybe they're just poking fun at themselves.

THE FREAK REVOLUTION

Jake Hall

Sunlight trickles in through the window as I sit at my dressing room table, the one that's been passed down by generations of my ancestors. Chuckles, Bozo, Doink; the *crème de la crème* of clownkind have all tucked their big-ass shoes under this rickety wooden stool, plastering their faces with bone-white greasepaint.

Today, I'm aiming for subtlety. Nothing ruins a clown's face like a too-wide smile, a too-dark shade of blood red. The devil is in the details, darling.

At least, that's what I tell myself. In truth, my makeup skills are shitty at best. I can't glue my eyebrows down to save my life. The legends of my trade would surely gasp in horror if they clocked my poor excuse of a mug, the red pockmarks and ashen hue of my god-given skin still visible through the barely-blended streaks of my clown white.

All I can think is that I am *fucked*. It's almost 2:00 PM, and I can hear the flustered tones of pissed-off moms rounding up their toddlers in the palatial garden. "Damnit Joanna, SIT DOWN," screams one, her voice notching quickly from concerned to feral. I hear a *crash* that rattles my bones. Through the audible chaos, I can discern that some nine-year-old asshole called Martha just ran headfirst into the buffet table, the manicured lawn now strewn with the ground-up mulch of corn dogs and chicken nuggets. Great, now I've smudged my eye makeup. *Fuck*.

Clowning is a dying industry, but it's the only one I've ever known. My earliest memories were made in a traveling circus. Every week, my family packed up their trapezes, hula hoops, and juggling swords, and they drove for miles. Interstates blurred into an amorphous whirl of gray asphalt glimpsed through dirt-streaked windows, and I spent these childhood voyages eagerly anticipating the next roadside diner we could all pile into. There are Polaroid photos of my chubby, grinning face stained with the syrup I smeared on top of waffles, my pale skin smudged with the red paint Mama Clown would rub off on me as she pinched my cheeks and kissed my face. We are a glorious troupe, a makeshift family made up of outcasts. We are queer, intersex, disabled. We are misfits in every sense of the word, a tight-knit community well-versed in turning shit to sugar.

Unsurprisingly, the world didn't view us so favorably. These weren't *all* happy memories.

Whenever we piled into the remote diners of Buttfuck Nowhere, every eye in the place would turn towards us, whether we liked it or not. Waitresses could barely disguise their cruel snickers, not even the lure of a tip incentive enough to treat us like humans. On more than one occasion we were told to fuck off, by strangers who hurled words like "freak" and "weirdo."

I should probably explain here that I wasn't actually related to anyone at the circus. I still don't know exactly what happened. My origin story is a mystery to everyone but those who birthed me and then left, the secrets of my past locked in their hearts and minds, gone from my life forever. All I know is that my biological parents abandoned me as a baby. Maybe they couldn't afford to take care of me? I convince myself that they didn't have the resources to raise me, that they were too preoccupied with the demons in their own heads to truly give me a childhood. This feels less painful than the possibility that I was unwanted from the get-go, that it wasn't an absence of resource but an absence of love that left me cast aside. I'm constantly writing and editing my origin story, tweaking the details to lessen the pain.

In my retelling, the story begins on the side of an interstate, where I was abandoned and left to die until Mama and Papa Clown spotted me and rushed out to rescue me. They are my lifetime guardians, the only parents I have ever known. They are flesh and blood and kindness and love, all wrapped up in harlequin costumes and white face paint. From this day onwards, I was adopted into their circus.

Growing up, "freak" became a word that we stole and subverted, one that we used for ourselves. We sucked the venom out of those five letters, sprinkled them with pride, and wore them like badges of honor. We had to. Objectively speaking, the definition fit. We made our living swallowing swords, dangling from the Big Top ceiling in skin-tight, sparkly leotards, blowing blue-licked flames from fuel-coated mouths.

But right now, none of that matters. Mrs. Mendleson doesn't give a shit about my identity, my sense of self, my thoughts or feelings on any of this. She doesn't care that I'm a person. All that she cares about is that I'm a source of cheap labor. All that she saw is my ad in the phone book—YOUNG CLOWN SEEKS WORK—and the fact that I'd be willing to entertain her sniveling kids for $50.

Despite my years of training and on-the-road education, I'm still new to clowning myself—and it shows. My first solo gig was a neighborhood barbeque. It was a shitshow. My big red nose fell off my face when I tried to honk it, my caked-on paint became blemished by the rivulets of sweat which trickled down my face as I realized I was surrounded, I was helpless. The kids, pouncing on a moment of weakness like jackals in the woods, dived to grab my fallen appendage as I chased after them, desperately willing my hand-me-down clown pants to not fall down. Public humiliation was one thing, public indecency was another. It's an experience that nearly broke me.

This is not what I signed up for. I grew up seeing black-and-white postcards of icons like Pierrot—a miserable fucker, but *damn* he can act!—and Canio, star of the 1892 opera *Pagliacci*. Spoiler alert: he's a jealous lover who eventually murders his wife. Not exactly a role model, but still, these guys were on-stage at the world's most revered operas and pantomimes. I find myself getting jealous of those horror film clowns, the ones with the creepy smiles and hidden knives. Some clowns hate them, thinking they give clowning a bad name. It's the age-old dilemma: tradition vs. modernity. Personally, the idea of being feared seems pretty damn appealing when the alternative is fighting for your life to make $50 in this god-awful gig economy, watching snot-nosed kids stamp on your feet and make private bets to see who can push you into the bushes the fastest. Many days, I'm tempted to go full Art the Clown and hack up the suburban family who treats you no better than a rat.

Humor me—wouldn't be it be kind of iconic? Me, a queer clown, taking revenge on the heteronormative cottage industry of bullshit garden parties organized by dissatisfied families with too much time on their hands? I could lead a queer clown revolution, one murder at a time!

Ok, I'm getting distracted. I guess I have anger issues—but really, who can blame me? Mama and Papa Clown worked tirelessly to make families across the country smile, and for what? What gratitude did they ever get? Those *dull* Neighborhood Watch associations used to make flyers warning of our arrival, especially when they learned that Mama and Papa Clown were actually queer. *Gasp!* A queer-owned circus? The horror! Those curtain-twitching fuckers made it their mission to launch a smear campaign against my family, rallying the support of every right-wing politician they could get hold of. They posted flyers far and wide, told schools we were a bunch of perverts hellbent on corrupting their kids. They made up grotesque lies and picketed the streets, waving dumbass placards with slogans like, DOWN WITH CLOWNS! Their marketing couldn't have been worse, and yet somehow, it worked. Word got out that we were "progressives." Audiences dwindled slowly. Our once-revered circus fell into disrepute, branded with a permanent black mark.

Times are bleak. I have a friend who became an influencer, and the thought of following in her footsteps chills me to the bone. Every day, she uploads makeup tutorials with clickbait headlines like, CUNTY CLOWNFACE 101 and HOW TO SERVE ART THE CLOWN REALNESS! She even went viral two years ago, with a video called KICKED OUT OF CLOWN COLLEGE. NOT CLICKBAIT! I'm happy for her—a little jealous, but happy deep down, I promise. Still, the thought of putting myself out there online makes me want to scream. TikTok teens flock to her page and leave comments like "slay queen!" and I honestly just *couldn't*, you know?

I grew up with generations of clowns who saw it go from a respected art form—you try driving one of those tiny cars and making that little flower actually shoot water—to a laughingstock, and we're not in on the joke. I literally saw a DoorDash ad with a clown driver the other day, and it made me want to die.

I'm too young to be this jaded. I'm two months into my clowning career, and I feel done. Like, so done. I'm shakily rounding off the corners of my bright red mouth—MAC lipliner, it's a godsend—as Mrs. Mendleson pokes her head around the door. Uh-oh. "When the hell are you coming out?" She practically froths at the mouth. Thankfully, she chooses not to comment on my mess of a face. I'm sure she's a nice person, deep down. I've just seen no evidence of it today, or in any of my interactions with her. In fact, I've seen her name crop up in the occasional anti-clown article, saying that *anybody* could be a clown, and that we're all talentless hacks. I've been choking down the urge to tell her that I know this about her, that I know how much she secretly hates me. Apparently, she'll buckle to the peer pressure of rabid children—but only when the clown comes cheap. I've even paid my own transport, and she hasn't so much as offered me a glass of water, only manhandled me into the garden to keep me a secret from the kids, like sneaking a clown into a children's party requires CIA levels of obfuscation. Fuck her.

"Ri-right," I stammer, picking up my red, curly wig and thinking of that legendary Jinkx Monsoon quote: *I tried to tease it, but I just pissed it off!* I think of making this joke to Mrs. Mendleson. I don't think she would appreciate it. Her sentences clash into a furied monologue. It turns out that really *was* the buffet table crashing to the ground, and a highly anxious child named Jonathan just slipped on a corn dog. That explains the crying.

I assure Mrs. Mendleson that I'm ready to go out, ready to jig and gesture and clown around for an audience that sees me as nothing more than an object, a novelty. Mrs. Mendleson purses her lips and nods curtly, before plastering the most impressive fake smile I ever have seen across her face. She could teach me a thing or two.

I take a deep breath, close my eyes, and say a silent prayer to all the clowns that came before me. All of the mavericks, the comedians, the downtrodden geniuses that paved the way for me to be here, in the suburbs, ready to give a garden full of kids a show that they will never forget.

I smooth down my ruffled collar, pat down my wig, and stuff the knife I brought into the pocket of my clown pants. I think of Mama and Papa Clown, the way their lives were destroyed by people just like Mrs. Mendleson—the "think of the kids" brigade perpetually ready to wage war on difference. I think of how my parents refuse to leave their home, twitching anxiously at the slightest sign of life on the driveway. I think of all the queer clowns that came before me, the freaks and weirdos chased out of roadside diners by the same bastards that ply their kids with Happy Meals, worshiping at the altar of the Golden Arches and their asshole mascot. I take a deep breath, contorting my face into the most sinister grimace I can manage. *This is for all of you*, I think. It's showtime.

ABOUT THE CLOWNS

Noel Alumit is a multidisciplinary artist based in Los Angeles. He wrote the novels *Letters to Montgomery Clift* and T*alking to the Moon*. His most recent book is the short story collection Music Heard in Hi-Fi.

Kate Bornstein is an author, actor, and performance artist who's been joyfully confusing people about gender for decades. Her books, like *Gender Outlaw*, *A Queer and Pleasant Danger*, and *Hello, Cruel World* teach readers how to clown around with identity without getting arrested. She's toured the world, played a clown on Broadway, and even snuck some nonbinary mischief onto NBC's *The Blacklist*.

Grace Byron is a writer from the Midwest based in Queens who writes for *The New Yorker, Frieze, GQ, Vogue, New York Magazine, The Nation,* and elsewhere. Her debut novel *Herculine* is out now from Simon and Schuster. @emotrophywife

Justin Chin was a crucial figure in the spoken word and literary scenes of San Francisco and beyond. His seven books explored his identity as a gay Asian-American with humor, gravitas, absurdity, and perversity. He died in December, 2015.

Jibz Cameron is a writer, performer, visual artist, and actor. She is most well known for her multi-media performance work as alter ego Dynasty Handbag, which has spanned over twenty years. Among many other esteemed accolades, Jibz is a 2022 Guggenheim Fellow, a 2021 United States Artist Award recipient, and a 2020 Creative Capital Grant awardee, and yet she still has herpes.

Lizzy Cooperman's a writer and performer who has written for shows on Comedy Central, Adult Swim, and Amazon Music. She hosted a year-long experimental podcast called *Lizzy Cooperman's In Your Hands*, produced by Starburns Audio, and her poetry has been published in Hotel Amerika and Harvard Review. She's appeared on HBO and Comedy Central and performs regularly in LA and beyond.

Marisa Crawford is the author of the poetry collections *Reversible*, *The Haunted House*, and, most recently, *DIARY*. She is the editor of *The Weird Sister Collection* (Feminist Press, 2024), and co-editor, with Megan Milks, of *We Are the Baby-Sitters Club: Essays & Artwork from Grown-Up Readers*. She lives in New York.

Devon Devine is an IndoRican witch, Polaroid artist, and zinemaker hailing from the Sunny Mission District of San Francisco, CA via Olympia, WA via Chicago, IL. You can find him documenting his best clown lifestyle on IG/Substack by following @devoncito

Dia Felix is a writer and media producer from California, now based in the Hudson Valley. She's the author of the Lambda-nominated experimental novel *Nochita*, poetry chapbook *YOU YOU YOU*, and Headlands Center for the Arts 2024 Wall Space Commission, *COOLEST MONTH*. Her interests include dairy, gossip, museums, mystics, and ending the internet.

Valentine Freeman's work has been published by *The Believer, Publication Studio, Rain Taxi, Good Press, Lost Horse, Ghost City Press,* and others. She lives on unceded Chumash land in California with her wife and dog.

Katie Fricas is a cartoonist and editor. Her comics have been in the *New York Times Book Review, The Guardian, the Los Angeles Review of Books*, and numerous anthologies. Her first graphic novel, *Checked Out*—about a queer library worker searching for love online, artistic validation in New York City, and the perfect book—was published by *Drawn & Quarterly* in May 2025. @cartoonfricassee

Harper Galvin is the author of *The Three Einsteins, Best Party of Our Lives*, and *Ugly Time*. They have contributed to *Vice Magazine, The Guardian*, and *The Stranger Newspaper*, and have an MFA in poetry from the University of Washington. They have both jumped out of and fallen into coffins during readings, and love winter clothes but run through the snow naked at every opportunity.

Nicole J. Georges is the author of the graphic memoirs *Calling Dr. Laura*, *Fetch: How a Bad Dog Brought Me Home*, and a collection called *Emotional Support Animals*. She teaches independent comics workshops and does a podcast called *Sagittarian Matters*.

Clement Goldberg is an award-winning Artist, Writer, Director, and Animator. Their satirical yet hopeful projects center collective grief rooted in climate crisis, cultural erasure, and extinction. Their film *Let Me Let You Go* received a Creative Capital Award and Clement's debut novel *New Mistakes* was published by DOPAMINE Press in 2024.

Jake Hall is the UK-based author of *The Art of Drag* (2020), an illustrated, in-depth history of drag, and *Shoulder to Shoulder* (2024), a love letter to queer solidarity movements. Jake aims to breathe life into marginalized histories, and to continue the fight for our collective liberation.

Samara (rhymes with mascara) Halperin's short films and videos have been making audiences laugh, cry, and scream in screenings from Amsterdam to Saskatchewan, since 1989. Samara is a filmmaker/professor/writer from NYC who lives in Oakland, California, where they make movies, teach filmmaking, learn rabbinics, and admire palm trees.

Scottie Harvey is a writer, performer, and animator living in Los Angeles, CA. She is writing a novel about the last Cold Stone Creamery.

Jennifer Hasegawa's latest poetry collection, *NAOMIE ANOMIE: A Biography of Infinite Desire*, is an experimental take on anti-memoir. Her debut collection, *La Chica's Field Guide to Banzai Living*, was long-listed for *The Believer* Book Award in Poetry. She was born and raised on the Big Island of Hawai'i and lives in San Francisco.

Alex Freeman Hischier is a writer based in a small, foggy town on the California coast. She recently finished a novel.

Tara Jepsen is a writer and comic living in Los Angeles. Her novel *Like a Dog* was published by Sister Spit/City Lights. She co-hosted legendary queer literary open mic, K'vetsh, for over ten years.

Jones is a nonbinary writer and award-winning drag king based in Los Angeles. Their work focuses on exploring and eradicating shame in the areas of mental illness, queerness, and the body.

Ely Kreimendahl is a writer, comedian, and podcaster, with the plot twist background of a long career as a psychotherapist. @elykreimendahl everywhere

Andrea Lawlor is the author of a novel, *Paul Takes the Form of a Mortal Girl* (Vintage), as well as two chapbooks, *Position Papers Vol.1* (Factory Hollow) & *Position Papers Vol.2* (Belladonna*). They teach creative writing at Mount Holyoke College.

Stella Leoni grew up in Paris, but spent the past decade in NYC and LA. Her writing is deeply influenced by the emotional undercurrents of works from all mediums—film, music, visual art, and literature alike. Her novel, *I'm Staying in Tonight*, was published in 2025.

Daniel LeVesque is the author of *Hairdresser on Fire: A Novel* (Manic D). He lives in Oakland, CA.

Julián Delgado Lopera is the author of *The New York Times* acclaimed novel *Fiebre Tropical* (Feminist Press 2020) and *¡Cuéntamelo!* (Aunt Lute 2017) an illustrated bilingual collection of oral histories by LGBT Latinx immigrants. Born and raised in Bogotá, Colombia, Julián currently resides in Brooklyn where he is an Assistant Professor of Creative Writing at CUNY. His second novel, *Pretend You're Dead and I Carry You*, is forthcoming in 2026 from Liveright, an imprint of Norton.

Sunny Lu lives in St. Louis. She reviews books on YouTube (a sunny book nook) and runs Lesbian Feminist Book Club.

Erin Markey is a writer, actor and creator of live performance works, often driven by original music. They live in Brooklyn, NY. "Mouth Tape" is an excerpt from their forthcoming book, *Psychosexual Production of a Classic.*

MariNaomi is a visual storyteller who splits their time between Nagoya, Japan and the San Francisco Bay Area. They are only slightly afraid of clowns. MariNaomi.com

Christina Catherine Martinez holds degrees from UC Berkeley and École Philippe Gaulier. One of them is a clown school, and the other one is in France.

Alistair McCartney is the author of *The Disintegrations* and *The End of the World Book. The Disintegrations* is the recipient of The Publishing Triangle's Ferro-Grumley Award for LGBTQ Fiction, and *TEOTWB* was a finalist for the PEN USA Fiction Award and the Edmund White debut fiction award. Originally from Australia, he lives in Los Angeles, where he is Teaching Faculty in Antioch University's MFA program.

Megan Milks is the author of *Margaret and the Mystery of the Missing Body*, *Slug and Other Stories*, and *Mega Milk: Essays*. They live in Brooklyn.

Maz Murray is an artist working in film, performance, writing, and installation. They had their first institutional solo show at Focal Point Gallery in 2024. His debut novel *Jaw Filler*, a collaboration with Charlie Markbreiter, is out December 2025 via Montez Press.

Deez Nutzian is an analog girl living in an AI world. She can be found writing about the trash and whimsy of years past from her current perch in the Bay Area.

jaz papadopoulos (they/them) is a queer writer, NSFW professional, and clown. They are interested in horticulture, nervous systems, erotics, kink, and romance. Their debut collection, *I Feel That Way Too*, is available through Nightwood Editions.

Page Person is a visual and performing artist who lives in Los Angeles. She hosts a monthly performance party called The End of the World.

Sophie Robinson is the author of the poetry collection *Rabbit* (2018) and the novel *Prairie Oyster* (2026). She also is the founder of Devotion, a radical and inclusive online creative writing school. She lives in Norwich and London.

Dorothy R. Santos, PhD (she/they) is a queer Filipino American writer, artist, and media scholar. They were born and raised in San Francisco, California. They love science fiction films, well written (and told) jokes, and reading tarot.

L Scully is a living writer.

Vivek Shraya is an artist whose body of work crosses the boundaries of music, literature, visual art, theatre, TV, film, and fashion. Her best-selling book *I'm Afraid of Men* was heralded by Vanity Fair as "cultural rocket fuel."

féi iká shumarí (b.1993, Chihuahua, Mexico) is a two spirit/trans woman, (un)documented writer, performance artist, and graphic designer. She is descendent of the Pi'ma, Rarámuri, and Cora peoples. For more of her projects, designs, services, and products visit: feiikashumari.com

Dr. Kelsey L. Smoot (they/he/Kelz) is a Tin House Workshop alum, a Pushcart Prize nominee, a Best of the Net nominee, and a Best New Poets nominee. Proudly, he is also the author of two chapbooks: *we was bois together* with CLASH! (An Imprint of Mouthfeel Press) and *Muse*, with Another New Calligraphy. Thrillingly, Kelz's debut full-length collection of poems, *SOULMATE AS A VERB* arrives in early 2026 with DOPAMINE/ Semiotext(e).

Bethy Squires is a writer living in Hollywood. Her work can be found on *Vulture* and *Vice*, and on shows like *Adam Ruins Everything* and *The History of Swear Words*. She's a double Gemini, but please don't hold that against her.

Michelle Tea is the author of many books and edited collections. She is the founding editor of DOPAMINE Books.

Joseph Earl Thomas is the author of *Sink*, a memoir, and the novel *God Bless You, Otis Spunkmeyer*, winner of the Center for Fiction First Novel rize. His work across genres has been published in *The Paris Review, The Verge, Harper's, VQR, The Yale Review* & elsewhere. A graduate of the University of Notre Dame's MFA program, he also earned his PhD in English at The University of Pennsylvania. He teaches writing at Sarah Lawrence College, and courses in Black Studies and Literature at The Brooklyn Institute for Social Research.

Chris E. Vargas is an artist and the Executive Director of the Museum of Trans Hirstory & Art (MOTHA), a critical and conceptual art & hirstory institution. He is the co-editor of the volume *Trans Hirstory in 99 Objects* (Hirmer, 2024).

Anya Ventura is a writer in Los Angeles.

Amanda Verwey is an artist and writer living in Los Angeles. @aaverwey

Riley Yaxley is most often a dinner party host, a fishkeeper, a beach rat, a flâneuse, a glutton, a flirt, a dancer, a delinquent daughter who forgets to call her mom; and she is also a writer and editor.

ALSO BY DOPAMINE BOOKS

SLUTS Anthology, edited by Michelle Tea.

NEW MISTAKES, by Clement Goldberg.

HOW TO FUCK LIKE A GIRL, by Vera Blossom.

DAYS RUNNING, by Shawn Stewart Ruff.

WITCH Anthology, edited by Michelle Tea.

SELF-ROMANCING, by L. Scully.

BARGAIN WITCH: ESSAYS IN SELF-INITIATION, by Brooke Palmieri.

SOULMATE AS A VERB, by Kelsey L. Smoot.

HELL IN A HANDBAG, by Jibz Cameron.

CLOWNS Anthology, edited by Michelle Tea.